THE FIRST
AMERICAN REVOLUTION

THE FIRST
AMERICAN REVOLUTION

Before Lexington and Concord

RAY RAPHAEL

The New Press, New York

Massachusetts map courtesy of Harvard Map Collection.

Published in the United States by The New Press, New York, 2002
Distributed by Perseus Distribution

LIBRARY OF CONGRESS CATALOGING-IN-PUBLICATION DATA
Raphael, Ray.
The first American revolution : before Lexington and Concord / Ray Raphael.
    p.   cm.
Includes bibliographical references and index.
ISBN 1-56584-730-X
1. Massachusetts—History—Revolution, 1775–1783—Causes.
2. United States—History—Revolution, 1775–1783—Causes.
3. Massachusetts—Politics and government—To 1775—Citizen participation.
4. Revolutionaries—Massachusetts—History—18th century.   5. Farmers—
Massachusetts—Political activity—History—18th century.   6. Artisans—
Massachusetts—Political activity—History—18th century.   7. Government,
Resistance to—Massachusetts—History—18th century.   8. Sedition—
Massachusetts—History—18th century.   I. Title.

E216 .R25 2002
973.3—dc21   2001044180

The New Press was established in 1990 as a not-for-profit alternative to the large,
commercial publishing houses currently dominating the book publishing industry.
The New Press operates in the public interest rather than for private gain, and is
committed to publishing, in innovative ways, works of educational, cultural, and
community value that are often deemed insufficiently profitable.

www.thenewpress.com

Printed in the United States of America

2   4   6   8   10   9   7   5   3   1

For Bill and Sharon, who know well that stories tell our lives.
And, as always, for Marie.

CONTENTS

ACKNOWLEDGMENTS

The preliminary research for this book was made possible through a fellowship from the National Endowment for the Humanities. The inspiration to tell this story came from my former teacher and good friend, Sheldon Wolin. I received excellent readings and many helpful suggestions from Holly V. Izard, Kenneth J. Moynihan, Marc Favreau, Cathy Dexter, and my wife, Marie Raphael. Holly Izard, Ken Moynihan, and Stephen Meunier filled many gaps in my knowledge of local Massachusetts history. The project would not have been possible without assistance from Julia Graham and Gloria Fulton of the Humboldt State University Interlibrary Loan Department, and from their counterparts in other libraries. I also wish to thank the many people who, through the years, have preserved valuable materials at the American Antiquarian Society in Worcester, the Worcester Historical Museum, the Forbes Library in Northampton, the Richard Salter Storrs Library in Longmeadow, the Massachusetts Historical Society, the New England Historic Genealogical Society, the Harvard Map Collection, the Connecticut Valley Historical Museum, and the New York Public Library.

VERMONT

NEW HA

NEW YORK

BERKSHIRE

HAMPSHIRE

WORCESTER

CONNECTICUT

RHODE

The STATE of

MASSACHUSETTS

from the best Information

1796

American Miles 69¼ to a Deg:

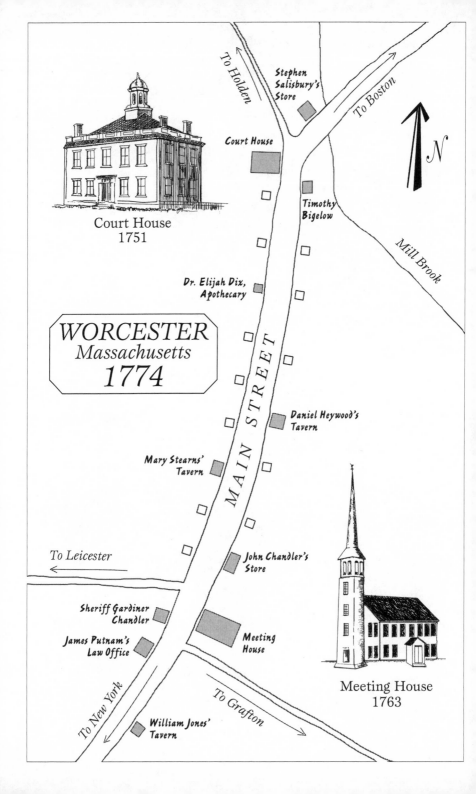

To Holden

Stephen
Salisbury's
Store

To Boston

N

Court House

Court House
1751

Timothy
Bigelow

Mill Brook

Dr. Elijah Dix,
Apothecary

WORCESTER
Massachusetts
1774

MAIN STREET

Daniel Heywood's
Tavern

Mary Stearns'
Tavern

To Leicester

John Chandler's
Store

Sheriff Gardiner
Chandler

James Putnam's
Law Office

Meeting
House

Meeting House
1763

To New York

To Grafton

William Jones'
Tavern

THE FIRST
AMERICAN REVOLUTION

INTRODUCTION

The American Revolution did not start with "the shot heard round the world" on the morning of April 19, 1775. When British Regulars fired upon a small group of hastily assembled patriots on the Lexington Green, they were attempting to regain control of a colony they had already lost. The real revolution, the transfer of political authority to the American patriots, occurred the previous summer when thousands upon thousands of farmers and artisans seized power from every Crown-appointed official in Massachusetts outside of Boston.

Starting in August 1774, each time a court was slated to meet under British authority in some Massachusetts town, great numbers of angry citizens made sure it did not. At Great Barrington, fifteen hundred patriots filled the courthouse to prevent the judges from entering. At Worcester, judges were made to read their recantations thirty times over, hats in hand, as they passed through 4,622 militiamen lined up along Main Street. So, too, at Springfield, where, "in a sandy, sultry place, exposed to the sun," once-important officials sweated under the burden of their heavy black suits. The functionaries of British rule cowered and collapsed, no match for the collective force of patriotic farmers. According to an eyewitness,

The people of each town being drawn into separate companies marched with staves & musick. The trumpets sounding, drums beating, fifes playing and Colours flying, struck the passions of the soul into a proper tone, and inspired martial courage into each.[1]

The governor's councilors, once elected but now appointed directly by the Crown, were also forced to resign. Thomas Oliver, lieutenant-governor of Massachusetts and a councilor as well, ceded to a crowd of four thousand assembled around his home in Cambridge. Timothy Paine of Worcester was visited by two thousand men who demanded his resignation. He told a committee he would comply, but his word would not suffice—the people wanted it in writing. Even that was not enough: the crowd demanded he come out of his house while a representative read his resignation aloud. Again Paine complied, and again the people wanted more: he would have to read his resignation himself, with his hat off, several times as he passed through the ranks. Nothing else would do.[2]

Through it all, the revolutionaries engaged in a participatory democracy which far outreached the intentions of the so-called "Founding Fathers." They gathered under no special leaders. Their ad hoc representatives, such as the five men elected to talk with Timothy Paine, operated according to instructions approved by the assembled crowd and reported back immediately to the body as a whole. Even the nighttime mobs (and there were many) maintained a democratic aspect. In Braintree, two hundred men gathered on a Sunday at around 8:00 P.M. to remove some gunpowder from the powder house and to make the local sheriff burn two warrants he was attempting to deliver. Successful in their missions, they wanted to celebrate with a loud "huzzah." But should they disturb the Sabbath? "They call'd a vote," wrote Abigail Adams, who observed the affair, and "it being Sunday evening it passed in the negative."[3]

By early October 1774, more than six months before the red dawn at Lexington, all Crown-appointed officials had been forced to disavow British authority or flee to Boston, which was still under military protection. "The Flames of Sedition," wrote Governor Thomas Gage, had "spread universally throughout the Country beyond Conception." [4] The British had lost all control of the Massachusetts countryside, and they would never get it back.

Scholars differ widely on how to define "revolution," but a good starting point, firmly-rooted in common usage, can be found in the *Random House Webster's College Dictionary* (1997): "a complete and forcible overthrow and replacement of an established government or political system by the people governed." In the late summer and early fall of 1774, the people of rural Massachusetts completely and forcibly overthrew the established government and began to set up their own. This was the first American Revolution. While a group of renowned lawyers, merchants, and slave-owning planters were meeting as a Continental Congress in Philadelphia to consider whether or not they should challenge British rule, the plain farmers and artisans of Massachusetts, guarding their liberties jealously and voting at every turn, wrested control from the most powerful empire on earth.

PART 1

BEFORE THE REVOLUTION

PEOPLE AND PLACE

On the eve of the Revolutionary War, 95 percent of the inhabitants of Massachusetts lived outside Boston.[1] Few of these people were involved in the Stamp Act protests, the Boston Massacre, or the Boston Tea Party—the signature events which define the prerevolutionary decade in the historical consciousness of most Americans. Some might have paid some attention to the growing rift between the British imperial government and the American Whigs, but for the most part they focused on personal and parochial concerns. For instance:

- Through the 1760s citizens of Worcester complained repeatedly about the law requiring them to support the Latin grammar school, which served college-bound sons of the elite. Education, they argued, should be open to all, and children should be taught in plain English.[2]

- In 1766 Springfield tanner Jedediah Bliss, to protest singing in church, read aloud from the Bible when the rest of the congregation broke into their hymn.[3]

- In 1768 farmers from the town of Deerfield mowed a thirty-acre meadow that was also claimed by the neighboring district of Greenfield; when men from both locales tried to cart off the hay, they wound up brawling with clubs and pitchforks.[4]

- In 1771 Worcester apothecary Elijah Dix was harassed by his outraged neighbors when they learned he was preserving the skeleton of a man who had just been hanged.[5]

- In 1773 and 1774 angry crowds in Worcester, Salem, and Marblehead protested against smallpox inoculations; men and women "of the poorer sorts" feared they would become exposed to the disease while "not being able to bear the expense of Inoculation" for themselves. Patriots from Salem complained that the concern over smallpox took precedence over all other important matters, including resistance to the king and Parliament.[6]

All this should come as no surprise. Local politics in colonial Massachusetts, like local politics everywhere, were dominated by affairs of school and church, by taxation and the division of land, by the construction and repair of roads, and by issues of health and public mores. When, in 1774, British policy would disenfranchise every citizen and undermine the autonomy of every community, the parochial concerns of separate localities would suddenly congeal—but until then, the political interests of ordinary farmers and artisans did not usually extend beyond the meeting houses of their own particular towns. Military mobilization and issues of monetary policy (such as the unsuccessful Land Bank scheme of 1740, which would have provided paper currency backed by land mortgages) were notable exceptions.

Colonial Massachusetts was overwhelmingly agrarian. Outside of the seaports, about two-thirds of the inhabitants owned their own farms. According to historian Jackson Turner Main, local communities such as Worcester were dominated by "a great middle class of small property owners."[7] Young men who did not yet possess land of their own often worked as farm laborers, and even many artisans and merchants kept gardens, poultry, and perhaps a cow.

An average farm—and most tended toward the average—consisted of 50 to 100 acres, about one-quarter of which were tilled, mowed, or pastured. The main field crops were flax (grown primarily for fiber) and Indian corn (the staple food for man and animal). Beans, squash, and potatoes grew in the gardens, while apples, to be made into cider, hung from the orchards. Depending on region and soil, farmers also planted wheat, rye, oats, or barley. They tilled the soil with wooden plows and flailed grain by hand.

The average family possessed a riding horse, a pair of work oxen, two or three milk cows, a handful of steers and heifers, perhaps half a dozen sheep, a pig or two, and a poultry flock.[8] Farmers probably spent more of their waking hours with animals than with people, and when socializing with their neighbors, they no doubt talked of livestock, crops, and the weather. Women spent most of their time processing the production of the farm: cooking, preserving, making butter and cheese, carding, spinning, weaving, sewing, knitting.

Most of the people lived in the countryside, yet each belonged to a small community called a "town." The typical town in colonial Massachusetts consisted of a meeting house with a nearby common (central square or grassy area) and burial ground, at least one tavern (and often more), one or two stores, and a handful of artisans' shops. Each county seat, or shiretown, also had a courthouse. Main Street in the town of Worcester was flanked by two centers—a meeting house and common to the south and a courthouse to the north—with taverns and stores, blacksmith shops, lawyers' offices, and residences in between.

People came to town not just to buy goods or services but to drink, to worship, to politic, or to drill for the militia. Stores, taverns, the meeting house (serving both as church and civic center), the town common—these were the venues for community activity.

Although the men and women of colonial Massachusetts labored on their separate farms and inside their separate homes, they placed a high value on social life and worship, which generally overlapped. They were not rugged individualists but congregationalists; they called their churches "meeting houses."[9] Attendance at services was required by law and absence was punishable by fine; although the law was rarely enforced to the letter, frequent absences provided grounds for rumor and suspicion. Social standing was reflected by the quantity and position of a family's pews. By the eve of the Revolution, the turmoil of the Great Awakening was well in the past—but even so, until 1774 the hiring and firing of a minister could disturb the tranquility of a community like no other issue.

Liquor was of great importance to these religious people, who gathered frequently in public houses (taverns) for drink and company. Historian David Conroy has calculated that Worcester and Middlesex Counties possessed one tavern for every forty or fifty adult males. Since each tavern for which he found data contained from sixteen to forty-four chairs, more than half the adult males of those counties could theoretically raise a toast at the same time while seated at some public house.[10] Local cider was the staple, but men also drank grain or potato whiskey, maple or cherry-flavored rum, peach brandy, and so on—whatever the innkeeper could muster up, perhaps from as far away as the West Indies.[11] All this public drinking, according to Conroy, would soon play a role in the growing challenge to established authority:

> Slowly, unevenly, but relentlessly a new political culture had emerged in colonial Massachusetts. The concept and practice of hierarchy had been strained, altered, and finally eroded by the restiveness, by the steady assertion of ordinary men shedding traditional constraints of their political behavior. They were most ready to do so in companies at taverns. . . . It was in taverns that men carried their examination of crown officials and policies to new levels of critical inspection. . . . [F]or the mass of male colonists, it was in taverns that they followed and acted on the unfolding drama with the crisis with England.[12]

Less frequently than for drinking or worshiping, people came together for purposes of self-government. Every March, inhabitants of each town gathered at the meeting house to elect officers for the year and to conduct community business. Additional meetings could be called by the selectmen, who were elected for one-year terms, or by a petition from ten citizens. Before each meeting, a warrant, or agenda, was posted in a public place, commonly on the meeting house door. Thus, the patriots who would overthrow British rule in 1774 received much training in the arts of democracy by their town meetings. They approached the Revolution well-versed in collective problem solving.

Participation in town meetings was open to most (but not all) adult male inhabitants. Any man whose property was assessed at over £20 could vote for local officers, while in elections for provincial representatives, a voter needed property which could yield 40 shillings in rent. According to historian Robert E. Brown, there was not much difference between these two qualifications, and over 90 percent of adult males in farming communities such as Worcester were entitled to vote. In seaport towns, with a greater proportion of landless laborers, the proportion of voters was considerably less. Even so, more than three of every four men in Massachusetts were enfranchised, and many of those who could not vote were still in their twenties, unmarried, and not yet living on their own. Colonial women, of course, were not allowed to vote.[13]

Elected town offices were many and varied: selectman, treasurer, clerk, constable, tithingman, road surveyor, fence viewer, hog reeve, deer reeve, hay warden, and so on. In Chesterfield, a newly created town in Hampshire County with only thirty families, twenty-one men were elected to at least one town office in 1762.[14] Most of these office holders received no recompense; they were simply performing their duty, as they did when working on roads. Men who refused to fulfill these civic responsibilities, like those not attending church, were subject to fines.

Adult males, in fulfillment of yet another obligation, came to town for militia days. Many of the men over age thirty had been in service during the Seven Years War with France, while some of those over fifty had seen action at Louisburg in 1745. Military training was an important ritual; when it came time to protect or defend, the men hoped to be ready.

Finally, in each shiretown, scores or even hundreds of men gathered for the county court sessions four times each year. When the courts convened, towns such as Worcester buzzed with excitement and gossip as men with property or reputations to protect came to plead their cases. In addition to probate courts, there were four components to the judicial system: justices of the peace, an Inferior Court of Common Pleas for each county, a Court of General Sessions of the Peace for each county, and the provincial Superior Court of Judicature. The workings of this multilayered judicial system, which reached deep into the everyday lives of colonial farmers, would constitute the primary bone of contention in the Revolution of 1774.

With no police force, the high sheriff and the justices of the peace did the daily dirty work of law enforcement. A justice of the peace had the authority to put libelers, drunks, or wife beaters in jail. He tried cases of profanity, fornication, and unnecessary absence from church. His word was law. If a defendant chose to dispute a justice's ruling, however, he could appeal the case and receive a jury trial at one of the county courts.

The Court of Common Pleas, composed of four judges appointed by the governor and a jury when needed, tried civil cases and received appeals from the justices of the peace. The court heard suits for the collection of debts and controversies over land title and boundaries; in rural Massachusetts, there was no shortage of either. The Court of Common Pleas, in the minds of ordinary farmers, possessed an awesome power: it could take your money, your cow, or perhaps even your land.

The Court of General Sessions of the Peace, meeting concurrently with the Court of Common Pleas, consisted of the four Common Pleas judges and other justices of the peace for the county. The Court of General Sessions heard criminal cases, often on appeal from the rulings of the justices of the peace. It also exercised several of the administrative functions of county government: it assessed the towns and allocated county expenditures, it ran the jails, it authorized the construction of county roads and bridges, and it granted liquor licenses to innkeepers and merchants.

The Superior Court of Judicature, composed of the Chief Justice of Massachusetts and four associate judges, heard both civil and criminal cases and received appeals from the county courts. Traveling twice a year to Worcester and other shiretowns, the judges embodied the authority of the Crown in local communities. When the Superior Court was about to convene, the local sheriff and his posse of notable citizens would meet the judges on the edge of town and escort them to their lodgings. The following day, with considerable pomp and circumstance, judges in their scarlet robes and long wigs would perch on a raised platform while barristers in black gowns and attorneys in plain black suits pleaded before them. "I saw the court when a boy," George Bliss once said, "and making all due allowance for the effect upon the mind of a child, I feel confident that no earthly tribunal could inspire greater reverence than its appearance did on my mind." [15]

The court system was an integral component of a multilayered governmental structure with numerous checks and balances. The ruling body of the province was the General Court, composed of three branches: the governor's office, the House of Representatives, and the Council. Each was charged with specific duties, and each had ways of limiting the power of the others.

The Crown appointed the governor, who in turn selected the judges, justices of the peace, militia officers, sheriffs, attorney-general, receiver-general (tax collector), and some other officials. According to the 1691 charter, however, all the governor's appointments had to be approved by his Council—and the Council in Massachusetts, unlike other colonies, was ultimately in the hands of the people.

The House of Representatives and the Council constituted the lower and upper bodies of the legislature. The House initiated taxation and had to approve all expenditures. The Council confirmed the business of the House and advised the governor. The voters of each town elected at least one representative to the House, with larger towns entitled to two. These representatives, serving one-year terms, were sometimes given detailed instructions by their constituents.

Every year the first business of the representatives was to meet with the twenty-eight members of the outgoing Council to select a Council for the upcoming session.

The Council's "advice" was in fact more than that. Because the Council had to approve all appointments, the governor did not have a free hand to engage in blatant patronage. Since the people chose their representatives, and since the representatives determined the Council, the people maintained some control over judges and other appointed officials. To some extent, they also exercised control over the governor himself. Since the General Court paid the governor's salary, and since there was no fixed amount according to law, the governor could not afford to ignore the wishes of the people he governed. Although the governor possessed the authority to prorogue the House of Representatives, he would need to reconvene it soon thereafter if he wanted to get paid.

Thus, on paper, the people maintained considerable control over the provincial government. But did they always exercise their power? Why, some historians have asked, did common farmers and laborers continually choose privileged gentlemen or lawyers to represent them? In practice, was political society in late colonial Massachusetts democratic or deferential?[16]

In many of the colony's farming communities, a handful of very powerful men—the "river gods" of Hampshire County, for instance—controlled the governmental apparatus. During the second quarter of the eighteenth century, John Stoddard of Northampton, son of the influential minister Solomon Stoddard, served as a justice of the peace, chief justice of the Court of Common Pleas, colonel of the Hampshire militia, commander-in-chief of the western forces, representative to the House, and member of the Council. Many of these positions he held concurrently. A rich land speculator, he used his political and military appointments to garner even greater wealth, prestige, and power. No county road could be laid without the approval of Colonel Stoddard, who would use his control over the Court of General Sessions to award the contract to a friend. Food for the militia would probably be purchased from someone he knew. When a gentleman's son was ready to embark on a career, John Stoddard, trusted friend to a succession of governors, was the man to procure him an appointment.

Upon Stoddard's death in 1748, his nephew Israel Williams, of Hatfield, assumed the role of kingmaker for Hampshire County. Williams, like his uncle John, graduated from Harvard College to take his place among the educated elite of Massachusetts. Williams was related to practically every government official in the county and to several of its most important ministers. His cousin Elijah Williams was patriarch of Deerfield, while his nephew William Williams had established his own domain in Pittsfield. He was related by marriage to other "river gods": John Worthington of Springfield and Joseph Hawley and the Dwight dynasty of Northampton. For several decades every justice of the Hampshire Court of Common Pleas and every officer of its Probate Court was related to Israel Williams. Like his uncle, Williams used both his own multifarious positions (the same as those once held by Stoddard) and his family web to wield power and influence. Nobody would ever dream of seeking an appointed political office in Hampshire County without his sponsorship.

Downriver at Springfield, John Worthington held sway. Worthington, a graduate of Yale, served as the king's attorney in all local cases. He was also a gentleman farmer, a land speculator, a money lender— and, of course, a holder of public office. He commanded local authority as justice of the peace, and he served frequently as Springfield's representative to the House. In 1767 and 1768 he was elected to the Council, and the following year he was offered the job of attorney-general for the province. (He declined the position, content with his immense power closer to home.) Often, while representing the Crown before the Court of General Sessions of the Peace, he would collect not only his attorney's fees but also payment for service as one of the court's justices.[17]

The plain of rich Massachusetts farmland in the Connecticut River Valley was more conducive to the accumulation of wealth than the hills and rocky soil so common in other regions of the state. This accumulation of wealth, in turn, facilitated an accumulation of power.

But even in other locations, a powerful elite sometimes came to domi-
nate public office.

In the town of Worcester, for instance, where small farmers accounted for the vast majority of the population, a handful of rich and
educated men, again interrelated, were able to establish a local dynasty. In 1731 John Chandler II, whose grandparents had settled in
Roxbury in 1637 and whose parents had settled in Woodstock, was appointed to serve as the first chief justice of the Court of Common
Pleas and the first judge of probate in Worcester County. His son,
John Chandler III, held virtually every possible governmental office:
he was elected to serve as town treasurer, selectman, representative to
the House, and member of the Council; he was appointed to the offices of court clerk, sheriff, register of probate, register of deeds,
judge of probate, chief justice of the Court of Common Pleas, and
colonel in the militia.

John Chandler III fathered two sons and seven daughters with his
first wife, Hannah Gardiner, and he helped raise the children of his
second wife, the wealthy widow Sarah Clark Paine. His daughters,
called the "seven stars" at the time, furthered the Chandler clan by
taking husbands from other prominent families.[18] His eldest son, John
IV, married his step sister, Dorothy Paine, while daughter Sarah married her step brother, Timothy Paine. (Later, a granddaughter of John
III married a grandson of his second wife, creating three generations
of Chandler-Paine alliances.) Members of this extended Chandler
family filled many of the public offices in Worcester in the decades
preceding the American Revolution. Historian Kevin MacWade has
calculated that of the ten men appointed to the most powerful offices
in Worcester County between 1750 and 1774, all but one (Thomas
Steel) were related to men who had held those offices before.[19]

Some of the outlying towns in Worcester County were dominated
by local patrons, much in the manner of English lords. In Rutland this
person was Scottish-born John Murray, married to one of the Chandler "seven stars." Physically, Murray stood head and shoulders
above the rest: at six foot three, he was even taller than George Washington.[20] He was also the wealthiest man of his region. A poor Rutland farmer who went into debt (as many did) had little choice but to

turn to John Murray, who alone accounted for more than 70 percent of the town's money lent out at interest.[21] Politically, John Murray ran the show as well, in grand style. According to a description of Murray penned in the early 1800s,

> [E]nterprising and prosperous, he became opulent and popular—being a large land-holder, [he] had some tenants and many debtors. On Representative day all his friends that could ride, walk, creep, or hobble were at the Polls. It was not his fault if they returned dry.[22]

In Hardwick, the prominent patron was Timothy Ruggles (Harvard, class of 1732), again connected to the Chandlers by marriage (his daughter Elizabeth married Gardiner Chandler, son of John IV). When Ruggles moved to Hardwick in 1754, he immediately became its first representative to the Massachusetts House of Representatives—a position he continued to hold until 1770. He was chosen to serve on the Council during that entire period, the longest tenure for any councilor in the province, and in 1762 he was elected speaker of the House. Ruggles achieved fame for his military achievements during the French and Indian War, and after the war he was rewarded with a large land grant and the position of brigadier-general.

"The Brigadier," as he came to be known, was one of the most important and influential men in prerevolutionary Massachusetts. He was also one of the most belligerent. John Adams, while apprenticing for the law in Worcester, came to know Ruggles personally and testified to his character:

> Ruggles's Grandeur consists in the quickness of his apprehension, Steadiness of his attention, the boldness and Strength of his Thoughts and Expressions, his strict Honour, conscious Superiority, Contempt of Meanness,* &c. People approach him with Dread and Terror.[23]

---

* The term "meanness" in this context does not connote a person who is unkind to others, but someone who is low in rank, station, or character.

These men were all very wealthy. Brigadier Ruggles's estate, confiscated during the Revolutionary War, included nine different farms totaling 1,670 acres—about twenty times the norm for Worcester County.[24] John Murray's confiscated estate was valued in excess of £26,000. John Chandler IV was richer yet, with an estate appraised at over £36,000; by contrast, 90 percent of the estates in Worcester during the revolutionary era amounted to less than £1,000.[25] Chandler owned property throughout the province, including nine working farms, one of the fanciest mansions in Worcester, three carriages, various shops and mills, five pews at the meeting house, and a slave.[26]

With wealth came social standing. When Timothy Paine, stepson of John Chandler III, graduated from Harvard in 1748, he was ranked fifth in his class. (Ranking, at that time, was strictly according to "dignity of family.") Rufus Chandler, son of John IV, graduated fourth in a class of forty in 1766, while his brother William made it to the top of the list in 1772. At Harvard, these young men were among the best that high society in Massachusetts had to offer.

At first glance, the political prominence of a rich and powerful elite seems to contradict the popular notion that town meetings, expressing the will of the people, set the tone for local politics in colonial Massachusetts. Historian J. R. Pole has labeled this apparent paradox "the problem of early American democracy." Although the institutions seemed democratic, Pole argued, modern observers should not impose current conceptions of democracy on colonial times; instead, they should try to set "the democratic elements in their proper place within a system conceived in another age, under a different inspiration." In this deferential society, when social rank meant far more than it does today, "democracy" had a different meaning. "If this was a democracy," Pole concluded, "it was a democracy that wore its cockade firmly pinned into its periwig."[27]

In fact, ordinary farmers had good, practical reasons for allowing the local elite to represent them in the General Court. Timothy Ruggles, John Murray, John Chandler, John Worthington, Israel Williams—powerful men with friends in high places—voted with the governor in provincial politics; in return, the governor granted them small favors. In the first year that Ruggles represented Hardwick, he pulled some strings to get the town's fines remitted; later, he sponsored a bill establishing an annual county fair in Hardwick.[28] When the inhabitants of Athol wished to establish their own town, they turned to John Murray, their man in the capital. Murray handled the petitions, drafted the legislation, and pushed it through the General Court; he even chaired the first town meeting.[29] Patrons with influence, these men knew how to get the job done. They could procure local contracts or intervene in times of need.

Common farmers did not hesitate to place their rich neighbors in local offices as well. The wealthy, who were literate and learned, could record deeds, take minutes at meetings, and guide ordinary folk through the legal system and an increasingly complex world of affairs. The elite had money, leisure, education, competence, and connections—all the requisites for public service in the colonial era. Common farmers possessed none of these.

Most of the time, common farmers in mid-eighteenth-century Massachusetts had little reason to quarrel with their representatives. It was of little import to them that Israel Williams or John Chandler voted with the governor on matters of no local interest. It mattered not that the men who moderated or recorded their town meetings possessed more than their share of wordly possessions. Indeed, the fact that prominent men participated actively in local politics added a certain status to the political domain. When farmers discussed what to do about pigs in the streets, their words were set to paper by men educated at Harvard.

Even so, there can be no doubt that a system based on patronage worked against town-based democracy. Men who had been placed in office by the governor owed their allegiance to him, not to the people they served—and the governor had no reason to complain if his underlings harassed or soaked the common folk. Appointed officials functioned as a class apart. "[T]he office of a justice of the peace is a great acquisition in the country," John Adams wrote, "and such a distinction to a man among his neighbors as is enough to purchase and corrupt almost any man." [30]

The precarious balance between town-meeting democracy and deferential politics—the two faces of government in colonial Massachusetts—would soon be tested by the political turbulence which followed in the wake of the French and Indian War. Starting in 1765, townspeople began to take more note of issues extending beyond their own parochial spheres. Provincial and imperial politics, once left to the elite, would soon be debated by yeomen and artisans in each and every meeting house in the colony. The tenuous truce between common folk and leaders would give way to conflict, and in 1774, ordinary citizens, defining themselves collectively and democratically, would settle the matter by force.

2

DIVISION

On the eve of the American Revolution, more than a century and a half had elapsed since the landing of the Pilgrims in 1620—a greater interval than that which separates us today from the Civil War. Pre-revolutionary Massachusetts was no fledgling society. In fact, it was old enough to show signs of wear.

For example, in colonial New England, few men bequeathed their land exclusively to their eldest sons. Since families tended to be rather large (double-digit offspring were not uncommon), significant estates were reduced to modest or meager proportions with the passing of generations. True, there was more land on the frontier for those who wished to move, but this was a close-knit society marked by strong community and familial bonds. Since most children, upon reaching maturity, preferred to remain close to home, farms became smaller and older townships became increasingly crowded.[1]

By the eighteenth century, inventories of estates in probate began to list "worn land."[2] Betty Hobbs Pruitt's analysis of the 1771 Massachusetts tax rolls revealed that about half of the farms had fewer than twenty acres of improved land, and almost half of these lacked either tillage, pasture, or hay land. Half of the small farmers possessed no horse, and almost two-thirds possessed no oxen to work the land. One-third had no milk cows or breeding swine. Many farmers, Pruitt and other scholars have concluded, were far from self-sufficient.[3]

The number of adults without any land at all was also on the rise. More men and women began to wander the countryside—the "strolling poor," they were called at the time. Each town, in order to avoid the obligation of supporting vagrants, "warned out" transients when they first showed up—and these warnings were on the rise in many communities. In Hampshire County, the official warnings for vagrancy increased by 248 percent from 1750–54 to 1760–64.[4] In the town of Worcester, there were seventeen warnings issued in the 1740s, thirty-one in the 1750s, and seventy-five in the 1760s.[5] The first poorhouse in Worcester was built in 1772.[6]

At least in some areas, the rich were getting richer as the poor were getting poorer. Historian Kenneth Lockridge has found that in the rural towns of Suffolk County, estates worth more than £900 increased dramatically from 4 percent in 1660 to 17 percent in 1765. (Estates valued at less than £100 also increased during this period, although only slightly—from 19 percent to 23 percent.) Increasingly, men leaving wills used the titles of "gentleman" or "Esquire." By the 1760s and 1770s, tax assessments listed several men with great amounts of money lent out at interest. The rich had money to lend; the poor were in need of borrowing. Economic class divisions were becoming more sharply defined.[7]

Struggling yeomen found it increasingly difficult to stay out of debt. Their income was seasonal, but their needs were constant. Farmers procured salt, sugar, or nails on credit from local merchants, and frequently (four times in ten, according to one historian), they settled their bills with farm produce or labor. If a farmer came up short at the annual accounting, the merchant or patron to whom he was indebted might agree to carry the credit to the following year—or he might try to collect through litigation.[8]

Lawsuits for the collection of debts were on the increase in the years preceding the Revolutionary War, signaling a partial unraveling of the tight-knit communities of rural Massachusetts.[9] From 1761 to 1765, the annual number of suits in five rural counties in Massachusetts amounted to 22 percent of the adult male population.[10] In Worcester, debt cases increased by 50 percent in the court sessions of

1773–74.[11] Typically, a creditor was listed in the court record as a "gentleman," while a debtor was a "yeoman."[12] If the judges decided in favor of the plaintiff, the defendant would have to pay court costs as well as the original debt; if and when he failed to meet this double obligation, the court was entitled to seize some of his property.

It would be easy to exaggerate the implications of poverty, debt, and litigation in rural Massachusetts. Several historians have suggested that the increasing discontent among the poor was a major cause of the American Revolution.[13] Jackson Turner Main, however, holds that only about 20 percent of the people in rural Massachusetts could be considered poor, while about 70 percent belonged to a propertied class of middling farmers.[14] Whatever the figures, it is difficult to imagine that Massachusetts farmers in the 1760s and 1770s were so impoverished that they would rally together and risk their lives in violent upheaval for reasons of economic hardship; most were not in such dire straits. These farmers were not peasants, nor were they ripe for a classic debtors' uprising.

This is not to say they had no worries. Each time an indebted farmer lost a case in court, his neighbors took note: they too were at risk. If they ever ran into debt—not an unlikely prospect—their status as freeholders might be threatened by merchants, money lenders, lawyers, and ultimately the court judges. Their hold on the good life was tenuous, dependent on the honor and integrity of men in wigs and robes who might one day determine their fates. Ordinary farmers who ran up small debts might lose livestock or land—whatever the judges decreed. Freeholders could become mere tenants. They might even join the "strolling poor." To lose their farms was to lose their freedom, and this was their worst fear.

In the early 1760s, Massachusetts farmers had little reason to suspect this might happen. By the summer of 1774, they had every reason to believe that it would.

In 1765, to help pay the debt incurred as a result of the French and Indian War, the British Parliament enacted a stamp tax on all official documents in its North American colonies. Many colonists resisted this "taxation without representation," as they called it. In Boston and other major cities, angry crowds hung effigies of stamp distributors. Rioters ransacked the houses of prominent officials, including Thomas Hutchinson, chief justice of the Superior Court of Judicature for Massachusetts. Stamps were destroyed and stamp distributors made to resign. Resistance was so forceful and widespread that the Stamp Act could not be enforced, and in 1766 it was repealed.

Rural communities in Massachusetts did not take the lead in the resistance movement, but some joined along. The Worcester County town of Leicester voiced concern that their "Darling Rights" were being threatened: "[W]e cannot but think, that the Sd Act is Contrary to the Rights of Mankind & Subversive of ye English Constitution & hath a Direct Tendency, to bring us into a State of abject Slavery & Vassalage." [15] Most towns, however, remained silent on the matter. Elite leaders no doubt tried to dampen resistance, although most stopped short of actively supporting the unpopular tax.

Throughout the province, courts closed their doors. Without stamps to affix to deeds, wills, orders, or judgments, they could conduct no legal business. In Hampshire County, Israel Williams, chief justice of the Court of Common Pleas, adjourned the fall session until February 1766, but even then no jury could be summoned for lack of a stamp on the writs. In Berkshire County, the probate judge William Williams, Israel's nephew, took the easy way out: claiming illness, he failed to show up for work.[16]

Some common farmers in Berkshire County put their own spin on the Stamp Act. On November 6, 1765, deputy sheriff John Morse tried to arrest Peter Curtis of Lanesborough for unpaid debts. Curtis resisted, but Morse overpowered him. Peter's friends, however, came to his aid and prevented Morse from taking his prisoner to jail. They told Morse it was unfair that Curtis should be arrested on an unstamped warrant dated before November 1, the day the Stamp Act took effect, since Curtis would be unable to procure bail for lack of stamps.

Having rescued Curtis for the moment, his friends then talked among themselves and decided that if any of them should be arrested, the rest would come to the prisoner's aid, as they had done for Curtis.

At a house-raising on November 26, most of the other men of Lanes-borough joined in the compact. That night, Morse, with a posse of five men and several warrants, entered the local tavern and tried to arrest Peter Curtis and another debtor named John Franklin, but a number of men from Lanesborough immediately made good on their pledge. According to one account, some "very angry, imprudent and profane language was uttered by both parties and they came to blows." The Lanesborough men prevailed, driving away the sheriff and his posse with clubs, staves, and stones. The rescuers warned Morse "that if he should come any more to take any person to gaol for debt before the times were altered, they would treat him again in like manner." [17]

Ten of the Lanesborough men (all but one were "yeomen") were later arrested for rioting. Nine pleaded guilty, but Seth Warren, with the help of Northampton attorney Joseph Hawley, defended his actions in court. Since Hawley was a famous and influential politician—something of a "river god" himself—the case became a *cause celebre*.

Those were troubled times, Hawley argued the following spring before the Superior Court. Because of the controversy around the Stamp Act, as well as the lack of required stamps for legal documents, "there was almost a total blank in the course of law, a chasm and gap in the administration of justice, when the King's writs did not run in the province," Hawley stated. He then asked rhetorically: "What then was the state and condition of the inhabitants of this province on the 26th of November 1765? Indeed little other than a state of absolute outlawry." Under such conditions, he argued, the normal rules of law did not apply. Seth Warren and the others "shewed themselves to be a sensible, discerning, judicious and courageous people" by resisting the incursions of Morse and his posse, who were backed by no legal sanction. [18]

This argument, with its profoundly revolutionary overtones, failed to convince Thomas Hutchinson and the other conservative judges. Warren was fined three pounds and charged four pounds, six shillings in court costs. Hawley himself was suspended from the bar.

The unpopular Stamp Act presented a problem for the elite: if they opposed it, they would alienate the men in high places who bestowed them favors, but if they supported it, they would enrage their constituents. Joseph Hawley was the exception in taking a stand against it; most of the others tried simply to wait it out. In Worcester, John Chandler and Timothy Paine judiciously refrained from taking any position on the matter, but this allowed other men to rise in political prominence. The Worcester town meeting broke its silence on provincial affairs by insisting that its new representative, Ephraim Doolittle, "Joyns In no Measures Countenancing ye Stamp Act." [19]

Timothy Ruggles, on the other hand, became deeply involved in the controversy. In October 1765, Massachusetts sent three representatives to the intercolonial Stamp Act Congress in New York: Brigadier Ruggles, the "river god" Oliver Partridge, and the firebrand James Otis, Jr. Ruggles was elected president of the Congress, outpolling Otis by one vote. There was only one problem: Ruggles, a "friend of government," did not really oppose the Stamp Act. The convention approved a statement which decried taxation without representation and claimed that the Stamp Act subverted "the rights and liberties of the colonists" [20]—but when it came time for the president to sign the declaration, he refused to do so. Ruggles suggested the document be sent back to the individual colonies for their consideration, but other delegates felt this weak response would negate the whole purpose of the Congress. Thomas McKean of Delaware upbraided Ruggles so vehemently that Ruggles, in the presence of the other delegates, challenged him to a duel. McKean later told John Adams that Ruggles "departed the next morning before day, without an adieu to any of his brethren." [21]

When he returned to Massachusetts, the Brigadier was taken to task for his refusal to sign. The House censured him and prohibited his explanatory statements from being printed in the official journal. John Adams, upon hearing of Ruggles's behavior at the Congress, noted in his diary: "This Ruggles has an inflexible Oddity about him, which has gained him a Character for Courage and Probity, but renders him a disagreeable Companion in Business." [22]

In Hardwick, his own people demanded an explanation. At the town meeting of March 3, 1766, the richest and most powerful man around—the Brigadier, the judge, and the only representative the town had ever sent to the General Court—was grilled by his humble neighbors. This time, Ruggles was able to wiggle his way out; his explanation, according to the town record, was "Sufficient to vindicate his Conduct." [23] In May, the people of Hardwick reelected Ruggles as their representative, but no longer was his rule unquestioned. Four years later the Brigadier would be voted out of office.

Not all members of the ruling elite weathered the Stamp Act storm. The names of thirty-two prominent Stamp Act supporters and plural officeholders were published in the *Boston Gazette* on March 31, 1766, and more than half of these were voted out of the House by the towns they represented.[24] The new House, now radicalized, failed to elect the usual suspects to the Council—government men like stamp master Andrew Oliver, treasurer Harrison Gray, and, most significantly, Chief Justice and Lieutenant-Governor Thomas Hutchinson. This political upheaval culminated in the election of James Otis as speaker of the House and Samuel Adams as clerk, although Governor Francis Bernard exercised his prerogative and vetoed Otis's election.[25]

The popular response to the Stamp Act altered the political landscape in Massachusetts. When Thomas Hutchinson and other victims of the 1765 rioting demanded compensation for the losses they had suffered, fellow conservatives tried to use this issue to win over moderates, who abhorred all rioting. But the radical Whigs, although publicly condemning the riots, opposed compensation. One prominent member of the Worcester County elite, Artemas Ward from Shrewsbury, joined Samuel Adams in writing arguments first against the Stamp Act itself and then against compensation. Tactically, representatives such as Adams, Ward, and Joseph Hawley were able to defeat compensation by coupling it with indemnity to all rioters (including Hawley's client from Berkshire County, Seth Warren). This, of course, was out of the question to conservatives, so Governor Bernard was forced to veto the measure. Afterward Bernard tried to punish Ward by withdrawing his commission as colonel in the militia. When Ward received Bernard's notice, he told the messenger:

> Give my compliments to the Governor, and say to him, I con-
> sider myself twice honored, but more in being superceded, than
> in having been commissioned, and I thank him for this, since the
> active that dictated it is evidence that I am, what he is not, a
> friend to my country.[26]

The defection of Joseph Hawley and Artemas Ward to the Whigs signaled a crack in the armor of the elite. No longer would common farmers look to a Chandler or a Williams for favors without at least questioning their politics. The elite, once invincible, had become vulnerable. Men who had been waiting in the wings now had a shot at challenging the entrenched leaders.

This was a major shift from just a few years earlier. Back in 1758, when John Adams was in Worcester training to be a lawyer under the tutelage of James Putnam, he had befriended two men—Ephraim Doolittle, a merchant and captain of the militia, and Nathan Baldwin, a saddler—because they were "great Talkers . . . and thinking Men" and because "there were no others in Town who were possessed of so much literature, Mr. Maccarty [the minister] and Mr. Putnam excepted." These "great Sticklers for Equality," Adams wrote in his autobiography, offered to sponsor Adams for the office of register of deeds. Since "the Chandler Family had engrossed almost all the public offices and Employment in the Town and County," Doolittle and Baldwin pleaded, "they wished to elect some Person qualified to share with them in these honors and Emoluments." But Adams declined: "My answer was that as the Chandlers were worthy people and discharged the Duties of their offices very well, I envied not their felicity and had no desire to sett myself in Opposition to them, and especially to Mr. Putnam who married a beautiful Daughter of that Family and had treated me with Civility and Kindness."[27] Doolittle and Baldwin had jumped the gun. The time was not quite ripe for an alternative to the Chandler dynasty in Worcester.

But after the Stamp Act crisis, conservative leaders like John Chandler became trapped by the contradiction of serving two masters: the people and the Crown. Every time one of the elite supported an unpopular British policy, he opened himself to criticism and ultimately condemnation by his constituents. Times were changing: people were beginning to voice their views on matters other than pigs and pews, to exercise their political rights as British citizens, and to use the powers granted them under the 1691 Massachusetts Charter.

Some men, Doolittle and Baldwin included, took steps to end the practice of patronage altogether. In 1766, when Ephraim Doolittle was elected to serve as Worcester's representative to the General Court, the town decided to instruct him with a strong political agenda (most likely drafted by his friend Nathan Baldwin):

- They called for an end to plural officeholding, stating in particular that nobody "holding any fee or military office whatsoever, especially Judges of the Superior Court, Judges of the Probate, Registers of Probate, Secretary, Clerk of either of the Courts, Sheriffs, or Province Treasurer, be chosen into his majesty's Council." This, in effect, would purge the Council of people like Chandler and Williams, who often held several of the offices enumerated.

- They suggested that "whenever any representative shall receive any office or commission from the Governor, he shall be dismissed from the house." A representative, they reasoned, was to serve the people who voted him into office, not the governor who granted him a commission.

- They pushed for open sessions of the General Court so people "may see and hear how affairs are conducted," and they urged the General Court to construct "a proper and convenient house" with room enough for spectators.

- They asked for "a new fee table" by which sheriffs and the various officers of the court received their recompense. The standard they suggested was a modest one: "neither more nor less than you would be willing to do the same service for yourself."

- Finally, they demanded "that a law be made to prevent bribery and corruption in the several towns in this province in the choice of representative." This might well have been aimed at John Murray of nearby Rutland, notorious for buying votes with liquor.[28]

The citizens of Worcester, in short, were calling for a sweeping reform of the governmental system. In their instructions to Doolittle they included two other measures: an end to excise taxes and tariffs (this would be the dominant theme of revolutionary politics over the next few years), and a repeal of the law requiring them to operate a Latin school (their children needed to learn "reading, writing, and arithmetic," not some dead language of no practical use for a farmer). The following year the town meeting added a new instruction: a call for the end of slavery. Again, this radical demand was targeted specifically at the elite, the only people in rural Massachusetts who owned any slaves.

In 1768 the British Parliament and the Crown, still intent on raising money from the colonies and protecting British industry, imposed a duty on goods exported to the colonies, such as glass, lead, paint, paper, and tea. This new wave of taxation, embodied in the Townshend Revenue Act, further fueled the political flames in Massachusetts. The House responded by discouraging British imports and encouraging home manufacture:

RESOLVED, that this house will use their utmost endeavors, and enforce their endeavors by example, in suppressing extravagance, idleness and vice, and in promoting industry, œconomy, and good morals in their respective towns.

And in order to prevent the unnecessary exportation of money, of which this province has of late been so much drain'd: It is further RESOLVED, that this house will, by all prudent

means, endeavor to discountenance the use of foreign super-
fluities, and to encourage the manufactures of this province.[29]

This was a hard program to oppose since it would simultaneously help
the balance of trade, force Parliament to take note of the colonists,
and encourage industry and moral fortitude on a personal level. Only
one of the eighty-two representatives voted against it: Timothy Ruggles, who feared that new local industries would hire farmhands and
thereby raise the price of agricultural labor.[30]

Various nonimportation agreements circulated among the citi-
zenry, with the signers pledging not to buy any goods from merchants
who peddled imported products. In Worcester, support for nonimportation was strong at the beginning, but it cooled when rumors, spread
by John Chandler among others, insinuated that the rich Boston merchants who initiated the agreements—men like John Hancock—were
smuggling contraband and hoarding imported goods to drive their
competitors out of business.[31]

In February 1768, the Massachusetts House of Representatives approved a circular letter, drafted by Samuel Adams and addressed to
the assemblies of each of the other colonies, which boldly declared
that the Townshend duties were unconstitutional. Since colonists
could not realistically be represented in Parliament, the letter argued,
they could not be taxed by it either.[32] Lord Hillsborough, England's
secretary of state for colonial affairs, took great offense. In February
he drafted his own circular letter to the royal governors, exhorting
them to press their respective assemblies "to take no notice" of the
original letter, thereby "treating it with the contempt it deserves."
Hillsborough also demanded that the Massachusetts House of Representatives rescind its letter, and he ordered Governor Bernard to dissolve the General Court if it failed to do so.[33]

The House voted 92 to 17 not to disavow its original letter. Within
patriot circles those who voted with the majority were eulogized and
the number "92" took on symbolic importance; the seventeen representatives who supported Hillsborough, on the other hand, became
demonized as "rescinders."[34] Of Worcester County's twelve repre-

sentatives, only Brigadier Ruggles voted to rescind. (Rutland's John
Murray was absent, perhaps by design, and John Chandler no longer
served in the House.) Four of the five representatives from the more
conservative Connecticut River Valley in Hampshire County (including Israel Williams) were rescinders, as were the two from Berkshire
County. These representatives, however, did not necessarily reflect
the views of their constituents. John Ashley, upon returning home,
was publicly rebuked by his neighbors in Great Barrington.[35]

The rift between so-called leaders and their constituents was
widening. After 1770 the people of Hardwick finally refused Timothy
Ruggles his perennial seat in the House. In Rutland, John Murray retained his seat, but no longer was he given free reign. Despite his "at-
tachment to the present measures of Administration," he was told by
his constituents, "you will make our Instructions the Rule of your
Conduct in Sd office."[36]

Political polarization subsided with the repeal of the Townshend
duties in 1770, but two years later the British administration provoked
a new wave of resistance when it decided that the salary of the governor would be paid by the Crown with money collected by customs
officials. Previously, the House of Representatives determined the
salary and paid the chief executive on an annual basis, thereby giving
the people a strong check against harsh or arbitrary rule; henceforth,
the governor would be responsible only to the British government on
the other side of the Atlantic, not to the people of Massachusetts. "An
INDEPENDENT ruler, a MONSTER in a free state," wrote March-
mont Nedham (John Adams) in the Boston Gazette, "rivet[s] the
chains of slavery."[37]

Worse yet, on September 28, 1772, the Boston Gazette reported that
the Crown had decided to pay the salaries of the chief justice of the
Superior Court (£400), the associate justices (£200), the attorney general (£150), and the solicitor general (£50). Everybody knew that
governors, in reality, did the bidding of kings, but judges, at least in
theory, were supposed to operate free of influence. Since colonial
judges served at the pleasure of the Crown, the only check the people
had on the Superior Court judges was through the local payment of

salaries.[38] Removal of this safeguard was an invitation to corruption. With no way of insuring judicial impartiality, the people of Massachusetts would be subject to arbitrary rulings and wicked designs on their property. This was "THE FINISHING STROKE," wrote "Oliver Cromwell" in the October 19 issue of the *Boston Gazette.* "[W]e are as compleat slaves as the inhabitants of Turkey or Japan."

Boston radicals—people like Samuel Adams, Joseph Warren, and Thomas Young, who had come to the fore as opponents to British imperial policy—capitalized on the moment. On November 2 the Boston Town Meeting appointed a Committee of Correspondence to write a letter to all 260 towns and districts in Massachusetts. The letter was "to state the Rights of the Colonists and of this Province in particular, as Men, as Christians, and as Subjects; to communicate and publish the same to the several Towns in this Province and to the World as the sense of this Town. . . . also requesting of each Town a free communication of their Sentiments on this Subject." [39] The committee, spearheaded by Samuel Adams, started drafting the document the next day. By the end of the month it had sent out the letter, popularly known as the "Boston Pamphlet," to the selectmen of each town and district in Massachusetts.

The Boston Pamphlet elucidated the many grievances the colonists harbored against their British rulers, in much the same manner as the Declaration of Independence a few years later, and it did so in flamboyant style: "Thus our houses and even our bed chambers, are exposed to be ransacked, our boxes, chests & trunks broke open, ravaged and plundered by wretches." Addressing the Crown's decision to pay judges' salaries from customs revenues, it prophesied doom: "We cannot, when we think on the depravity of mankind, avoid looking with horror on the danger to which we are exposed." [40]

How would the people in the rural hinterland, presumably less advanced in their thinking, respond to such rhetoric? Or would they bother to respond at all?

The returns soon flooded in: from at least 119 towns early in 1773 and from another 25 by the end of the summer. (There might well have been more, for the surviving minutes of the Boston Committee of Correspondence are not necessarily complete.) More towns responded to the Boston Pamphlet than sent representatives to the General Court.[41] Of the minority that failed to respond, most were small or recently organized communities with no representatives. A few, such as Springfield, seem to have been towns with conservative selectmen like John Worthington, who either suppressed the Boston Pamphlet or argued successfully against it.[42]

With just a handful of exceptions, the replies were favorable, even effusive. In their own words and their own style, the country folk matched or surpassed the passion of the Boston pamphleteers. "We seem to have a Solon or Lycurgus in every second or third town and district," commented one of the authors of the original pamphlet. In the words of historian Richard Bushman, "In the smallest town there was at least one individual who could discourse on the British Constitution even if he could not spell."[43]

The reply from Hubbardston, a small community in Worcester County with a total population of only 300, was typical. It started with a forthright declaration of Lockean principles:

> We are of the opinion that Rulers first Derive their Power from the Ruled by Certain Laws and Ruls agreed upon by Ruler and Ruled, and when a Ruler Breaks over Such Laws and Rules as agreed to by Ruler and Ruled and makes new ones that then the Ruled have a Right to Refuse Such new Laws and that the Ruled have a Right to Judge for themselves when Rulers Transgress.

The letter then complained that taxation by "Parliment" and the Crown's payment of judicial salaries "appears to us so big with Slavery that we think it enough to arouse Every Individual (that has any Ideas of arbitrary Power above the Brutal Creation) to use his utmost indeavors in a lawfull way to Seek Redress for our Injured Rights and Priveleges." The people, it concluded, had a right to resist "in the most firm, but the most peaceable manner."[44]

These letters demonstrated that discontent with imperial policies was not limited to Boston. People with influence in the towns, and possibly other citizens as well, cared deeply about issues of imperial policy. Men who had signed nonimportation agreements in response to the Stamp Act and Townshend Acts, or older men who had been active in the Land Bank controversy three decades before, were already primed for political action. The Boston Pamphlet presented them with an opportunity to voice their opinions.[45]

Even more important, the towns were ready to act. Almost half of those which responded established standing committees of correspondence—the beginnings of a revolutionary infrastructure which would facilitate the flow of information over the next few years. From now on, the people would be informed of all the latest developments in the rapidly unfolding political drama. In the words of historian Richard Bushman, "The network of activists meant that revolutionary language by 1773 was sounding in virtually every adult ear in Massachusetts, and that there was a fluid continuum of discourse joining the Boston press and town meeting and the talk in meetings and taverns throughout the Province." [46]

In the town of Worcester, forty-one men submitted a petition requesting that the Boston Pamphlet be presented at the annual town meeting in March 1773. "[A]fter Some Debate thereon," the motion to read the tract out loud "Passed in ye affirmative." We can only imagine what John Chandler, the moderator, thought of the inflammatory rhetoric, but we do know that most of the other men in attendance approved. They selected a committee of five to draft a response: former selectmen William Young, Samuel Curtis, and David Bancroft; a prominent merchant, Stephen Salisbury; and a blacksmith, Timothy Bigelow.

It was Timothy Bigelow, age forty-two at the time, who would soon hobknob with the Boston Whigs and lead his townsmen onto the battlefield. Bigelow came from a long line of artisan-farmers. His great-grandfather was a blacksmith with a large farm and "extensive tracts of land" as yet undeveloped; his father was a cordwainer and "substantial farmer"; his brother and uncle were carpenters; and his father-in-law, Samuel Andrews, was a prosperous tanner with a large house in town which eventually became the home of Timothy and his wife, Anna. Timothy was the fifth of six children, but one died in infancy and another was scalded to death at the age of three. He received no formal education beyond the district school, but he possessed a library and presumably discoursed in a knowledgeable fashion with men like Nathan Baldwin and Ephraim Doolittle. He was a man of moderate means: his thirteen acres and a blacksmith shop on Main Street were assessed in 1771 at £6 in annual worth of the whole real estate. (John Chandler, by contrast, possessed seven times this much in the town of Worcester alone. The mean annual worth in Worcester was £4.5, and the median £3. Bigelow was not among the top quarter in wealth, but he did claim two of Worcester's seventeen "servants for life.")[47]

Bigelow had served his town as one of six "Hogreaves" in 1763, one of two "Tything men" in 1766, one of eleven "Surveyors of Highways & Collectors of ye Highway Taxes" in 1769, and one of two "fence Viewers" (the other was his brother Daniel) in 1771.[48] His appointment to the letter-writing committee in 1773 would prove his major breakthrough into politics on a larger scale.

The task faced by Bigelow and his fellow committee members was to draft a reply strong enough to reflect the patriotic sentiments of the town's majority yet not so shrill as to alienate the conservative minority. They came up with a wordy document heavy in Whig philosophy but light in particulars. The letter commenced:

It is our opinion that mankind are by Nature free, and the End and Designe of forming Social compacts, and entering into civil Society, was that each member of that Society, might enjoy his liberty and property, and live in the free exercise of his Rights, both civil and Religious, which God and Nature gave; except such as are expresly given up by compact. This we apprehend to be the Scope of that noble System of Government, the English Constitution, The Great Wisdom in giving so just a ballance of Power, through all its parts, very justly excites admiration: and when we apprehend a Designe to overthrow the Same in one part by any person or persons, (by Distroying Dependance of one of the Community, on the other, and Substituting, in its room, a crafty, or political Dependance, the former being as much Superior to the Crafty Designes of wicked corrupt plunderers of mankind) it is our duty, to exert ourselves against it to the utmost of our power for by Nature, and the Charter of this Province, we are intitled to all the Rights, and privelages, of the above Constitutions, as though we were born within the Realm of England: and it is . . .[49]

So it continued in a similar vein, almost two thousand words in scarcely a dozen sentences. The handful of specific complaints dealt only with the troubles in Boston. At the May meeting the draft was approved with no record of debate or dissent. Worcester's Tories seemed to have held their tongues, outvoted but not overly distressed by the proceedings. Patriots had been mouthing off at British policies for years. For the moment, there was no reason to suppose that the letter to Boston would result in any significant harm.

But the response to the Boston Pamphlet was only the beginning. To stay abreast of the growing crisis, the town meeting appointed Timothy Bigelow, William Young, and John Smith to serve as a standing committee of correspondence.[50] The sanctioning of a committee to communicate with radicals in other areas was of more lasting significance than the letter itself. Surely this must have rankled local Tories—and there were many of them, albeit not enough to constitute a majority. While most towns in the county had but few members of the officeholding elite, Worcester, the shiretown, was home to a significant number of powerful men. There was John Chandler IV and his fifteen offspring; John's brother Gardiner, the high sheriff, with his six offspring; Timothy Paine, with his ten offspring; James Putnam, the influential attorney who had taught law to John Adams; and others.[51] These people were not about to surrender to upstart radicals who threatened traditional hierarchies by challenging British rule. If Chandler and company did not yet fight back in public, they grumbled among themselves. Dr. William Paine, one of Timothy's sons and John Chandler's nephews, confided to a friend that the radicals in

Worcester were "Devils" and a "Sett of Cussed Venal Worthless Raskalls." [52] Such feelings were doubtless shared by others. An ugly cleavage in the community of Worcester, barely concealed under a veil of civility, awaited only a precipitating event to tear the town apart.

When news of the Boston Tea Party reached Worcester during the third week of December 1773, local patriots began to prepare for the next stage in the escalating confrontation. On the afternoon of December 27, Timothy Bigelow, his cousin Joshua Bigelow, fellow members of the committee of correspondence John Smith and William Young, his friend Nathan Baldwin, and more than two dozen others met at the home of Asa Ward to found the American Political Society (APS). (Baldwin's associate Ephraim Doolittle had recently moved to Petersham.) As a private political club, the APS would not have to measure its words to meet the approval of the sizable Tory minority at the town meeting. It was free to organize, inflame, and even prepare for war.

Joshua Bigelow, the town's representative to the General Court for the previous seven years, was elected APS chairman, and Timothy Bigelow, Nathan Baldwin, and Samuel Curtis were assigned the task of drafting a code of rules and regulations. On January 3, 1774, the group presented its draft to the overall membership, which the body adopted. In the preamble, the members spelled out their reason for coming together: to oppose "the machinations of some designing persons in this Province, who are grasping at power, and the property of their neighbors." These "designing persons" created a problem not just for "the good people of this country in general," but for "the town of Worcester in particular." [53]

Clearly, in the minds of the Worcester radicals, the "enemy" was not just the British Parliament on the other side of the Atlantic. The enemy was also at home, right there in Worcester County: creditors such as John Chandler and John Murray, lawyers such as James Putnam, and judges such as Timothy Ruggles, who presided over the Inferior Court of Common Pleas. Working in concert, these powerful men posed a threat to the property of small farmers and artisans. To counter this threat, the rules and regulations required that members of the American Political Society bypass the legal system and "avoid all law suits with all men." Any disputes arising between members of the Society were to be submitted to arbitration, and anyone failing to abide by this measure would be expelled. This in fact was the second rule listed, preceded only by a pledge of secrecy.

The membership of the American Political Society soon grew to seventy-one. Members pledged to meet once a month, with a sixpence fine for unexcused absences. They agreed to limit monthly meetings to four hours, although there was no time limitation for quarterly meetings. They also agreed "that in all and every of our monthly meetings, our expenses for liquor, &c., shall not exceed sixpence per man upon an average, and in our quarterly meeting, it shall not exceed two shillings per man." These men might drink, but not to excess: they had important business to attend to.

During its brief existence, the American Political Society exerted a powerful influence on politics in Worcester. Its members could be counted upon to show up at every town meeting, effectively ensuring a majority. It placed items on the agenda and determined the actions the town meeting was to take. As the majority caucus, it more or less ran the town.

At the annual town meeting held on March 7, 1774, the citizens of Worcester chose three members of the American Political Society, plus Timothy Paine, to serve as selectmen. The inclusion of Paine, a moderate among the elite, was no doubt a show of nonpartisanship. Even so, there could be no doubt that this was a new day in Worcester: for the first time in twenty-six years, John Chandler was not among the selectmen.

Responding to "a Request of Twenty-seven of the Freeholders and other inhabitants," the town at this time addressed the two most pressing issues facing the people of Massachusetts: the tax on tea and the Crown's payment of executive and judicial salaries. Timothy Bigelow, William Young, and Josiah Pierce drafted a strongly worded statement, which the meeting approved by a narrow margin. In it, the

town resolved not to purchase imported tea and also promoted a sec-
ondary boycott: anybody who sold contraband tea, the citizens declared, had "justly merited our Indignation, and Contempt, and must
be considered, and treated by us, as enimys and trators to their Country."[54] The statement attacked the Crown's payment of judicial
salaries in equally forceful terms:

> [T]o have these who are to judge, and Determin, on our lives,
> property, paid by a foreign State, immediately Destroy, that nat-
> ural dependance which ought to Subsist between a people, and
> their officers, and of consequence, destructive of liberty: For
> which reason, we are of the opinion, that we are not in the least
> bound in duty to Submit, to the ordering and Determining of
> Such officers as not dependent on the Grants of this people for
> their pay.[55]

These provocative words proved too much for some of the local
Tories to bear. Were merchants who sold tea and other goods to be
considered "enimys" and "trators"? Were the people of Worcester
about to resist orders issued by the courts? According to local folklore, attorney James Putnam, John Chandler's brother-in-law, carried
the standard for the opposition, but the blacksmith Timothy Bigelow
successfully opposed him. Eighty-six years later, local historian
Charles Hersey, who had listened to the tales of aging revolutionaries
when he was a young man, wrote of the incident:

> "When these resolutions were read," said an eye witness of the
> scene to the writer, ". . . the tories were pale with rage." After a
> few moments, James Putnam, the leader of the tories, arose.
> Putnam was said to be "the best lawyer in North America. His
> arguments were marked by strong and clear reasoning, logical
> precision and arrangement, and that sound judgment whose
> conclusions were presented so forcibly as to command assent."
> He made such a speech against the resolutions as had never be-
> fore been heard in Worcester; and when he sat down, the same

informant said that "not a man of the whig party thought a single word could be said,—and that old Putnam, the tory, had wiped them all out." Timothy Bigelow at length arose, without learning, without practice in public speaking, without wealth,— the tories of Worcester had, at that day, most of the wealth and learning,—but there he stood upon the floor of the Old South Church, met the Goliath of the day, and vanquished him.[56]

James Putnam was not willing to concede defeat. He and twenty-five others, including John Chandler and Dr. William Paine, signed a "desent & Protest." (Timothy Paine, moderator of the March meeting, was not among the signatories.) This was the first time the town records of Worcester indicated a dissent on any issue. As the patriots increased their rhetoric, the Tories of Worcester began to organize a cohesive opposition, a counterweight to the American Political Society.

Locally, the issue of judicial salaries came to a head on April 19, the date the Superior Court was slated to convene in Worcester. Feeling intense pressure from people throughout the province, four of the five Superior Court judges had already refused "the bribe offered them by the Crown," to use the words of the Worcester town meeting. Only Peter Oliver, the chief justice, said he would accept payment from the Crown under the new law. The Massachusetts House of Representatives had impeached Chief Justice Oliver a month before the Worcester annual meeting, but before Oliver could be tried by the Council, Thomas Hutchinson, now the governor, had dissolved the General Court. The impeachment was left hanging.

This impeachment drama would soon be played out in Worcester. If Peter Oliver showed up at Superior Court on April 19, local activists vowed they would shut the court down. This they could do, for much of the court's business required the participation of local grand jurors. On April 4 the American Political Society instructed Joshua and Timothy Bigelow to refuse to serve as grand jurors if the chief justice sat on the bench "before he is lawfully tried and acquitted from the high crimes and charges for which he now stands impeached." If the Bigelows were fined for their refusal to answer the summons, the Society agreed to pay their fines.[57]

On April 19, Joshua and Timothy Bigelow, Ephraim Doolittle from Petersham, and a dozen other grand jurors from Worcester County arrived at the courthouse with a prepared statement: "[W]e apprehend it would be highly injurious," they announced, "to subject a fellow countryman to trial at a bar, where one of the judges is not only disqualified, . . . but . . . stands convicted, in the minds of the people, of a crime more heinous, in all probability, than any that might come before him."[58] The jurors declared they would not serve if Oliver showed up. But when the sheriff reported that the chief justice had failed to meet him on the outskirts of town, as was the custom, and when the other judges told the court they doubted Oliver would show up, the grand jurors agreed to serve. They had made their point— they had kept the chief justice for the province of Massachusetts from showing up for work.[59]

At the regularly scheduled town meeting the following month, the chasm between local Whigs and Tories deepened. Not everybody wanted this to happen. When the meeting convened on May 16, the majority of citizens chose John Chandler, now in the minority, to serve as moderator—just as he had done so many times in the past. Chandler consented, an indication that the tear in Worcester society was not yet beyond repair. John Chandler also continued to be entrusted with the job of town treasurer, while his son Clark still served as town clerk.

The main item on the agenda was to issue instructions to Joshua Bigelow, the man they chose to represent them at the General Court. Six of the seven members of the committee charged with preparing the draft of the instructions belonged to the American Political Society: Timothy Bigelow, Samuel Curtis, Josiah Pierce, Edward Crafts, John Kelso, and Joshua Whitney. The seventh, merchant Stephen Salisbury, was a moderate Whig.[60] Needless to say, the document they reported out to the body of the whole on May 20 reflected the sentiments of the town radicals, with nary a nod to the concerns of conservatives. It decried the recent closure of the Boston port, and it directed Joshua

Bigelow "that whatever measures great Britain may take to Distress us . . . you be not in the least Intimidated . . . But to the utmost of your power Resist the most Distant approaches of Slavery." It issued "the Streckest Injunction" not to approve compensation for the tea dumped into the Boston harbor; it told him to use his "utmost Endeavors" to convene "a general Congress" of the committees of correspondence from throughout the colonies; it urged him to pursue the impeachment of Chief Justice Oliver to its conclusion.[61]

The Tory minority aggressively pursued its opposition to this draft, led once again by James Putnam. When it came time to vote, however, Timothy Bigelow and the American Political Society still prevailed: the instructions were adopted without alteration.

But Putnam, along with William Paine, did not let the matter rest. Immediately following adjournment, Putnam and Paine gathered forty-three signatures on a petition that called for a special town meeting to reconsider the previous votes. The good people of "many Towns & Places within the Province," the petition claimed, had been "so far seduced" by the "artfull Practices" of the so-called patriots of Boston "that they have unwarrantably adopted measures Subversive of publick Liberty and the good order of the State." Specifically, it stated that "at the annual meeting in Worcester in march last certain resolves were passed, and Voted to be Entered on the Records of the Town of Worcester against the Express will and opinion of the respectable Inhabitants of the Town then assembled, and had not the members of the Comittee themselves who made or copied these resolves Voted for their being accepted and recorded there would have been a majority of the Town against the acceptance of them." (The insinuation that the resolves had been "copied" was a particularly nasty dig at local radicals, who were presumed to do the bidding of more learned leaders in Boston.) The petitioners also objected to the town's sponsorship of the committee of correspondence, and they demanded at the very least that the proceedings of this quasi-public body be made available for all to see.[62]

By law, the selectmen were required to honor this petition and call a special town meeting. And so it was, on June 20, that both sides mustered their forces for a final showdown. Although Putnam and William Paine had gathered every "friend of government" they could, there were simply not enough of them in Worcester. Once more the radicals prevailed.

Outvoted, the Tories drafted a dissent which they hoped to register in the town record. When the patriot majority denied them this courtesy, Clark Chandler, the town clerk, entered the dissent in the record nonetheless. This Tory "Protest," as it came to be called, also found its way into the Boston newspapers, much to the chagrin of the patriots. The tone of the Protest was bitter indeed:

> We, . . . thinking it our indispensable duty, in these times of discord and confusion in too many of the towns within this Province, to bear testimony in the most open and unreserved manner against all riotous, disorderly and seditious practices, must therefore now declare, that it is with the deepest concern for public peace and order, that we behold so many whom we used to esteem sober, peaceable men, so far deceived, deluded and led astray, by the artful, crafty and insidious practices of some evil-minded and ill-disposed persons, who, under the disguise of patriotism, and falsely styling themselves the friends of liberty, some of them neglecting their own proper business and occupation, in which they ought to be employed for the support of their families, spending their time in discoursing of matters they do not understand, raising and propagating falsehoods and calumnies of those men they look up to with envy, and on whose fall and ruin they wish to rise, intend to reduce all things to a state of tumult, discord and confusion. . . .
>
> [A]s it appears to us that many of this town seem led by strange opinions, and . . . as the town has refused to dismiss the persons styling themselves the Committee of Correspondence for the town, and has also refused so much as to call on them to render an account of their past dark and pernicious proceedings:
>
> We therefore, whose names are hereunto Subscribed, do each of us declare and protest, it is our firm opinion, that the Com-

mittees of Correspondence in the several towns of this Province, being creatures of modern invention, and constituted as they be, are a legal grievance, having no legal foundation, contrived by a junto to serve particular designs and purposes of their own, and that they . . . are a nuisance. . . .

It is by these committees . . . that papers have been lately published, and are now circulating through the Province, inviting and wickedly tempting all persons to join them, fully implying, if not expressly denouncing the destruction of all that refuse to subscribe those unlawful combinations, tending directly to sedition, civil war and rebellion.

These and all such enormities, we detest and abhor, and the authors of them we esteem enemies to our King and country, violators of all law and civil liberty, the malevolent disturbers of the peace of society, subverters of the established constitution, and enemies of mankind.[63]

Fifty-two inhabitants of Worcester—the "Protestors," as they would be called—affixed their names to these vitriolic words. (In a town with fewer than 250 eligible voters, this constituted a sizable minority.) Worcester was more divided than ever. By the early summer of 1774, it seemed unlikely that conservatives such as James Putnam, William Paine, John Chandler, and the rest of the Protestors would ever settle their differences with radicals Timothy Bigelow, Joshua Bigelow, Nathan Baldwin, and other members of the American Political Society. With compromise out of the question, the only resolution was for one side or the other to prevail.

In May 1774, two momentous events widened the political schism in Massachusetts even further: first, news arrived that Parliament, under the advice of the British ministry, had decided to punish the colonists for the Tea Party by closing the port of Boston, and second, a new governor took the reins of government.

The Port Bill, effective June 1, was expected to lead Massachusetts into dire straits, and the arrival of the new governor signaled trouble as well. There had been no love lost between the patriot majority and the old governor, Thomas Hutchinson, particularly following the publication of letters sent to London in which Hutchinson stated that "government had been too long in the hands of the people in Massachusetts" and urged "an abridgement of what are called English liberties." But the patriots had a serious problem with Hutchinson's replacement, General Thomas Gage, even before his arrival, for Gage served also as commander-in-chief of the British armed forces in North America. Did this presage an end to civil government?

Immediately upon hearing that the port was to be closed, the Boston Committee of Correspondence sent out another circular letter to the towns of Massachusetts, and to the other colonies as well.[64] Again, many towns responded by echoing the rage of the Boston committee and by offering support to the beleaguered people of Massachusetts' major city. Citizens of Leicester argued that if the Crown claimed "the right to dispose of private property" by closing the port of Boston, it might also prohibit "any town or husbandman from sowing grain, mowing grass, and feeding his pastures, so long as his majesty thinks proper."[65] Chelmsford respondents wrote: "It is the opinion of this Town, that the Present Day is as Dark and Distressing a Day as this Country ever experienced. . . . [T]he Question is, wether we Submit to the arbitrary, lawless, tyrannical will of a minister, or by using those Powers given us by the god of nature, . . . prevent So awful a Catastrophe."[66] These sentiments were expressed less formally in public houses scattered throughout the countryside. John Adams recalled a conversation he overheard while passing the night at a Shrewsbury inn during this time:

> [A]s I was cold and wet, I sat down at a good fire in the bar-room to dry my great coat and saddle-bags till a fire could be made in my chamber. There presently came in, one after another, half a dozen, or half a score, substantial yeomen of the neighborhood, who, sitting down to the fire after lighting their pipes, began a lively conversation upon politics. As I believed I was unknown to all of them, I sat in total silence to hear them.

One said, "The people of Boston are distracted!"

Another answered, "No wonder the people of Boston are distracted. Oppression will make wise men mad."

A third said, "What would you say, if a fellow should come to your house and tell you he was come to take a list of your cattle, that parliament might tax you for them at so much a head? And how should you feel, if he was to go and break open your barn, to take down your oxen, cows, horses, and sheep?"

"What I should say," replied the first; "I would knock him in the head."

"Well," said a fourth, "if parliament can take away Mr. Hancock's wharf and Mr. Rowe's wharf, they can take away your barn and my house."

After much more reasoning in this style, a fifth, who had as yet been silent, broke out, "Well, it is high time for us to rebel; we must rebel some time or other, and we had better rebel now than at any time to come. If we put it off for ten or twenty years, and let them go on as they have begun, they will get a strong party among us, and plague us a great deal more than they can now." [67]

This was tavern talk. Most of the country people were not actually ready to rebel, but many did sign a strongly worded boycott agreement called a Solemn League and Covenant. (There were actually two versions, one written by the Boston committee and the other by the Worcester committee.) [68] Boycotts had worked twice in the past, forcing the repeal of both the Stamp Act and the Townshend Acts. This time the stakes seemed higher, but the old tools were brought back into play. Perhaps, the people reasoned, economic pressure could force Parliament to reopen the port.

Governor Gage, like the Port Bill, was not well received. There would be no honeymoon between the commander-in-chief of the army which occupied Boston and the patriots who controlled the General Court. Gage's first act as governor was to reject thirteen of the twenty-eight men whom the House had selected to serve on the

Council.[69] The remaining members of the Council responded with a "welcoming" address which was not very welcoming. The Council suggested to Gage that "your Administration in the Principles and general Conduct of it, may be a happy Contrast to that of your two immediate Predecessors," and they went on to blame "the Disunion between Britain and the Colonies" exclusively on the "Machinations" of former governors.[70] Gage offered a terse response:

> Gentlemen of the Council,
> I cannot receive an Address which contains indecent Reflections on my Predecessors. . . . I consider this Address as an Insult upon his Majesty and the Lords of his Privy-Council, and an Affront to myself.
> T. GAGE [71]

The General Court proceeded with its business: it called for towns to come to the relief of Boston, it endorsed the boycott of tea, and, most significantly, it elected representatives to a Continental Congress, slated to meet at the end of the summer in Philadelphia. The new governor correctly perceived that the patriot-dominated General Court could do him no good, and it might do him much harm. On June 17, the day the House selected delegates to the Continental Congress, Gage dissolved the General Court—or at least he tried to:

> His Excellency the Governor, having directed the Secretary to acquaint the two Houses [the House of Representatives and the Council] it was his Excellency's pleasure the General Assembly should be dissolved and to declare the same dissolved accordingly; the Secretary went to the Court House and finding the Door of the Representatives Chamber locked, directed the Messenger to go in and acquaint the Speaker that the Secretary had a Message from his Excellency to the Hon. House, and desired he might be admitted to deliver it; the Messenger returned, and said he had acquainted the Speaker therewith, who mentioned it to the House, and their Orders were to keep the Door fast.[72]

The secretary posted the notice on the outside of the door, but the men within continued to meet. Legally, the General Court was dissolved; in practice, patriots during the summer and fall of 1774 would meet with each other in town meetings, committees of correspondence, county conventions, and eventually a Provincial Congress—and no Crown-appointed governor could stop them.

On the surface, Gage's rejecting of council members and his dissolution of the General Court might appear as rash and arbitrary acts which directly precipitated the Revolution. But we need to place his actions in context: governors in Massachusetts and other colonies had been vetoing council-member appointments and dissolving assemblies throughout the late colonial era.[73] To some extent, this was politics as usual. It was not the dissolution of the General Court that triggered the Revolution, nor was it the oft-cited Boston Port Bill. The people of Massachusetts—not just the political leaders and patriotic activists who had been writing letters and petitions—were about to rise up and rebel because of a lesser-known bill which, if enforced, would deprive them of any effective voice in their government.

On June 6, 1774, the *Boston Gazette* published the full texts of two acts recently passed by Parliament. The first, entitled *A Bill for the impartial Administration of Justice in the Cases of Persons questioned for any Acts done by them in the Execution of the Law, or for the Suppression of Riots and Tumults, in the Province of the Massachusetts-Bay in New England,* stated that no officer of the Crown would have to stand trial in Massachusetts for murders committed in the line of duty. If soldiers fired into crowds of rioters, as they did in the Boston Massacre, they would not be subjected to local juries who might take offense with their actions. Its opponents called this "The Murder Act," since it appeared to sanction the killing of civilians.

The second act, *A Bill for the better regulating the Government of the Province of the Massachusetts-Bay in North America,* was far more sweeping in scope. There were four key provisions:

- All judges, justices of the peace, sheriffs, marshals, and other officers of the courts would be appointed by the governor,

without the consent of the Council, and would serve at his
pleasure alone. Previously, with the approval of the Council
required for all appointments and dismissals, the people had
some check on the judiciary and the machinery of law
enforcement. Now, they would have none. The governor was
free to appoint whomever he wanted. Patronage could easily
run rampant. Without any recourse, the people might well be
sucked dry by corrupt officials.

• The Council—the upper branch of the legislature, advisor
  to the governor, and in many ways the administrator of
  the law—would henceforth be appointed directly by the
  Crown, to serve at his pleasure. Previously, councilors had
  been elected each year by a joint meeting of the incoming
  representatives in the House and the outgoing Council.
  Since the people chose their representatives, they had
  considerable say in the make-up of the Council as well. Now,
  they would have no say whatsoever. And since the governor
  was no longer dependent on elected representatives for his
  salary, two of the three arms of the General Court had no
  reason at all to pay the least credence to the will of the
  people.

• Each agenda item at every town meeting in Massachusetts
  would have to be submitted in writing to the governor and
  meet with his approval. The people could elect their town
  officials in March, and they would be permitted to meet one
  more time to choose their representative, but beyond these,
  no meeting could be called without the prior consent of the
  governor. Needless to say, there would be no more
  declarations about rights and liberties, no more committees
  of correspondence, no more boycotts or provocative
  measures of any kind. In fact, people would be effectively
  barred from even talking about these things at town
  meetings.

- All jurors would be appointed by the sheriffs, who were themselves appointed by the governor. Under the old system, jurors were chosen from a list that the towns themselves provided; in the future, ordinary farmers and artisans would have no say at all in selecting the men who could seize their property or send them to jail. Once the new law was in effect, all jurors might be selected from among the propertied elite, men who would not hesitate to deal harshly with those who had fallen into debt.[74]

All this was in direct contradiction to the 1691 charter. The Massachusetts Government Act (often called simply "the Act") went far beyond the "better regulation" of the government and disenfranchised the citizens of Massachusetts. Yes, they could elect town officers—but if they wanted to decide whether the hogs could roam free, they would have to consult the governor. Yes, they could still vote for their representatives—but these men no longer had any control over the actions of governmental officials (judges, justices of the peace, sheriffs) who had the power to alter the lives of ordinary people. Nor did representatives have the least bit of influence with the governor or his councilors. And if the people didn't like any of this, they could say nothing about it in their town meetings.

Patriots in Massachusetts had been sparring with royal officials for almost a decade, but prior to the Act, the resistance had always been centered in Boston. Conservatives had contended that discontent was a localized phenomenon: it was the Boston "mob," led by Samuel Adams and the Boston "faction," that accounted for the Stamp Act riots, the skirmishes with soldiers culminating in the Boston Massacre, and the Boston Tea Party. The Boston Committee of Correspondence had sent out letters to the towns, and the towns had fallen into line behind the leadership in the colony's queen city. Since the problem could thus be easily pinpointed, according the conservative perception, it might be contained and eventually eradicated.

Not so any more. The passage of the Massachusetts Government Act affected every man who could vote in every town in the province, from Cape Cod to the Berkshires. In rural areas such as Worcester, where an overwhelming plurality of adult males possessed the right to vote, the threat of disenfranchisement provoked an unparalleled reaction. In the summer of 1774, the focus of the rebellion shifted suddenly from the metropolis to the countryside.

In the sharply divided town of Worcester, the Act proved the decisive factor in determining which party would prevail. In March, patriots had won a key vote at the town meeting by only a slim margin, and in May, James Putnam, an astute politician, thought he could muster enough votes to reverse the patriots' victory.[75] By the end of the summer, however, the handful of Tory holdouts in Worcester would be massively outnumbered and publicly humiliated. Local farmers might have been divided as to whether it was proper for the men in Boston to dump tea into the water, but there was no debating the evils of the Massachusetts Government Act. No rational man—not even James Putnam—could maintain that the Act boded well for the people of Worcester. It took little prodding for common farmers and artisans to see that their freedom was on the line.

And so it went throughout the province. Even in Springfield, the conservative stronghold of John Worthington, people took notice of the ominous turn of events. At the town meeting of July 12, citizens declared they should not be "dissiez'd of our Property, or any way Punish'd, without the judgment of our Peers." They voiced this concern twice, a clear indication that the new method of choosing juries bothered them. Three times they referred to their "Sacred" charter, which had been superceded by the Act. They declared that "the propos'd new System of Government, Virtually Annihilating our most Essential Charter Rights, added to the Boston Port Act, gives us such apprehensions of the designs of Administration against our Liberties, as we have never before allowed ourselves to entertain."

Indeed, this was the first time the town of Springfield, as a body, registered anything resembling patriotic sympathies. Worthington and the conservatives did manage to get the meeting to express "great deference and respect" to "the wisdom of the British Parliament" and to oppose any "Insult upon that respectable body," but these words, included in the interests of compromise, could not mask the fact that political sentiments in Springfield were shifting toward the radicals. River gods such as John Worthington and Israel Williams had hitherto been able to keep a lid on rebellious actions or pronouncements in much of the Connecticut River Valley, but even men such as these did not have the power to convince the people that the Massachusetts Government Act would do no harm.[76]

Increasingly during the summer of 1774, staunch Tories throughout the Massachusetts countryside felt themselves isolated. The Act had rendered their position untenable. Their basic principle, obedience to government, could now be construed only as *blind* obedience, and few men who did not have vested interests with the Crown were willing to defer so totally.

Men who had once wielded power lost even the power to influence. Governor Thomas Gage, commander-in-chief of the North American forces and nominally the most powerful Englishman in the Western Hemisphere, found that few would abide by his pronouncements. On June 29 he tried to outlaw the Solemn League and Covenant, ordering magistrates "to apprehend and secure for Trial, all and every Person who may hereafter presume to publish, or offer to others to be signed, or shall themselves sign the aforesaid, or a similar Covenant."[77] Did Gage truly think this order would lead to arrests and convictions? If so, he wasn't paying close enough attention.

But what else could he do to stem the tide? Short of calling forth the army, he could do little more than issue declarations. On July 21, ten days before the Act was to take effect, he tried to appeal to the religious sentiments of the people:

MASSACHUSETTS-BAY

By the GOVERNOR

A PROCLAMATION

For the Encouragement of Piety and Virtue, and for preventing and punishing of Vice, Profanity and Immorality.

In humble Imitation of the laudable example of our most gracious Sovereign GEORGE the Third, who in the first Year of his Reign was pleased to issue his Royal Proclamation for the Encouragement of Piety and Virtue, and for preventing of Vice and Immorality, in which he declares his Royal Purpose to punish all Persons guilty thereof; and upon all Occasions to bestow Marks of his Royal Favour on Persons distinguished for their Piety and Virtue:

I therefore, by and with the advice of his Majesty's council, publish this Proclamation, exhorting all his Majesty's Subjects to avoid all Hypocrisy, Sedition, Licentiousness, and all other Immoralities, and to have a grateful Sense of all God's Mercies, making the divine Laws the Rule of their Conduct.

I therefore, command all Judges, Justices, Sheriffs, and other officers, to use their utmost Endeavors to enforce the Laws for promoting Religion and Virtue, and restraining all Vice and Sedition; and I earnestly recommend to all Ministers of the Gospel that they be vigilant and active in inculcating a due Submission to the Laws of God and Man: and I exhort all the People of this Province, by every Means in their Power, to contribute what they can towards a general Reformation of Manners, Restitution of Peace and good Order, and a proper subjection to the Laws, as they expect the Blessing of Heaven.[78]

This one last plea for the people to behave themselves was all the governor of Massachusetts could muster, and he had no good reason to suppose that his words would make a difference.

Privately, Gage expressed great concern. In a letter to Lord Dartmouth, Lord Hillsborough's replacement as secretary of state for the colonies, he did not exude the confidence of a commander-in-chief. He suggested the Act would serve as "a Kind of Test of People's Conduct," and he anticipated significant problems in trying to implement it. "I imagine they propose to intimidate the new Counsellors from accepting their Commissions," he warned. Even worse, he reported that the "staunch Friends of Government" were already so intimidated by "their Opponents and their Mobs" that they exhibited "Timidity and Backwardness."[79]

As well they should, for an overwhelming majority of the people of Massachusetts were greatly enraged. Tory fears were certainly well-founded. There was no telling how far angry farmers might go after August 1, the day the Massachusetts Government Act was scheduled to take effect.

PART 2

THE REVOLUTION OF 1774

3

INTIMIDATION

On August 6, 1774, Governor Gage received his official instructions to implement the provisions of the Massachusetts Government Act. The king had chosen thirty-six men to sit on the Council—"mandamus counsellors" they were called at the time, since they derived their authority from an official writ of the Crown. Only three of the thirty-six had been elected to the 1774 Council, recently dissolved. Fourteen others were former councilors who had been deposed because of their conservative political orientation.[1] By selecting men whom the people had specifically rejected, the Crown was directly repudiating the electoral process established by the 1691 charter. This would quickly backfire.

Four of the "mandamus counsellors" came from Worcester County. Three of these—Timothy Paine, John Murray, and Abijah Willard—were brothers-in-law to John Chandler and partners in land speculation.[2] (It remains unclear why the king overlooked Chandler himself.) The fourth was Brigadier Timothy Ruggles, perhaps the most notorious Tory in the province outside of Boston.

Two of the councilors were prominent "river gods" from Hampshire County—John Worthington and Israel Williams—while no councilors were appointed from Berkshire County. The three western counties, accounting for over half the contiguous area of Massachusetts, would be represented on the Council by six members of the conservative elite.

Governor Gage wasted no time in trying to put the Act into effect. On Sunday, August 7, he ignored the Sabbath and sent messages to each of the newly appointed councilors, summoning them to Salem the following morning. The sooner they signed on, Gage must have reasoned, the less likely they would be to succumb to pressure exerted by the patriots.

Only eleven of the thirty-six showed up to take their oaths on Monday—a less than overwhelming demonstration of support. According to John Andrews, an astute political observer, three more accepted but for some reason were not sworn in, while two declined and four others "took time to consider of it." The remaining sixteen, "being at a distance about the country," could not be notified in time.[3] In name at least, a new Council had been formed—albeit with minimal participation. Governor Gage had implemented the first provision of the Act.

The patriots of Worcester County, like Governor Gage, responded immediately to the arrival of the Act. On Tuesday, August 9, 1774, fifty-two members of the committees of correspondence from twenty-two towns assembled hastily at Mary Stearns' tavern in Worcester, across Main Street and a few up down from the meeting house. (Mary's husband, Thomas, had recently died, but Mary continued to run the business on her own.)[4]

The meeting opened, as all gatherings did, with a "solemn prayer." A committee was appointed to count the votes, and elections were held for chairman and clerk. (As with town meetings, committees of correspondence had no permanent chairmen.) A committee of ten was then appointed to draw up resolutions. Timothy Bigelow, Joshua Bigelow, and John Smith from the town of Worcester, along with Ephraim Doolittle, Joseph Henshaw, Samuel Ward, Luke Drury, Edward Rawson, Paul Mandell, and Jonathan Holman from other towns, left the meeting room to draft resolutions and letters, while the rest of the men talked politics and drank rum. (Unlike the meetings of the

American Political Society, this gathering imposed no limits on alcohol consumption. "I retail'd a whole barrel [of rum] yesterday," wrote the storekeeper Stephen Salisbury on August 10. "Such is the Demand.")[5]

That afternoon the committee presented its drafts. The delegates discussed, debated, and fine-tuned the various resolutions, but they took no action during the opening day of the convention. The stakes were too high to transact business without full consideration.

The meeting reconvened at widow Mary Stearns' tavern the following morning at 7 o'clock—a common starting time for these farmers, who rose early. The delegates first approved two letters: one addressed to the Massachusetts delegates to the Continental Congress, "to inform them of the sense of the county respecting our public affairs," and the other to the committees of correspondence in Worcester County which were not represented at the current meeting. "Since all that is valuable in this life is at stake," they wrote, "the united wisdom and aid of the whole are wanting, to oppose the torrent of tyranny rushing upon us." At the next county convention, to be held three weeks later, they hoped all the towns would send delegates.

After discussing the current crisis formally within the meeting and informally the previous evening, the delegates voted on their resolutions. Each item was considered separately, and each passed unanimously. These resolutions, a tightly reasoned application of Lockean principles, opened with the traditional pledge of loyalty to the king, but the patriots of Worcester County were quick to qualify the extent of their allegiance:

> Resolved, That we bear all true allegiance to his majesty king George the third, and that we will, to the utmost of our power, defend his person, crown, and dignity, but at the same time, we disclaim any jurisdiction in the commons of Great Britain over his majesty's subjects in America.

Next, they observed that the contractual obligations existing between themselves and the king were based on the 1691 charter, in which the king promised "to protect and defend us, his American subjects, in the free will and full enjoyment of each and every right and liberty enjoyed by his subjects in Great Britain." But if the contract between themselves and the Crown were ever to be broken, they reasoned, both parties would be freed from its obligations. The consequences were monumental:

> Resolved, that an attempt to vacate said charter, by either party, without the consent of the other, has a tendency to dissolve the union between Great Britain and this province, to destroy the allegiance we owe to the king, and to set aside the sacred obligations he is under to his subjects here.

The Massachusetts Government Act, by unilaterally revoking the 1691 charter, constituted "a great and high-handed claim of arbitrary power" which absolved the colonists of any further obligations to Great Britain. Instead, they concluded, the people of Massachusetts had an obligation only to themselves:

> Resolved, that it is the indisputable duty of every American, and more especially in this province, to unite in every virtuous opposition that can be devised, in order to save ourselves and posterity from inevitable ruin.

It was a powerful argument, to be repeated countless times throughout Massachusetts in the following months. Almost two years later, Thomas Jefferson would use identical reasoning in the Declaration of Independence.

But the implication was frightening: a total break with Great Britain. Less than two months later, the town meeting of Worcester would be able to embrace this logic and advocate independence, but for now, this Worcester County Convention came up a bit short. The only "virtuous oppositions" they could conjure up were the nonconsumption of British goods and a censure of the local judges who had offered a favorable address to Governor Gage. A weak climax, after such a strong start.

Even if they failed for the moment to embrace the full extent of their own argument, and even if they proved less than creative in their tactical suggestions, these patriots did point in a direction with profound revolutionary consequences. Opposition, they said, would have to start at the town level and include the whole body of the people, not just fifty-two political activists gathered at Mary Stearns' tavern:

> Voted, That we most earnestly recommend it to the several towns in this county, (and if it should not be thought too arrogant,) to every town in the province, to meet and adopt some wise, prudent, and spirited measures, in order to prevent the execution of those most alarming acts of parliament, respecting our constitution.

This may not sound like much; it certainly has less of a dramatic flare than most revolutionary directives. But that's exactly what happened in the end: each town adopted its own "spirited measures," which, in sum, proved sufficient to bury the Massachusetts Government Act. In the absence of any centralized leadership, it was a multitude of these local actions that would drive the British from power.

Convention delegates looked ahead to the next scheduled session of the Inferior Court of Common Pleas of Worcester County, slated to meet four weeks later on September 6. That would be a likely time to engage in some form of protest, since the court would be meeting under the authority of the Act. The convention consequently adjourned until August 30, one week prior to the court's opening session—plenty of time for every town in the county to meet, elect delegates, and give instructions. Perhaps by then the patriots of Worcester County might be able to come up with a few "spirited measures" suitable for the occasion.

The Inferior Court of Common Pleas for Berkshire County was scheduled to meet on August 16, 1774, in Great Barrington, the shiretown. Here at the westernmost edge of the province, at least a three-day ride from Boston, suits were to be decided for the first time by officials appointed under the Massachusetts Government Act.

Berkshire County, only recently separated from Hampshire County, was not in the political vanguard. The elected representatives had voted conservatively during the preceding decade of revolutionary activity, while common farmers who debated the affairs of the empire did so for parochial reasons.[6] Even so, patriotic fervor had reached into the Berkshires in the wake of the Boston Tea Party, and on July 6, 1774, sixty political activists from around the county had met at Stockbridge to express their concern over the Intolerable Acts.

The primary response of this county convention, typical for the times, was to promote a Solemn League and Covenant. Although the covenant would not take effect until October 1, its political impact would be felt much earlier: as of August 1, "any trader or shop-keeper in this county" would have only forty-eight hours to sign the agreement if he wanted to avoid a boycott of his store.[7]

Although the county convention passed the measure unanimously, patriots faced opposition from outside. A score of local Tories, including several justices of the peace and the county sheriff, had tried in vain to keep the meeting from happening, and three of these men complained to Governor Gage on July 15 that they were "being threatened to have our Houses rifled, tarred, feathered, etc. and upon all Occasions insulted." Supporters of the government, they reported, were in a distinct minority, for the Solemn League and Covenant had "captivated almost the whole County."[8]

Perhaps the most outspoken of the Tories was David Ingersoll, a Yale graduate who had been practicing law in Great Barrington for a decade and who had served his community as justice of the peace, captain in the militia, and representative to the General Court. Ingersoll reported to Gage that, before sunrise on August 2, "a vast concourse of people" armed with clubs surrounded his house and demanded he arise from his bed. At first Ingersoll "utterly refused to comply with their insolent requisition," but after the men broke into his house and threatened his family, he obeyed.

The "ruffians," as he called the intruders, placed Ingersoll and his servant on horses and took them to the town of Canaan, just over the Connecticut border and fourteen miles from Great Barrington, where they had erected a "pompous Liberty pole." They accused him of many "crimes," including his support for the Massachusetts Government Act and his opposition to the Berkshire covenant. They demanded he sign and seal an oath, but he refused. He suggested instead that they give him half an hour to compose a statement he could sign in good faith. The "ruffians," by Ingersoll's own admission, were quite democratic, for they passed "Several votes one way and another" before letting him off with his revised oath and sending him home.[9] They did not have to inflict any bodily damage to convey their message; threats and innuendo would suffice. By the time the rumors reached Boston, Ingersoll was said to have been covered with grease ("for want of tar") and feathers, "put down an empty well," and kept there overnight.[10]

These political strategies—nonimportation covenants and the mob intimidation of individual Tories—had been employed for nearly a decade, ever since the Stamp Act crisis of 1765. But late in July 1774, the patriots of Pittsfield, one of the larger towns in Berkshire County, proposed a new and more direct method for opposing British policy: Why not close down the courts? Since the weight of governmental authority was experienced most directly and frequently through the judicial system, closing the courts would effectively bring the Massachusetts Government Act to a halt.

While this idea was probably in circulation in Worcester, and possibly elsewhere, the first recorded mention of it appears in a letter from the Pittsfield Committee of Correspondence to the Boston Committee of Correspondence, dated July 25: "[W]e are persuaded that no business can be transacted at said Court," they wrote. "We expect to get it adjourned unless we should hear from you. We thought it highly expedient to know your Thoughts on so interesting an Occasion."[11] The Pittsfield committee, while appearing to act deferentially towards the revolutionary leaders in Boston, had in fact seized the initiative. On July 31, the Boston committee responded: "We acknowledge ourselves deeply indebted to your wisdom. . . . [N]othing in our opinion could be better concerted than the measures come into by your County to prevent the Court's sitting."[12]

The Berkshire County patriots held another county convention on August 4, but no records or descriptions of the event survive. However, we do have a petition composed by a town meeting held in Pittsfield on August 15, the day before the opening of the court:

> To the Honorable His Majesty's Justices of the Inferior Court of Common Pleas for the County of Berkshire:
>
> . . . We view it of the greatest importance to the well-being of this Province, that the people of it utterly refuse the least submission to the said acts, and on no consideration to yield obedience to them; or directly or indirectly to countenance the taking place of those acts amongst us, but resist them to the last extremity.
>
> In order in the safest manner to avoid this threatening calamity, it is, in our opinion, highly necessary that no business be transacted in the law, but that the courts of justice immediately cease, and the people of this Province fall into a state of nature until our grievances are fully redressed by a final repeal of these injurious, oppressive, and unconstitutional acts. . . . We do therefore remonstrate against the holding any courts in this county until those acts shall be repealed; and we hope your honors will not be of a different opinion from the good people in this county.[13]

Early the following morning, Tuesday, August 16, while the judges and magistrates powdered their wigs in preparation for the court (to nobody's surprise, they had not heeded Pittsfield's petition), some fifteen hundred unarmed men gathered at the Berkshire County courthouse, a one-and-a-half-story wooden structure, "plain and unpainted, . . . destitute of architectural pretention or adornment, save a semi-circular window in its eastern gable and some little carved wood work about the front door." A symbol of civil authority, the courthouse protruded into Main Street—"a conspicuous object in the ill-kept and untidy village," according to a history of Great Barrington written in 1882.[14] When the judges arrived for work, according to an eyewitness account, they discovered that the patriots had filled the Court-House and Avenues to the Seat of Justice, so full, that no Passage could be found for the Justices to take their Places. The Sheriff commanded them to make way for the court; but they gave him to understand that they knew no court on any other establishment than the ancient laws and usages of their country, & to none other would they submit or give way on any terms.[15]

The court never did open for business; in fact, it would never meet again under British rule. With no choice but to submit to the will of the people, the judges retreated. Chief Justice William Williams, at the age of sixty-four, had sense enough to do so quietly. Israel Stoddard expressed "a manly remonstrance" before giving in.[16]

Conservative attorney David Ingersoll, who must have had business before the court, wisely decided not to attend. After the judges had departed, many among the energized crowd made an appearance at Ingersoll's house, but the hated Tory had already "repaired to the Wilderness," where he would spend the night in the muggy August heat. According to Ingersoll's declaration to Governor Gage, the patriots "attacked his house and office, broke and Entered both of them, destroyed his Yard fences, his Garden, and greatly damaged his House, papers, &c." They then pursued Ingersoll into the woods.

The following day, Ingersoll "procured a number of armed men to protect him," but he finally set out for Boston, realizing he would never find peace in Berkshire County. When he arrived at Chesterfield, some thirty-five miles away, he was confronted by another crowd of two hundred men who demanded that he sign the Berkshire covenant; this time they would not let him go until he did. Again at Hatfield he was "surrounded by about 200 men who ordered him to decamp within a few minutes." Finally, by travelling through the woods and along back roads, he made his way to Boston, where he could receive the protection of British troops.[17]

Berkshire was the first county to close its courts; others would soon do likewise. Governor Gage, in reference to the Berkshire court closure, wrote that "popular Rage has appeared at the Extremity of the

Province, abetted by Connecticut, . . . and makes its way rapidly to the rest." [18] But Gage was only partially correct; the rage was not making its way from one location to another, it was erupting everywhere at once. Conservatives like Gage preferred to see it otherwise: by speaking of the *spread* or *diffusion* of unrest, they implicitly denied the validity of local protest. Boston's John Andrews described the mood of the times more accurately when he wrote on August 18, before he had heard about the happenings at Great Barrington, that "The inhabitants of the country towns . . . are prodigiously vex'd." [19] The common farmers of Massachusetts, all faced with disenfranchisement, were responding with a strong and nearly unanimous voice.

Back in Boston on August 16, 1774—the same day that patriots were taking command at Great Barrington—Governor Gage was administering the oaths to thirteen more "mandamus counsellors," including all four from Worcester County: Timothy Ruggles, Timothy Paine, John Murray, and Abijah Willard. Boston merchant Samuel Salisbury wrote to his brother Stephen in Worcester: "I had the disagreeable sight of the Governour and Councill walking in procession among whom was our friend Mr. Pain[e], which I was sorry to see as I conclude from that he has taken the oath." [20] Gage boasted to Lord Dartmouth that twenty-four of the thirty-six councilors had now signed on, but his boasting was premature: What would happen when the councilors returned to their hometowns?

One of them, Daniel Leonard, known for his fancy attire ("he wore a broad gold lace round the rim of his hat; he made his cloak glitter with laces still broader"), traveled from Boston to his home in Taunton on Saturday, August 20. [21] The following morning he made the simple mistake of attending church, thereby announcing to his neighbors he was back in town. Immediately, "a paper was posted up by the meeting-house door, requesting the inhabitants to assemble the next day on the green." [22] On Monday, according to John Andrews,

> upwards of two thousand men met on the green in that town [Taunton], and but for the expestulations of Leonard's father

(who disapproved of his Son's being a Councellor, and promis'd
to use his influence with him that he should resign) would have
pulled his house down.[23]

The crowd was temporarily appeased. "There was not the least Disorder or appearance of Violence in any of the Assembly," said one of
the newspaper accounts.[24]

But the matter did not end there. In a letter to Governor Gage,
Leonard explained how the patriots continued their intimidation:

> On Sunday noon I received intelligence that the People were
> much exasperated at me, and the Town of Taunton, with the
> neighbouring towns, were to asemble the next day to *deal with
> me* (that was the expression) for accepting a Seat at the Board,
> that it was expected they would begin with remonstrance and
> entreaty, and if that proved sufficient to obtain an engagement
> on my part to resign my Seat, all would be well, if not, that a
> number had determined to proceed to violence. Such was the in-
> telligence I received and could depend on. Many things ren-
> dered it impracticable for me to make any resistance in my own
> house, one of which I beg leave to mention, the situation of my
> wife, who was pregnant.
>
> I accordingly came as far as Stoughton that day, and the next
> to Boston, supposing that the People would disperse without
> giving my family any trouble, when it should be known that I
> was absent. But I was mistaken: on the next day which was the
> 22d Instant, about five hundred persons assembled, many of
> them Freeholders and some of them Officers in the Militia, and
> formed themselves into a Battalion before my house; they had
> then no Fire-arms, but generally had clubs. Some of the princi-
> pal persons came to my house with a message that the People
> were much incensed at my accepting a Seat at the Board, and
> begged I would resign it. Upon being informed that I was not at
> home, they returned to the main Body, who dispersed before
> night, after having been treated with rum by their Principals.[25]

By day, the crowd acted peacefully—but once the sun was down, some of the patriots took their concerns to the next level:

> My Family supposing all would remain quiet, went to bed at their usual hour; at 11 o'Clock in the evening a Party fired upon the house with small arms and run off; how many they consisted of is uncertain, I suppose not many; four bullets and some Swanshot entered the house at the windows, part in a lower room and part in the chamber above, where one Capt. Job Williams lodged. . . .
>
> Capt. Williams at whom the firing seems to have directed, was the person that furnished me with the intelligence that the People were to assemble, and who pulled down and tore in pieces a written notification that was fixed on the Meeting House for the People to assemble; wherefore I conclude it probable that the attack upon the house was principally designed for him. However that may be, my family were exposed by it, and I have received repeated advices from my friends at Taunton, since I arrived at Boston, that my life will be in danger if I return.[26]

The patriots of Taunton, striking fear by the light of a full moon, had driven Daniel Leonard from his home. Perhaps wisely, he remained for the while in Boston, where he continued to serve on the governor's council and to pen polemical letters to the Boston papers, writing under the name of "Novanglus." Leonard hoped to return to Taunton once the troubles had passed—but the troubles never did pass. This formerly prominent citizen, accustomed to riding about in one of the few coaches in rural Massachusetts, had become a refugee.

The abrasive Timothy Ruggles encountered difficulty even before taking the oath. Departing Hardwick on his way to Boston, he had to travel "on the Road near Worcester," where "a Number of People collected . . . to stop him, but he made his Way through them."[27] After arriving safely, he marched in the grand procession on August 16 to become one of the governor's councilors. Perhaps hesitant to face his constituents in Worcester County, Ruggles tarried for a few days in Boston. On August 19 Daniel Oliver, a young justice of the peace in Hardwick, wrote to Ruggles: "There are those here, who I am satisfied thirst for your blood, and they have influence enough over the others to put them upon spilling it." [28]

So instead of going home, Ruggles traveled to Dartmouth to visit a friend. But the Brigadier was well known throughout the province, and patriots would not tolerate his presence *anywhere* once he had accepted a position on the Council. The following week the *Boston Evening Post* published a letter from Taunton dated August 25:

> We hear that Brigadier Ruggles, one of the new made Counsellors, being at Col. Toby's at Dartmouth, the People assembled there one Day this Week, and ordered him to depart forthwith; upon which the Colonel promised them he would go the next Morning by Sun an Hour high; but before that time the Brigadier's Horse had his Mane and Tail cut off, and his Body painted all over. [29]

The day following, the letter reported, a crowd of two to three thousand was expected to assemble to force the resignation of the local sheriff, and "also to desire Brigadier Ruggles to depart the County immediately." The letter concluded, "Such is the Spirit of this County—they seem to be quite awake, and to have awoke in a Passion. It is more dangerous being a Tory here than in Boston, even if no Troops were there."

Where was Ruggles to go? Certainly not home to Hardwick, where his neighbors thirsted for his blood, nor even to some other town, where the Brigadier himself, instead of his prize horse, might come to some harm. In the past, local jurisdictions in Massachusetts had "warned out" the transient poor; now, they were warning out hated Tories. The only safety an official of the new government could find was behind British lines. [30]

Abijah Willard, a "large and portly" Tory from Lancaster in northeastern Worcester County, also traveled about after taking his oath as a councilor. [31] Instead of returning straight home after the ceremony on August 16, Willard journeyed to Union, Connecticut, supposedly on some sort of business. But even in a different colony, he could not escape the charged political climate. The patriots in the border town of Union captured Willard, made him spend a night in jail, and then returned him to Massachusetts. In Brimfield, the first town over the border, he was placed in the hands of four hundred patriots. According to a contemporary account, this crowd, once again acting democratically,

> called a Council of themselves, and Condemned Colonel Willard to Newgate Prison, in Symsbury; and a number set off and carried him six miles on the way thither. Colonel Willard then submitted to take the oath . . . , on which they dismissed him. One Captain Davis of Brimfield was present, who showing resentment, and treating the people with bad language, was stripped, and honored with the new fashion dress of tar and feathers; a proof this, *that the act for tarring and feathering is not repealed.*[32]

Willard's resignation was published in the Boston papers:

> Whereas I, Abijah Willard of Lancaster, have been appointed by Mandamus a Counsellor for this Province, and having without due Consideration taken the Oath, [I] do now freely and solemnly declare that I am sorry that I have taken the said oath, and do hereby solemnly and in good faith promise and engage that I will not sit or act in said Council, . . . and do hereby ask forgiveness of all honest, worthy gentlemen that I have offended.[33]

But Willard's resignation, by any objective assessment, had hardly been offered "freely."

In the town of Worcester, the ongoing struggle for local power was nearing its end. With a town meeting scheduled for Monday,

August 22, 1774, the American Political Society convened the preceding Thursday to decide how the town was to proceed. Acting under no legal authority, the APS determined that Nathan Perry was to serve as moderator for the forthcoming town meeting—the first time in living memory that neither John Chandler nor Timothy Paine held that office. The APS also directed seven of its members to draft articles of surrender which the fifty-two men who had protested the results of the June meeting (the "Protestors") would be forced to sign. Finally, and most audaciously, it commanded "the Selectmen of Worcester" to "forthwith make Search and examine the Town Stock of Ammunition and see if the Quality and Quantity be as the Law Directs." [34]

Clearly, the patriots had taken over the town. Most of the Protestors, sensing defeat and worried for their safety, gathered on Sunday evening at Mary Stearns' tavern (still called by some the "King's Arms") and professed their willingness to recant. But the patriot majority wanted it in writing. At the official town meeting the next day, Nathan Perry was indeed elected moderator, and the committee of seven selected by the APS was officially charged with preparing a formal apology for the conservatives to sign. At the core of the recantation, later printed in the Boston papers, was a declaration that the Worcester patriots were not a mob, and their actions were not to be construed as riots:

> [W]e the subscribers, have given the good people of this Province in general, and the inhabitants of the town of Worcester in particular, just cause to be offended with each of us. . . . [W]e acknowledge we have cast cruel aspersions upon the town of Worcester and upon the Committee of Correspondence for said town, and upon all Committees of Correspondence throughout the Province, for which we are sorry, and take this opportunity publicly to manifest it, and declare we did not so well consider the contents, and that we had no other intention than to bear our testimony against mobs and riots. . . . [T]o the best of our knowledge we declare that the present generation in this town has never been concerned in any mobs or riots in this

or any other place. And we hereby beg their forgiveness, and all others we may have offended.[35]

Although begging forgiveness was not their style, most of the Protestors—including John Chandler and his sons Clark, William, and Rufus—saw no choice but to submit. Of the fifty-two Protestors, only James Putnam, William Paine, and three others held firm and announced they would not recant.

The forced and formal apology, however humiliating, was still not enough to satisfy the patriots. Unhappy with even the appearance of dissent, they admonished town clerk Clark Chandler for entering the original Protest in the official records. At the continuation of the town meeting on Wednesday, they passed an intriguing resolve:

> Voted, that the town clerk do, in presence of the town, obliterate, erase, or otherwise deface the said recorded protest, and the names thereto subscribed, so that it may become utterly illegible and unintelligible.[36]

Dutifully, Clark Chandler inked his pen and drew it across the entire Protest, line by line, in full public view.

But even that would not suffice. A few words could still be deciphered in the record book, the patriots claimed, so they made him do it again—this time with continuous loops of tight spirals, which rendered the Protest unintelligible. While this should have ended the matter, it didn't. We do not know exactly what triggered the last dramatic humiliation, but we do know that on August 24, 1774, the clerk for the town of Worcester—John Chandler's son—was forced to dip his own fingers in a well of ink and drag them over the first page of the Protest. Today, if you go to the clerk's office in the Worcester City Hall and ask to view volume 4, page 21 of the Town Records, you will see the horizontal lines, the spiraling loops, and several finger-sized smudges of ink drawn sloppily across the yellow, aging paper. The longest of these defacements has short, irregular changes in direction, clear indication of a forced hand. The only words peeking out through all the markings are "some evil minded," an appropriate summation for the mood of the day.[37]

On page 23, the third and final page of the Protest, the signatures have been crossed out, but this time the lines are all different: some straight, others looped, and each with a slightly different stroke. This was not the work of one man. It would appear that each of the Protestors was called forth to strike his own name from the record, the final act in this dramatization of the transfer of power in Worcester.

The patriots of Worcester, although flush with victory, still had to deal with two major items of unfinished business: the Inferior Court of Common Pleas, which was due to convene on September 6, and the three local councilors who had not yet resigned—Timothy Ruggles, Timothy Paine, and John Murray.

They started with Paine. He wasn't the worst of the three; in fact, mild-mannered Timothy Paine had been elected to several offices in recent years, and he had even been trusted with the role of moderator at the turbulent March, May, and June town meetings. (On the other hand "Madame Paine"—Timothy's wife and John Chandler's sister—was "perhaps the most outspoken Loyalist of either the Chandler or Paine families.")[38] Perhaps the patriots started with Paine because they thought they might be able to reason with him—or simply because he was local they knew he was at home. Unlike Leonard, Ruggles, and Willard, Paine had chosen not to run. "I had some private notice of it," he later wrote, "but upon the whole I thought it not best to go out of the way, and determined to stay and see how far they intended to carry matters."[39] In any case, the patriots of Worcester, fired up by the ink incident earlier in the week, hatched a plan which targeted Timothy Paine.

On Friday, August 26, riders fanned out from Worcester to alert the surrounding towns of the impending action. In Leicester, Spencer, Brookfield, Rutland, Westborough, Shrewsbury, Grafton, Sutton, Oxford, and points beyond, farmers mustered quickly and prepared to travel to Worcester.[40] The ones coming from farthest away had to travel on Friday and spend the night; the others arose before dawn to ride into town by daybreak.

Although the town of Worcester contained fewer than 350 adult males, inclusive of all the farmers within the township, a crowd estimated variously at fifteen hundred, two thousand, and three thousand gathered on the Worcester Common on the morning of August 27.[41] We have three detailed accounts of what occurred: two reports to newspapers and a letter by Paine to Governor Gage. All three are in basic agreement, differing only as to the size of the crowd. According to Paine:

> The people began to assemble so early as Seven o'Clock in the morning, and by Nine, by the best computation, more than *Two Thousand men* were paraded on our Common. They were led into town by particular persons chosen for that purpose, many were Officers of the Militia, and marched in at the head of their companies. Being so assembled they chose a large Committee from the whole body, which Committee chose a Sub Committee to wait upon me. . . .
>
> I received them first at my Chamber Window, but upon assurance from them they had no design to treat me ill, I admitted them into my house. They then informed me of their business, that they were a Committee chosen by a large body of People assembled on the Common to wait upon me to resign my Seat at the Council Board. I endeavored to convince them of the ill consequences that would ensue upon the measures they were taking, . . . but all to no purpose, they insisting that the measures were peaceable, and that nothing would satisfy the Assembly unless I resigned, and that they would not answer for the consequences if I did not. Thus surrounded on every side, without any protection, I found myself under a necessity of complying, and prepared and signed a resignation, which the Committee refused to accept, and after making alteration according to their own minds they accepted the following form, vizt.

"To Messrs Joshua Bigelow, Thomas Denny, Joseph Gilbert, Edward Rawson and John Goulding,

"GENTLEMEN, As you have waited upon me as a Committee chosen by a large body of People now assembled on the Common in Worcester, desiring that I now resign my Seat at the Council Board; my Appointment was without sollicitation, and am very sorry I accepted, and thereby given any uneasiness to the People of the County, from whom I have received many favors, and take this opportunity to thank them: and I do hereby assure you that I will not take a Seat at the Board unless it is agreeable to the Charter of this Province."[42]

At this point Paine thought his written recantation would suffice, but he was mistaken. According to one of the newspaper accounts,

[Paine] then asked if that was satisfactory? They replied he must wait on the people, which he thought unreasonable, after he had complied with their demand; but they said it was in vain, unless he made his personal appearance, the people would not be satisfied; and after their promising to protect him from insult, he waited on them to the body of the people.[43]

Timothy Paine, although living only a short walk from the courthouse, always preferred to make the journey in his "handsome green coach, trimmed with gilding and lined with satin."[44] Not this time. Led by the committee, he was ushered through the lines of Worcester County yeomen waiting along Main Street. Once he and the committee were situated in the heart of the crowd, Thomas Denny "read his resignation, with which numbers were dissatisfied, requiring that Mr. Paine should read it himself, and that with his hat off."[45]

Again Paine thought he was through, but he was not. Only a small portion of the people had heard his resignation, and the rest wanted to hear it as well. For the assembled patriots, this was a moment to be milked. The crowd "drawed up in two bodies, making a lane between them, through which the committee and he passed and read divers times as they passed along, the said acknowledgment." [46] Finally, the people were satisfied: Timothy Paine, duly humbled, had resigned—not in private and not only once, but repeatedly in public. One version of the story, part of Worcester's enduring folklore, holds that

> in the excitement attendant on the scene, Mr. Paine's wig was either knocked off or fell off. Be that as it may, from that day he abjured *wigs*, as much as he had done *whigs*, and never wore one again. The now dishonored wig in question, he gave to one of his negro slaves, named "Worcester." [47]

Was Timothy Paine mistreated by the crowd? Not likely. Paine himself stated, "I met with no insult excepting they obliged me to walk with my Hat off when I passed through them." Yet Gage wrote to Lord Dartmouth that Paine "was seized and roughly treated." [48] The British would have liked to portray the Worcester crowd as a "mob," but according to firsthand sources, including Paine himself, the crowd was orderly and even respectful, albeit forceful in their demands.

This was no accident. These citizens took special care to distance themselves from any intimations that they might be a "mob." In their view, they had acted like model citizens. The crowd conducted all its business according to strict democratic principles: ad hoc delegates were elected to conduct negotiations, while all decisions were put to a vote of the entire body. There were no "leaders" empowered to issue orders from above. Even the insistence that Paine read his resignation repeatedly was inspired by democratic concerns: nobody wanted to be left out of the drama.

Paine himself was certainly impressed by this showing. He concluded his letter to Gage:

> Thus Sir you see an open opposition has taken place to the Acts of the British Parliament. I dread the consequence of enforcing them by a military Power; people's spirits are so raised they

seem determined to risque their lives and every thing dear to
them in the opposition, and prevent any person from executing
any commission he may receive under the present administration. They give out that Brigadier Ruggles shall not sit as a
Judge in our County Court, and that the Court shall not be held
here.

Paine had witnessed the power of the people firsthand. His advice
to avoid the use of military force was heartfelt—not written under the
gaze of patriots but in a private letter. Rumors abounded, with much
foundation, that Gage was poised to send troops to keep the court
open on September 6. Paine had heard these rumors; he might even
have had some communication from Gage himself, perhaps an offer
of military support. Paine undoubtedly hoped that his letter to Gage,
if the General took it seriously, might prevent a bloodbath.

The action against Timothy Paine had taken the better part of the
morning, but the business of the day was not over. There were two
more councilors to visit, and since those councilors lived in other
towns, the patriots wasted no time. By noon, Paine wrote, Main Street
in Worcester "was all still."

John Murray was next. About five hundred of the men who had
visited Paine headed toward Murray's home in Rutland, some fifteen
miles northwest of the town of Worcester, where they were joined by
"about one thousand more from towns above." [49] But Murray was not
at home. John and his son Daniel, who was studying to be a doctor,
had tarried in Boston for a week after the administration of oaths on
August 16. They finally headed home a week later, "being both well
armed and resolute," according to John Andrews. "I imagine they are
determin'd to stand a brush, if opposed," Andrews added, "being
both very stout men, near or quite as large as a Forrest." But they did
not travel too quickly, for the next day Andrews wrote:

Col. Murray halted yesterday at Cambridge, least too great pre-
cipitancy in so bold an enterprise should prove fatal. He has
behav'd like an experienc'd commander, and sent to reconnoitre

before he advances, with a view to better inform himself of the hostile disposition of his townsmen.[50]

On Thursday, August 25, the Murrays made their final advance. Daniel went home to stay, but his father packed up his belongings and left the same night.[51] So when fifteen hundred aroused citizens of Worcester County came to his home two days later to demand that he resign from the council, they came up empty.

At first, the crowd did not accept Daniel's word that his father was away. The men "insisted upon searching the house, which was thoroughly done, as also the barns, out houses and stables."[52] They had heard Murray was back home from Boston; they did not yet know he had just moved out. When they failed to unearth the object of their search, some became angry. This crowd, acting later in the day and against a more hated adversary, seems to have behaved more aggressively than the one in Worcester. According to Daniel Murray, most of the men were "armed with sticks in general heavy enough to have levelled a man at a stroke."[53] (In 1864, Lorenzo Sabine claimed that a John Singleton Copley portrait of John Murray in formal attire—at that time in the possession of Murray's grandson—had a hole punched through the wig. Family tradition, wrote Sabine, held that "a party who sought the Colonel at his house after his flight, vexed because he had eluded them, vowed they would leave their mark behind them, and accordingly pierced the canvas with a bayonet.")[54]

How would the patriots proceed, with Murray nowhere to be found? They decided to post a letter in the Boston newspapers, which they composed on the spot and published soon thereafter:

To John Murray, Esq:
Sir,
    As you have proved yourself to be an open Enemy to this
Province, by your Conduct in general, and in particular in
accepting of the late Appointment as an unconstitutional
Counsellor, in Consequence whereof, a large Number of Men

from several Towns are assembled, who are fully determined to
prevent your holding said Office as Counsellor, at the Risque of
our Lives and Fortunes; and not finding you at Home, think
proper to propose to your serious consideration: the following
viz:

That you make an immediate Resignation of your Office, as
a Counsellor.

Your compliance as above, published in each of the Boston
News Prints by the Tenth Day of September next, will save the
People of this County the Trouble of waiting on you
immediately afterwards.

In the Name and Behalf of the whole Assembly now present,
Willard Moore[55]

Despite the threat, Murray refused to resign. Along with fourteen
other councilors who held firm, he continued to serve at the governor's pleasure—but he never did return to his home in Rutland. Only
the presence of the British army in Boston saved him from the wrath
of his countrymen. The following year, when Daniel requested permission from the revolutionary government to visit his father in
Boston, his request was denied.

On the evening of August 27, the patriots had one more visit to
make: to the Brigadier from Hardwick. Some ventured there, but
most, believing that Ruggles was on the run, dispersed.

Timothy Ruggles, like John Murray, was conveniently away from
home. We do not know for sure whether the diehards who continued
to Hardwick took any aggressive actions that night, for the Brigadier
was hounded so often by patriots that the incidents were blurred together in the reporting. A few months later, a Loyalist's letter complained that Ruggles

had his arms taken from his dwelling-house in Hardwick, all of
which are not yet returned. He had at another time a very valuable English horse, which was kept as a stallion, poisoned, his
family disturbed, and himself obliged to take refuge in Boston,

after having been insulted in his own house, and twice on his way, by a mob.[56]

Perhaps his guns were seized, his horse poisoned, or his family disturbed on the night of August 27, or perhaps these transgressions occurred at some other time. In any case, Ruggles, like Murray, had no life left at home. Unlike the more flexible Timothy Paine, Tories who stood by their beliefs—particularly those continuing to hold office under the Massachusetts Government Act—were unwelcome in the Massachusetts countryside in the late summer of 1774.

The blacksmith Timothy Bigelow, who was elected to almost every revolutionary committee in Worcester, was not among the five men selected to negotiate with Timothy Paine on August 27 because on that day he and Ephraim Doolittle were meeting at Faneuil Hall in Boston with delegates of the committees of correspondence from Suffolk (which included Boston), Middlesex, and Essex Counties. The meeting had been called on the request of radicals from Worcester. On August 15 they had written to the Boston committee suggesting an intercounty gathering; two days later the Boston committee had responded positively and scheduled the meeting for August 26 and 27.

Until the summer of 1774, the Boston committee had assumed the leadership role among Massachusetts patriots. It was the Boston committee that sent out letters to towns, and when one of the other towns had something to contribute, it would run the idea through Boston first. Many responses to the Boston Pamphlet had even displayed a deferential attitude toward Boston committee members. Now, although Boston was still the focus of correspondence, the outlying districts were seizing the initiative. Berkshire County had suggested closing the courts, and Worcester County was asking for the counties to meet together.[57]

Worcester's motivation for suggesting the multicounty meeting is not stated directly in the records, but it is easy to surmise. On August 13, two days before writing to the Boston committee, William Henshaw of Leicester had received intelligence that Commander-in-Chief Gage, embarrassed by the treatment the Superior Court had received in Worcester on April 19, might be sending a regiment of troops to Worcester to protect the court on September 6.[58] This was a scary prospect, and patriots from around the county, at their town meetings and caucuses, nervously discussed what could happen when they tried to close the courts. If Worcester patriots stood alone against British Regulars, they might well be crushed, but if they gained the assistance of freedom fighters from elsewhere, they would stand more of a chance. This need to garner support was the not-so-hidden agenda of Timothy Bigelow and Ephraim Doolittle in their meeting with a score of well-known patriots including Joseph Warren, Benjamin Church, William Molineaux, and Elbridge Gerry.

On Friday, August 26, the assembly appointed a subcommittee to draft resolutions: Thomas Young and Joseph Greenleaf of Boston, Elbridge Gerry of Marblehead, Thomas Gardner of Cambridge, and Timothy Bigelow of Worcester. The subcommittee was charged with considering "what Measures are necessary to be taken respecting our novel and unconstitutional Courts of Justice."[59] The group presented their preliminary draft the next day; after much debate and some alteration, a final report was drawn up and accepted by the entire gathering.

The language of the final report was strong, as Worcester delegates must have hoped: "[N]o power on Earth, hath a Right without the consent of this Province to alter the minutest title of its Charter," it stated. Unlike most public pronouncements of the time, it dispensed with the usual opening courtesies to the king; instead, it claimed boldly that Massachusetts citizens were "intitled to life, liberty, and the means of sustenance by the grace of Heaven and without the King's leave." It asked that each county oppose the courts to be held within it, and it called for the convening of a Provincial Congress which would establish "Referee Committees" to help settle disputes if and when the courts were closed. "[E]very Officer belonging to the Courts" who acted under the authority of the Massachusetts Government Act was to be considered "a Traitor cloaked with the pretext of law," and they "ought to be held in the highest detestations by the People, as common Plunderers." Finally, the report called for the people to learn "the Military Art according to the Norfolk Plan . . . as necessary means to secure their Liberties against the designs of Enemies whether Foreign or Domestick." [60]

From a preliminary draft of the document penned in the hand of Elbridge Gerry, we can glean some sense of the discussion by the delegates. A few of the original words were made more dramatic in the final version: "usurpers" became "daring usurpations," and "deprived" became "robbed." An entire paragraph that suggested that officials be shunned in their religious "connections" as well as their financial and social dealings was dropped to avoid dissent. Most significantly, the early draft contained a clause stating that the courts should be opposed "in every Way that shall not be productive of Carnage and Bloodshed." As before, the patriots did not wish to be associated with mobs or riots, but the wording must have been troublesome to the delegates from Worcester: how could they guarantee there would be no bloodshed if British troops came to Worcester? The final draft said simply that the courts should be "properly opposed in the Counties wherein they shall be attempted to be held." This open-ended language was less restrictive of revolutionary activity.[61] Worcester radicals were left free to oppose the courts in any manner they saw fit.

Come September 6, they would certainly try. And now, it was clear, their cause would be embraced by the mainstream of political protest in revolutionary Massachusetts.

Local communities in colonial New England knew how to apply pressure on deviant individuals, whether heretics or Tories. This pressure could be brought to bear on several levels: economic, social, or religious. In close-knit towns with only one church, Sunday meetings provided excellent venues for humiliation. Although disavowed by the gathering of the committees of correspondence in Boston, ostracism from the community of worship served as a potent revolutionary tool, as evidenced by the case of George Watson.

Returning home to Plymouth after taking his oath as a councilor,

George Watson, like Daniel Leonard, went to church as usual. The *Boston Evening-Post* reported what happened:

> [W]hen he came into the House of publick Worship, a great number of the principal Inhabitants of that Town left the Meeting-House immediately upon his entering it; "being determined not to worship in fellowship with one, who has sworn to support that change of our constitution, which professedly establishes despotism among us." [62]

Josiah Edson, another councilor, had a similar experience. "[H]is townsmen at Bridgewater, after some exhortation," wrote John Andrews, "thought proper to *send him to Coventry*, nor would they even deign to sing ye psalm after his reading it, being deacon of the parish." [63]

Watson and Edson responded differently to the pressure. Edson, like Ruggles, Murray, and Leonard, retreated quickly to Boston, where he served on the governor's council; Watson, like Willard and Paine, chose to resign. In a letter to Gage, he explained why:

> By my accepting of this Appointment, I find that I have rendered myself very obnoxious, not only to the inhabitants of this place, but also to those of the neighboring towns. On my business as a Merchant I depend, for the support of myself and Family, and of this I must be intirely deprived, in short, I am reduced to the alternative of resigning my Seat at the Council Board, or quitting this, the place of my Nativity, which will be attended with the most fatal Consequences to myself, and family. Necessity therefore obliges me to ask Permission of your Excellencey to resign my Seat at the Board, and I trust, that when your Excellency considers my Situation, I shall not be censured. [64]

Watson's statement was honest: he could not endure isolation from his community. The resignation of Andrew Oliver, on the other hand, was something of an evasion: he claimed he could not legally serve,

since he owned significant property in Connecticut.[65] The most intriguing resignation came from Thomas Hutchinson, Jr., son of the
previous governor. If he did not resign, Hutchinson stated, his neighbors would drive him from his home, and this would present a hardship to others:

> [I]t would be exceedingly inconvenient for me to change the
> place of my residence, or submit to any kind of restraint of my
> person, being the only one of Governor Hutchinson's family
> now in the country, and having the care of his affairs here, as
> well as those of the late Lieut. Governor Oliver, both of which I
> apprehend will suffer greatly by my being under any personal
> restraint. I am sensible these reasons are of a private nature, but
> as they relate to the concerns of others more than my own, I
> hope your Excellency will think them sufficient to induce you to
> accept the Resignation of my trust as one of His Majesty's
> Council for this Province.[66]

Often, patriots could force resignations or make officials toe the
line merely by the threat of ostracism, but certain individuals, such as
David Ingersoll and Timothy Ruggles, seemed to provoke genuine
wrath not easily contained within reputable forms of protest. Despite
the repeated efforts of the patriots to distance themselves from
"mobs" and "riots," crowds forming at night instilled great terror. In
Roxbury, Joshua Loring—known as "the Commodore" because of
his service on the Great Lakes during the French and Indian War—
was the object of mob action:

> At 12 o'Clock in the night of the 29th Instant I was awaked by a
> very hard knocking at my door; immediately I jumped out of
> bed and threw up the window, when I saw five men disguised,
> their faces black'd, hatts flap'd, and with cutlasses in their hands.
> I ask'd them who they were, they answered they came from a
> Mob. I then asked them what they wanted; they told me they
> came to know if I would resign my Seat at the Board. I answer'd

I would not, and went into some discourse with them, asking what right they had to make such a demand on me or any other man. They told me they did not come to talk, they came to act, and that they wanted my answer: I replied that they had got it already. They then told me they would give me till tomorrow night to consider of it, and then the speaker gave orders to a large party who were in the road, to discharge their pieces, which they accordingly did, and which I took to be pistols. They then told me my house should be safe till tomorrow night, and went off in number about sixty.

The next night being the 30th I thought it most prudent to leave my house, and my son went out to it to receive the Mob. He informs me as follows:—that in the evening about 1/2 past 8 o'Clock his mother came home much affrighted, and told him at or near Liberty Tree in Roxbury, she saw about fifty men assembled, who immediately on knowing the carriage began to huzza scream and whistle, and called out to the Coachman to stop, but he continued on, and they followed the carriage in this manner for near a mile, and were then close at hand.

About 9 o'Clock he heard their noise, and in a few minutes they were up to the house, and immediately knocked at the door; he went to it and found five men disguised, their faces black'd and cutlasses in their hands: they order'd the candle to be put out, and then asked for the Commodore, and said they came for his answer. He told them he was gone to Boston, and then endeavored to reason with them against their demand, but to no purpose; they said this was the second time they had come, and to beware of the third, that if he would publish in the Thursdays News Paper a Recantation, it would be well, if not, he must abide by the consequences, which would be very severe, that his house would be levelled to the ground, and many other of the like threats; and then these Five who seemed to have the direction, I can't say command, of the Mob who were at the gate, retired to them, and during all this time they kept laying on the board fence with clubs, and crying out Don't fire, for God's sake don't fire, keep back, keep back: but the People did not seem to mind them, and continued their hallowing and knocking on the fence with their clubs: all of which was designed to intimidate.

They soon went off, and, as he was informed, to the house of Mr. Pepperell, who not being home, they returned again within the space of half an hour, and in the same tumultuous manner halted in the road opposite the house, and all at once were very silent, occasioned, as he was informed, by some friends speaking to them; a few minutes after they set up their hallowing &c again, and went off. And as it was a very dark night he could not judge of their numbers, but was told they were about two hundred.[67]

The men who shot into Daniel Leonard's house, slashed John Murray's portrait, and brandished cutlasses at Commodore Loring's family in the dead of night were fewer in number than the vast crowds of freeholders who met by the light of day on the village greens, but their political effect was the same: the Crown-appointed councilors were compelled by fear to submit or retreat. Commodore Loring, like Brigadier Ruggles and Colonel Murray, chose to retreat. "I have always eaten the King's bread, and I always intend to," he wrote. (Joshua Loring, Jr., soon followed his father's lead and sought the protection of British troops. In 1775 the younger Loring purchased the office of Suffolk County sheriff in occupied Boston for £500, and in 1777, after fleeing to Halifax, he was placed in charge of patriot prisoners-of-war.)[68]

William Pepperell, mentioned in Loring's narrative, also fled his home on the night of August 30. "[M]y servant brought me intelligence from the country," he wrote the following day, "that a large number of men, in disguise, came to my house last evening and inquired for me, and being informed that I was in town, they ordered my servant to come to me this morning and tell me that I must resign my Seat at the Council Board or take the consequence of a refusal."[69]

Pepperell never returned home. If he had, he would likely have suffered harm, for patriots had a particular quarrel with this particular councilor. His grandfather of the same name had been a great hero, the conqueror of the French fortress at Louisbourg in 1745. Without a surviving son, the elder William Pepperell bequeathed his name and his immense estate in Maine to his daughter's son. Legally, this required the approval of the legislature, which was granted. At the time of the patriots' visit to his home, the younger William Pepperell was in the process of seeking his grandfather's British title of baronet. Pepperell, who owed his wealth and standing to a venerable grandfather and to the people of Massachusetts, was viewed by neighbors as disgracing his heritage by accepting an appointment to the Council in order to keep favor with the Crown. "[T]he time will come, Sir," wrote "a Yorkshireman" in the *Boston Gazette,* "when the character of your father shall cease to protect you, your estate be plundered, your purse . . . be exhausted; your country detest and despise you.—Then, Sir, enjoy the title of a Baronet, like a King without Subjects." [70]

By the end of August 1774, none of the "mandamus councellors" commanded any authority beyond the limits of Boston; indeed, those who lived past city limits could not even set foot in their own homes. Even within Boston they were hounded. They received some protection from the British troops who occupied their lodgings, but when a councilor ventured outside, Whig craftsmen and shopowners rang bells to alert the people that one of the hated Tories was in their midst. [71]

The intimidation of individual councilors was having some effect, but the true test of the incipient Revolution would come with closing the courts. On August 30 Hampshire County's Inferior Court for Common Pleas and the Court of General Sessions of the Peace were scheduled to convene in Springfield. A week later courts would try to open in Worcester. Within a month after that, the inferior courts in all nine contiguous mainland counties were to convene. And on September 20, the Superior Court of Judicature for the province of Massachusetts Bay was slated to meet in Worcester, the very heart of resistance.

Governor and commander-in-chief General Thomas Gage had promised to send troops to protect the courts, at least in Worcester; the patriots, on the other hand, had vowed that the courts would never sit under the authority of the Massachusetts Government Act. Something would have to give.

4

CONFRONTATION

During the later part of August 1774, patriots and British officials geared up for the court openings. While farmers-turned-activists spoke with their neighbors—formally at meetings and informally in taverns—about the evils of the Massachusetts Government Act, General Gage received reinforcements: the Fifty-Ninth Regiment from Halifax and the "Royal Welch Fusileers" from New York.[1] It seemed unlikely that Gage would send troops all the way to Springfield on August 30, but few doubted he would try to protect the court at Worcester on September 6.

The first big test of power, however, came unexpectedly in the town of Salem on Wednesday, August 24, when local leaders called a town meeting to elect delegates for an upcoming countywide convention. There was nothing unusual in this; towns throughout the province were holding meetings without the governor's consent, in defiance of the Massachusetts Government Act. A few towns, including Boston, tried to circumvent the Act: the citizens would adjourn each session to some future date, thus eliminating the need to call a "new" meeting. (The people of Marblehead adjourned the same meeting forty-six times.)[2] Most towns, however, turned their illegally convened meetings into conscious acts of civil disobedience. "The towns through the country are so far from being intimidated," wrote

John Andrews, "that a day in the week does not pass without one or more having meetings, in direct contempt of the Act; which they regard as a blank piece of paper and not more." [3]

Salem, however, was in a unique situation: as the seat of the provincial government, would it too flout the law?

It did. On Saturday, August 20, the Salem Committee of Correspondence (not the selectmen, as was customary) posted notices about town:

> The committee of correspondence desire the merchants, freeholders and other inhabitants of this town to meet at the town house chamber next Wednesday, at nine o'clock in the morning to appoint five or more deputies, to meet at Ipswich, on the sixth of September next, with the deputies which shall be appointed by the other towns in this county, to consider of and determine on such measures as the late acts of parliament and our other grievances render necessary and expedient. [4]

Then on Tuesday, the day before the meeting, Governor Gage issued a proclamation:

> [W]hereas by a late Act of Parliament, all Town-Meetings called without the consent of the Governor (except the annual Meetings, in the Months of March and May) are illegal, I do hereby strictly prohibit all Persons from attending . . . any Meeting not warned by law, as they will be chargeable with all the ill Consequences that may follow thereon, and answer the same at their utmost Peril. [5]

It is doubtful whether Gage expected anyone to heed this warning, but he was compelled to give it nonetheless. Meanwhile, acting on the likelihood that the meeting would still be held, Gage readied his troops.

At 8:00 Wednesday morning the governor summoned the leaders

of the Salem committee to meet him an hour later—the exact time of the scheduled town meeting. Perhaps Gage thought the meeting would flounder without its leaders; if so, he was mistaken, for the meeting went on as planned. In a letter to the Boston committee, Salem committee members described what happened when they answered Gage's summons:

> He asked if we avowed those notifications. It was answered by one of the comtee. that it was well known that the comtee. of correspondence ordered the notifications for the meeting. He then desired us to disperse the people immediately; for as we were the source of the meeting, we must abide by the consequences. It was answered, that the inhabitants being assembled, they would act as they thought fit, we could not oblige them to disperse; that we did not think we acted in opposition even to an act of parliament, much less to the laws of this province. He told us he should not enter into a discourse about the matter, he came here to execute the laws, not dispute about them. . . . He concluded by telling us if the people did not disperse, the Sheriff would go first; and if he was disregarded, and needed support, that he would support him. This he uttered with much vehemence.[6]

Even as the governor was meeting with the committee, two companies from the Fifty-Ninth Regiment were marching to the entrance of town. There they halted and loaded their guns. Eighty soldiers then continued toward the courthouse. But the troops, "equipped as if for battle," were too late: the meeting had already done its business and disbanded, having elected six representatives to the county convention.

As threatened, Gage pressed the issue. He ordered Judge Peter Frye to issue warrants for the arrest of the committee members who had called the meeting, charging them with "seditiously and unlawfully causing the town to be assembled by those notifications, without leave from the governour, in open contempt of the laws, against the peace, and the late statute."[7] The first two patriots brought into custody posted bail, but the next five refused, defiantly telling Gage "if the ninetieth part of a farthing would be taken as bail, they would not give it." They then returned the governor's previous threat: "If he committed them, *he must abide by the consequences.* "[8]

Judge Frye soon released his prisoners without bail, no doubt influenced by a huge outpouring of popular pressure. John Andrews reported on Friday, August 26:

> The affair at Salem is the only topic of speculation this day. The latest accounts we have had from there was at ten o'clock P.M. [probably Thursday evening], when there was upwards of three thousand men assembled there from the adjacent towns, with full determination to rescue the Committee if they should be sent to prison, even if they were oblig'd to repel force with force, being sufficiently provided for such a purpose; as indeed they are all through the country—every male above the age of 16 possessing a firelock with double the quantity of powder and ball enjoin'd by law.[9]

Thus, seven months and twenty-four days before the famous showdown between British Regulars and colonial farmers on the Lexington Green, Governor Gage was faced with a decision of staggering proportions: Should he force the issue? If he did not, he would be failing to enforce British law—but if he did, blood would flow.

Gage's first response was to issue an ultimatum: committee members, although temporarily freed on their own honor, had until 4:00 P.M. Thursday to post the bail that was originally demanded of them. The governor's ultimatum, of course, was ignored. Faced with over three thousand armed and angry patriots that night, Gage finally decided to back down. "[H]is Excellency has suspended the matter at Salem by dropping the prosecution," Andrews wrote the following day. "[S]eeing them resolute and the people so determinate, he was willing to give up a point rather than push matters to extremities."[10]

The patriots, on the other hand, pushed the issue even further: Why had Frye, justice for the Inferior Court of the County of Essex, agreed to do the bidding of Governor Gage? Indeed, why should he conduct any business at all under the new Act?

Gage knew that Frye was vulnerable. Fearing for the judge's well-being, he offered protection: "If you are in any Apprehensions for the safety of your House, you will put in it as many Soldiers as you think Necessary for your Defence." [11] But protection would not be enough. Peter Frye, a resident of Salem, would have to live side-by-side with his neighbors long after this incident had passed. "He and his family were in danger of starving," wrote John Andrews, "for the country people would not sell him any provisions, and the [town] inhabitants, however well dispos'd any might be to him, dare not procure him any." When the county convention of September 6 and 7 formalized measures to isolate Frye, he finally "resign'd all his posts of *honor* and *profit*." [12] We do not know the precise actions taken by the convention for the "fourth resolve, which respected Peter Frye, Esq.," was stricken from the record after he withdrew the outstanding warrants and offered his "frank and generous" resignation. [13] "I hope to be restored to that Friendship & Regard with my Fellow-Citizens and Countrymen which I heretofore enjoyed," Frye pleaded, giving up his office and promising "not to do any Thing either in my public or private Capacity" to execute the Massachusettss Government Act." [14]

Here at the seat of provincial government, patriots without fame had openly turned the Massachusetts Government Act into "a blank piece of paper and not more." It was a significant precedent. A few days later, in nearby Danvers (formerly Salem Village), the people held another meeting. As reported by John Andrews:

> Notwithstanding all the parade the governor made at Salem on account of their meeting, they had another one directly under his nose at Danvers, and continued it two or three howers longer than was necessary, to see if he would interrupt 'em. He was acquainted with it, but reply'd—"Damn 'em! I won't do any thing about it unless his Majesty sends me more troops." [15]

Now, having backed down twice in his own backyard, how could Gage expect to enforce the law in Springfield, Worcester, or other provincial towns?

On August 30, both the General Sessions of the Peace and the Inferior Court of Common Pleas for Hampshire County were slated to convene in Springfield. The Hampshire courts, far removed from Boston, would probably not receive support from British troops, but it was not a foregone conclusion that radicals could muster enough support to close the courts down. On the one hand, judging by the voting patterns of its representatives to the General Court, the political orientation of Hampshire County had been relatively conservative during the previous decade.[16] (An exception was Joseph Hawley, the representative from Northampton, who associated with the likes of Joseph Warren, John Adams, and Samuel Adams.) But on the other hand, common farmers were beginning to turn away from conservative leaders of the past and act according to their own interests. Israel Williams and John Worthington, the most powerful of the "river gods," were among the first "mandamus counsellors" to resign their posts.[17] Clearly, Tory elites were already feeling pressure in the Connecticut River Valley.[18]

In anticipation of the upcoming court session, the various towns elected delegates to convene on Friday, August 26, in Hadley—home of a recently erected liberty pole measuring 130 feet, thought to be the tallest in the province. When representatives from twenty-five towns and districts gathered there to consider whether the upcoming courts should be allowed to sit, they faced various options: they could petition the judges to adjourn; they could disrupt the court physically; or they could try to convince the judges to meet under the authority of the old charter instead of the Massachusetts Government Act. "After mature deliberation and passing of sundry votes," they decided to ask the judges themselves: under what authority did they hold their offices? This was a loaded question. Only by claiming they held office by the old charter would the judges have any hope of satisfying the patriots.[19]

As the radicals revved up for confrontation in Springfield, conservatives shuddered. The Reverend Stephen Williams of Longmeadow, uncle of Israel Williams, wrote in his journal on August 26: "I am in fear & concern, what things will come to—oh that God would graciously appear for our help." The following day, after hearing the news from Hadley, he wrote:

> Clouds & thick darkness are round about us—great tumults & uproars among people, complainings in our Streets, murmurings and a resolution (tis said) among many, that our courts Shall not Sit: I have this to comfort me, that the Lord reigns; the Lord G,d who is infinitely wise and powerfull, mercifull & just, he Governs O: I humbly request of him to pity this people; reform them, pardon them, and in thy great mercy, be pleasd to help us.[20]

Israel Williams, meanwhile, was conspicuously absent from the meeting at Hadley, even though he had dominated politics in Hampshire County for decades. In fact, he was conveniently out of the county, supposedly visiting his sick daughter in Pittsfield. Like Timothy Ruggles and Abijah Willard, however, he found no refuge while on the road. A crowd discovered his presence and accosted him, demanding that he resign his post on the council. He willingly complied, since he had already proffered his resignation. The crowd also demanded that he not interfere with the nonimportation agreement; here he complied begrudgingly. Finally, they demanded he not sit as a judge at the upcoming court session in Springfield. He refused, but the crowd determined he had conceded enough and they let him go his way.[21] Israel Williams would not always be able to talk his way out so easily. The following Tuesday, he would have to face the folks back home.

By Monday night, the judges, justices of the peace, lawyers, and various officials with business before the court had arrived in Springfield. Before the judges could don their suits and wigs and get to the courthouse early Tuesday morning, they heard the tolling of the West

Springfield bell—the signal for patriots to gather.[22] Two to four thousand men, many carrying white staves, soon mustered about the courthouse, where they hoisted a black flag to threaten the judges away.[23]

The message was clear. The judges and justices bypassed the courthouse and convened at a "publick house" nearby, where they received a committee of delegates from the demonstrators. The delegates asked them: How did they hold their authority, by the Charter or by the Act? However conservative in political philosophy, the officials knew how they must respond: "We consider and judge ourselves to hold our offices . . . by virtue and force of the Charter," they stated. But they did hedge: "The late act of Parliament," they claimed, had not made a significant "alteration" in their authority. Were they implying that they regarded the Act as consistent with the Charter?

The delegates took the justices' reply outside, where they read it "three times distinctly . . . to the people assembled." The people talked, discussed, debated, and finally concluded by a vote that the answer was not satisfactory. Then they took another vote: "Whether this Assembly be willing that the said Courts should sit." They decided it should not. The delegates went back to announce to the justices "that they would not sit contrary to the minds of the people."[24]

At this point, faced with a hostile crowd of thousands, the officials conceded the issue: they would not hold court under the Act. The patriot press reported the incident without going into great depth:

On Tuesday the 30th of August, the Day the County Court was to set at Springfield, a great concourse of People, judg'd about 3000, assembled at the Court-House in that place, and appointed a Committee to wait on the Court and request their appearance amongst the People, which they immediately complied with; when they very willingly signed the following Engagement, viz.

"We, the Subscribers, do severally promise and solemnly engage to all People now assembled, in the County of Hampshire, on the 30th Day of August 1774, that we will never take, hold, execute, or exercise any Commission, Office, or Employment whatsoever, under, or in Virtue of or in any Manner derived from any Authority, pretended or attempted to be given by a late Act of Parliament, entitled, 'An Act for better regulating the Government of the Province of Massachusetts-Bay, in New England.' "

[Signed] Israel Williams, Oliver Partridge, Timothy Dwight, Thomas Williams, John Worthington, Joseph Hawley, William Williams, Simeon Strong, Moses Bliss, Jonathan Ashley, Elisha Porter, William Billings, John Phelps, Solomon Stoddard, Justus Ely, Caleb Strong, Samuel Fowler, Jonathan Bliss.[25]

The newspaper account reveals little of the human drama, but we can learn more about what happened that day from a letter written by Joseph Clarke of Northampton, Joseph Hawley's adopted son, to an unidentified friend, addressing not only the substance but the tone of the Springfield demonstration. The people, according to Clarke, marched proudly about "with staves and musick" as they brought Crown-appointed officials to their knees:

Springfield, Aug. 30th, 1774.

We arrived in town about noon this day and found all the people gathered before us. A committee from the body of the county had just waited upon the court to demand a satisfactory answer, that is, whether they meant to hold their commissions and exercise their authority according to the new act of parliament for altering the constitution of the province, which being answered in the negative, It was put to vote after the Sd message & answer were read to the people assembled before the meeting house, whether they were willing the Court should sit; it passed in the negative.

Then the people paraded before Mr. Parson's [a large tavern on the southeast corner of the courthouse square], from thence marched back again to the meeting-house and demanded the appearance of the judges. The judges came according to their desire, and amidst the Crowd in a sandy, sultry place, exposed to the sun as far as they were able in such circumstances, gave a reasonable, &, to the major part, a satisfactory answer to such questions as were asked.

It was also demanded of them that they should make a declaration in writing, signed by all the justices and lawyers in the County, renouncing in the most express terms any commission which should be given out to them or either of them under the new arrangement, which was immediately complied with and executed accordingly.

The People then reassembled before Mr. Parson's house. Your uncle Catlin falling into a personal quarrel, at length gained the attention of the people. They considered him as an object worthy of their malice, as he was an officer of the court. He was treated with candor and too mildly to make any complaint. His boasted heroism failed him in the day of trial, and vanished like a puf of smoak. He and O. Warner, who came to his assistance in the quarrel, made such declarations as were requested of them, and then were dismissed, unhurt, and in peace. Your uncle may say what he pleases with regard to their abuse of him, but I was an eye witness to the whole, and you I believe will be satisfied that no abuse was intended when I tell you what easy terms they requested & were satisfied with, namely, only a declaration that he would not hold any office under the new act of parliament.

Col. Worthington was next brought upon the board. The sight of him flashed lightening from their eyes. Their spirits were already raised and the sight of this object gave them additional force. He had not refused his new office of counsellor. [According to Governor Gage, Worthington had in fact already resigned, but he had not yet published his resignation.] For that reason especially he was very obnoxious. But the people kept their tempers. He attempted to harangue them in mittigation of his conduct, but he was soon obliged to desist. The people were not to be dallied with. Nothing would satisfy them but a renunciation in writing of his office as Counsellor and a recantation of his address to Gov. Gage, which last was likewise signed by Jona. Bliss & Caleb Strong, Jun.

Jonathan Bliss next came upon the floor, he was very humble and the people were very credulous. He asked their pardon for all he had said or done which was contrary to their opinions; and as he depended for his support upon the people, he beged to stand well in their favor.

Mr. Moses Bliss was brought into the ring, but the accusation against him was not well supported, and he passed off in silence. The Sheriff was the next who was demanded; he accordingly appeared. He was charged with saying some imprudent things, but none of them were proved, & he departed.

Col. Williams took the next turn. He went round the ring and vindicated himself from some accusations thrown upon him and denied some things that were laid to his charge. He declared in my hearing that "altho' he had heretofore differed from the people in opinion with regard to the mode of obtaining redress, he would, hereafter, heartily acquiesce in any measures, that they should take for that purpose, and join with them in the common cause. He considered his interest as embarked in the same bottom with theirs, and hoped to leave it in peace to his Children."

Capt. Merrick of Munson was next treated with for uttering imprudent expressions. I thought they would have tarred & feathered him, and I thought he almost deserved it. He was very stubborn, as long as he dare be, but at length he made some concessions. But not till after they had carted him. No man received the least injury, but the strictest order of justice were observed. The people to their honor behaved with the greatest order & regularity, a few individuals excepted, and avoided, as much as possible, confusion.

The people of each town being drawn into separate companies marched with staves & musick. The trumpets sounding, drums beating, fifes playing and Colours flying, struck the passions of the soul into a proper tone, and inspired martial courage into each.

I kept all the time amongst the people, and observed their temper and dispositions, which I shall be better able to inform by word of mouth than otherwise.

Another incident I will relate and then I have done. Mr. Stearns, by imprudent expressions, raised their indignation. They marched in a body to Col. Worthington's and demanded him. Mrs. Worthington assured them he was not in the house. But they were by no means satisfied. They entered the house. She was fright, delivered up all her keys, begged of them to accept of their property, but spare their lives, and took her two youngest daughters in her arms and fled out into the fields. The people searched the house, but not finding Stearns they returned peaceably.

The people will probably be condemned for preventing the sitting of the court but their conduct yet is comendable. I wait till morning, hope nothing will be transacted rashly tonight, for it is given out by the fearful that there is a number looking.[26]

And so it was, in a "sandy, sultry place, exposed to the sun," that British authority was overthrown in Hampshire County. The imposing black suits and weighty offices of the judges offered no protection from men with "lightning" in their eyes. When John Worthington tried to bicker, the people made it clear they "were not to be dallied with."[27] Having seen what had happened to Worthington, Israel Williams, the most powerful man in western Massachusetts, was reduced to groveling. His apologies notwithstanding, he would continue to be hounded mercilessly by the plain farmers over whom he had once lorded.

Yet there had been no violence. The handful of unarmed officials, with few (if any) allies in the crowd, would have been foolish to take on three thousand men, organized into military companies. A smaller crowd might have had to play all their cards to force submission, but not here. The force implicit in such an overwhelming majority was too strong to permit resistance, and without resistance no blood would be shed.

According to Clarke, the crowd adjusted its behavior according to individual personalities. Those smart enough to submit without a quarrel were quickly dismissed; those who needed more coaxing were treated to additional displays of the people's power. In either case, the victims were dismissed as soon as they resigned. This was a purposive event with a definite goal, not an exercise in vengeance or retribution.

Clarke's description, although written only to a friend and not intended for public view, abounded with praise for the restraint of the crowd. This was certainly no mob, he wanted to believe: Catlin was treated "mildly"; the people "kept their tempers" with Worthington; "the strictest order of justice was observed." Some suspects were even released for lack of evidence—hardly a trademark of mobs.

Joseph Clarke, it would seem, had good reason to praise the events of the day, but he also had good reason to express, in his closing remark, fear of the events that might transpire that night. Might not their newly acquired power make the farmers heady? To what lengths might the triumphant rebels go, fueled by liquor after such a day as this?

As it turns out, there were no reports of mob action that night, nothing "transacted rashly." [28] There can be little doubt, however, that the public houses of Hampshire County came to life on the evening of August 30, 1774. Imagine the feeling of power the men had felt outside the courthouse, marching to martial music as the mighty were pulled down. And imagine the toasts that evening, with hearty "huzzahs" following each one—thirty, fifty, perhaps a hundred or more deep male voices echoing from the walls of every tavern in the vicinity of Springfield. This was the stuff of revolution.

The old order was crumbling. The worst fears of the conservatives were being realized. The Reverend Stephen Williams wrote on August 30:

this is a memoriable day—the court was to Set—the populace met in Grat Numbers—& hinderd them, yea tis said brot ye judges to make Declarations, & promises—thus we are brot to

Anarchy—but I will yet comfort myself, that ye Lord Reigns—Zion/King Sits in Heaven—tis a time, I believe fer ye prudent to Keep Silence.[29]

And Southampton's Jonathan Judd, Jr., recorded in his journal:

Wednesday. 31. hear this Morning that 3, or 4,000 People were collected that they would not let the Court Sit. afterwards they trimed some of the Court. all opposition was in vain every Body submitted to our Sovereign Lord the Mob—Now we are reduced to a State of Anarchy. have neither Law nor any other Rule except the Law of Nature which much vitiated and Darkened to go by. . . .

Saturday. 3. nothing new unless that the Mob Party are likes to be the Strongest what is like to be the event of these things none knows. the most miserable Situation is probable. people seem to be infatuated to our Destruction.[30]

Yes, the people *were* infatuated with the destruction of the British-controlled government, which had been administered by family and friends of Williams and Judd. And yes, as Williams cautioned, it would be prudent for those who opposed the rebels to remain silent. The insurgents, secure in their numbers and aroused to action, were indeed a force "not to be dallied with."

Also on August 30, 150 delegates from "from every town and district" in Middlesex County gathered at Concord "to consult upon measures proper to be taken at the present very important day." The first item on the agenda was to read "the Act for better regulating the Government of the Province of Massachusetts Bay" in its entirety. The convention then chose a committee of nine to draft an appropriate response.[31]

The preamble to the committee's report, one of the most literate and powerful expressions of the radical sentiments of the time, established the urgency of the moment, but it also called for a reasonable and mature "mode of conduct":

> It is evident to every attentive mind, that this province is in a very dangerous and alarming situation. We are obliged to say, however painful it may be to us, that the question now is, whether, by a submission to some late acts of parliament of Great Britain, we are contented to be the most abject slaves, and entail that slavery on posterity after us, or by a manly, joint, and virtuous opposition, assert and support our freedom. There is a mode of conduct, which in our very critical circumstances, we would wish to adopt; a conduct, on the one hand, never tamely submissive to tyranny and oppression, on the other, never degenerating into rage, passion, and confusion. This is a spirit which we revere, as we find it exhibited in former ages, and will command applause to the latest posterity.

The resolutions followed the same line of reasoning as the Worcester convention of August 9 and 10: the 1691 charter had been a contract, which Parliament violated when it passed the Massachusetts Government Act. With a touch of irony, the report stated "that a debtor may as justly refuse to pay his debts, because it is inexpedient for him, as the parliament of Great Britain deprive us of our charter privileges, because it is inexpedient to a corrupt administration for us to enjoy them." With great attention to detail, the report then elucidated the ways in which the citizens of Massachusetts would be disenfranchised if the Act were allowed to take effect: the governor's Council, formerly elected, would be appointed by the king; court judges and local officials would be appointed by the governor and serve at his pleasure, "without consent of council"; jurors would be summoned by sheriffs, who answered only to the governor; town meetings, "the scaffolding of English freedom," would be prohibited. The provisions of the Act, they concluded, "if quietly submitted to, will annihilate the last vestiges of liberty in this province, and therefore we must be justified by God and the world, in never submitting to them."

To oppose the Act, the report recommended that the people "yield no obedience" to any government official who "shall accept a commission under the present plan of arbitrary government." (It mentioned, in particular, Samuel Danforth and Joseph Lee, who had taken their oaths to sit on the Council.) It recommended convening a Provincial Congress, just as Timothy Bigelow and the joint committees of correspondence had suggested three days earlier, and it pledged itself to abide by the determinations of the Continental Congress, soon to meet in Philadelphia. Most significantly, it stated that "we will not submit to courts" constituted under the Act, and that "all business at the inferior court of common pleas and court of general sessions of the peace, next to be holden at Concord, must cease."

This report, after debate, was adopted by the Middlesex County Convention by a vote of 146 to 4. The stage was set for a showdown in Concord on September 13.

Simultaneous with the Hampshire court closure in Springfield and the Middlesex convention in Concord, patriots from throughout Worcester County met in the town of Worcester on Tuesday, August 30. One hundred and thirty men attended, more than double the turnout for the previous convention on August 9 and 10. In fact, the gathering was too large to be contained within the confines of Mary Stearns' tavern. After the opening prayer, the first item of business was "[b]y reason of the straitness of the place, and the many attending, to adjourn to the county court house." [32]

Timothy Bigelow and Ephraim Doolittle, recently returned from Boston, were among the committee of nine chosen to draft the resolutions. The following morning at 7:00, when the meeting of the whole reconvened at the courthouse, the first thing discussed was how to proceed with debate:

Voted, That every person who speaks in this meeting shall rise up, and, after he is done speaking, shall sit down, and not speak more than twice on the same subject, without obtaining leave, and shall not speak irrelevantly.

Here in the heartland of New England, where citizens were well versed in the art of conducting meetings, patriots imbued with a democratic spirit wanted to insure against domination by a few individuals.

The committee's draft was read and debated throughout the morning. In the afternoon each resolution was voted on separately, and some were altered significantly before being approved. Again, the format favored a full and detailed discussion of the issues.

The final draft included more than rhetoric. In addition to presenting the case against the Act, delegates addressed issues of local and practical concern. If they meant to close the courts, exactly how would they pull it off? And how would they govern themselves afterward, with no recourse to the official administration of justice?

The first resolution stated point-blank "that it is the indispensable duty of the inhabitants of this county, by the best ways and means, to prevent the sitting of the respective courts." To achieve this, the convention "recommended to the inhabitants of this county, to attend, in person," the court session starting on September 6. In order that the protest remain orderly, delegates "recommended to the several towns, that they choose proper and suitable officers, and a sufficient number, to regulate the movements of each town, and prevent any disorder which might otherwise happen." Again, these freehold farmers, artisans, and other respectable folk did not wish to be construed as a mob, despite their advocacy of mass demonstrations:

> Resolved, That as the dark and gloomy aspect of our public affairs has thrown this province into great convulsions, and the minds of the people are greatly agitated with the near view of impending ruin, we earnestly recommend to every one, and we engage ourselves, to use the utmost influence in suppressing all riotous and disorderly proceedings in our respective towns.

Since "the ordinary course of justice must be stayed," the men reasoned, each individual should "pay his just debts as soon as may be possible, without any disputes or litigation." During an indeterminate period wherein there would be no civil authority, certain routine functions of government—in particular, the licensing of "innholders and retailers"—would revert to the towns. (The regulation of the sale of alcoholic beverages in hard-drinking but God-fearing New England was always a hot local issue.) This interim period, delegates hoped, would not last for long. Each town was urged to elect representatives to "one general provincial convention, to be convened at Concord, on the second Tuesday of October next, to devise ways and means to resume our original mode of government." The need for a Provincial Congress had been discussed before; now, after the multicounty meeting three days earlier in Boston, a date and place had been set.

The cornerstone of government, both old and new, had to be the town meeting: towns should "pay no regard to the late act of parliament, respecting the calling of town meetings, but, to proceed in their usual manner." Towns were also urged to "indemnify their constables for neglecting to return lists of persons qualified to serve as jurors."

Finally, the delegates addressed the most pressing matter of the moment: a call to arms. The first draft of the resolutions read:

That whereas, it is generally expected, that the governor will send one or more regiments to enforce the execution of the acts of parliament, on the 6th of September, that it be recommended to the inhabitants of this county, if there is intelligence, that troops are on their march to Worcester, to attend, properly armed, in order to repel any hostile force which may be employed for that purpose.

Some delegates must have wondered: Why protect only the town of Worcester? The original motion was withdrawn in favor of one more universally applicable:

That if there is an invasion, or danger of an invasion, in any town in this county, then such town as is invaded, or being in danger thereof, shall, by their committees of correspondence, or some other proper persons, send letters, by express posts, imme-

diately, to the committees of the adjoining towns, who shall send
to other committees in the towns adjoining them, that they all
come properly armed and accoutred to protect and defend the
place invaded.

What counted most, however, were the accompanying measures:

> *Voted,* That it be recommended to each town of the county, to
> retain in their own hands, what moneys may be due from them
> severally to the province treasury. . . .
> *Voted,* That each member will purchase at least two pounds of
> powder in addition to any he may have on hand, and will use all
> his exertions to supply his neighbors fully.
> *Voted,* That the members and delegates endeavor to ascertain
> what number of guns are deficient to arm the people in case of
> invasion.

The citizens of Worcester County were preparing for war. On July
4 the American Political Society had declared "that each, and every,
member of our Society, be forth with Provided, with Two Pounds of
Gun Powder each 12 Flints and Led Answerable thereunto," and
thirty-five of the men present promptly agreed to "take and pay for"
between two and six pounds of powder each.[33] On July 22 merchant
Stephen Salisbury told his brother Samuel that although business was
slow, he was completely out of gunpowder; the demand was so great,
in fact, that he was thinking of building his own powderhouse. On
August 20 he wrote, "Guns are in good demand as well as powder. I
would therefore have you send me all the Longest guns that you
have." On August 25 he asked Samuel to send him, along with choco-
late, pepper, and Spanish indigo, some "Barr Lead," "Gun Locks,"
and "Bullets—25 to the pound." [34]

At some point—we don't know exactly when—members of the
American Political Society managed to smuggle four cannons out
of Boston.[35] "Blood will too probably be spilt in this contest," wrote
"A. P." in the *Massachusetts Spy* on August 25, but "to suffer these

novel courts to go on and establish themselves is treasonably to give up our constitution; to spill our dearest blood in its defence is . . . a duty for the neglect of which we demerit ETERNAL DAMNATION." [36]

On August 27, three days before the county convention in Worcester, General Gage wrote to Lord Dartmouth:

> In Worcester, they keep no Terms, openly threaten Resistance by Arms, have been purchasing Arms, preparing them, casting Ball, and providing Powder, and threaten to attack any Troops who dare to oppose them. Mr. Ruggles of the new Council is afraid to take his Seat as Judge of the inferior Court, which sits at Worcester on the 7th [actually the 6th] of next Month, and I apprehend that I shall soon be obliged to march a Body of Troops into that Township, and perhaps into others, as occasion happens, to preserve the Peace. [37]

During the week prior to the convening of the Worcester court, as Commander-in-Chief Thomas Gage prepared his troops, Governor Thomas Gage tried to act as if he still commanded political authority over the province of Massachusetts. On Tuesday, August 30—the day of the court closure at Springfield and the Worcester and Middlesex county conventions—Gage attended the opening of the Superior Court of Judicature in Boston, in Suffolk County, the only place where it could safely convene.

Traditionally, sessions of the Superior Court were replete with pomp and circumstance, and despite the political turmoil, the ceremonious court was to proceed as usual. The *Boston Gazette* reported:

> Last Tuesday being the day the Superior Court was to be holden here, the Chief Justice, Peter Oliver, Esq., and the other Justices of said Court, together with a number of gentlemen of the bar, attended by the High and Deputy Sheriffs, walked in procession from the state-house to the court-house, in Queen-street. When the Court were seated and the usual proclamations made, a list of

the names of the gentlemen returned to serve as Grand Jurors, was presented to them, and the Court appointed Mr. Ebenezer Hancock, Foreman.[38]

There were no mass demonstrations against the court on the streets of Boston, but when Ebenezer Hancock rose to be sworn in, he declined. One by one, each of the twenty-two grand jurors refused to take the oath. When asked why, each referred to a prepared written document, which made the usual case against Peter Oliver sitting as chief justice and the usual argument against the Massachusetts Government Act. This was a politically orchestrated event. It is unlikely that all the jurors, selected by the governor and his appointed sheriff, agreed with the statement of resignation they had just signed, but all felt compelled to go along.

In addition to the twenty-two grand jurors, all thirty-three of the petit jurors tendered their resignations. Chief Justice Oliver, after urging the jurors to reconsider, adjourned the court until the following day. Perhaps Gage, Oliver, and the other judges thought they could apply some countervailing pressure on the jurors out of chambers, but it was to no avail. When the court reconvened at 10:00 the next morning, all jurors were absent. So was Peter Oliver. Perhaps he had been told to stay home to entice the jurors to return, but even that didn't work. Not a single one of the jurors dared defy popular sentiment.

The Superior Court of Judicature for Suffolk County, minus its jurors, continued to meet through Friday, conducting "such business as is usually transacted, without Juries."[39] Since it decided a number of cases, Gage could point to at least one governmental body that continued to function, however minimally. This was enough to needle the patriots, who felt that *any* session of *any* court which met under the authority of the Massachusetts Government Act was anathema to the cause of freedom. The decision of the Superior Court judges to continue the session, according to the *Boston Gazette*, caused "inexpressible grief" for "their fellow citizens."[40]

On Wednesday, August 31, Gage tried to convene his council. Two days later, Gage wrote to Dartmouth, "I ordered a Council to assemble, but upon their Representation, that they shou'd be watched, stopped, and insulted on the Road to Salem, [they desired] to be assembled here [in Boston]." [41] Only fifteen of the original thirty-six attended, but, as with the Superior Court, Gage proceeded with business nonetheless. He told the Council why so few members had attended (as if the remaining councilors did not already know), and then he asked for their input on a pressing decision he had to make within the next week:

> . . . whether they would advise to the sending of any troops into the County of Worcester, or any other County in the Province, for the protection of the Judges and other Officers of the Courts of Justice. Whereupon several Gentlemen of the Council expressed their Opinions, that inasmuch as the opposition to the execution of any part of the late Acts of Parliament relating to this Province, was so general, they apprehended it would not be for His Majesty's service to send any Troops into the interior parts of the Province, but that the main body continue in the Town of Boston, which might be strengthened by the addition of other Troops, to be improved as circumstances may occur, and be a place of safe retreat for all those who may find it necessary to remove thither. [42]

As much as Brigadier Ruggles, "Commodo." Loring, "Colo." Murray, "Colo." Leonard, "Colo." Edson, and Mr. Pepperell (as they were listed in the minutes) wanted to return to their homes outside Boston, they knew it wasn't feasible. Having directly encountered the power of the patriots, they offered sound advice to their governor: Keep your army in Boston.

But would he listen? On September 2, Gage wrote to Dartmouth:

> I came here [to Boston] to attend the superior Court, and in the Intention to send a Body of Troops to Worcester, to protect the Courts there, and if wanted to send Parties to the Houses of

some of the Counsellors who dwell in that County, but [I heard]
from undoubted Authorities, that the Flames of Sedition had
spread universally throughout the Country beyond Conception, the Counsellors already drove away, and that no Courts
could proceed on Business. . . .

The Council was of Opinion that it was very improper to
weaken the troops here by any Detachments whatever, as they
could not be of any Use to the Courts, as no Jurors wou'd appear, and by that Means defeat their Proceedings, and that Dis-
turbance being so general, and not confined to any particular
spot, there was no knowing where to send them to be of Use.[43]

Four days before the Worcester court was to convene, Gage
seemed to be having second thoughts about his plan to send troops.
Within a matter of hours, he would have additional cause for concern.
Even as he penned his letter to Dartmouth, events were transpiring in
nearby Cambridge that would help him make up his mind.

On the evening of Wednesday, August 31, Boston patriots noticed
some movement among the British Regulars. Sources near the governor reported that Gage was still upset about the events in Salem the
previous week, and they feared he might be sending troops to imprison the members of the Salem Committee. At 10:00 the Boston
committee sent an express message to Salem, warning patriots there
of the troop movements. The Salem committee, by return express,
replied that they were ready "to receive any attack they might be exposed to for acting in pursuance to the laws and interest of their country, as became men and christians." [44]

But the troops didn't go to Salem. According to the *Boston Evening-
Post,*

On Thursday Morning, half after four, about 260 Troops embarked on board 13 Boats at the Long Wharf, and proceeded up
Mystic River to Temple's Farm, where they landed, and went to
the Powder-House on Quarry Hill, in Charleston Bounds,

where they took 212 Half Barrels of Powder [the *Boston Gazette* said 250], the whole Store there, and conveyed it to Castle-William. A detachment from this corps went to Cambridge and brought off two field pieces.[45]

Thomas Gage, in his own way, was heeding the advice his Council had just given him. Instead of sending troops deep into the heart of the province, or even to rebellious Salem, he managed to seize the offensive by acting more locally. By ten in the morning the mission had been accomplished, without meeting any resistance.

Gage had good reason to go after the powder. Four days earlier, on August 27, he had received a letter from Brigadier-General William Brattle:

This morning the Select Men of Medford, came and received their Town Stock of Powder, which was in the Arsenal on Quarry-Hill, so that there is now therein, the King's Powder only, which shall remain there as a sacred Deposition till ordered out by the Capt. General.[46]

The men from Medford had taken only what was their due, but they could have taken more; as confrontations escalated, Gage reasoned, they might well seize the king's powder as well. The general was making a preemptive strike. He was also initiating a military maneuver, however modest, that he could win.

But the military gain—some powder and two field pieces—came at an enormous political price.

On Thursday morning, September 1, a crowd began to gather at the windowless stone tower at Quarry Hill, which had one of Ben Franklin's new lightening rods extending from the roof. By the time they arrived, however, the British troops had already departed. There would be no direct confrontation that day, but the crowd was clearly upset at Gage's initiative. Even if it was the king's own powder, this *felt* like a hostile act.

As local townsmen and farmers talked about how they might respond, councilors Samuel Danforth and Joseph Lee from Cambridge, in Middlesex County, became anxious. They had not attended the meeting of the Council the day before, but neither had they tendered their resignations. With hundreds of angry men lolling about nearby, and more pouring in steadily, their moment of truth had arrived. They both decided to concede. That very day, each wrote to Gage, saying that in light of the circumstances, it would be prudent not serve on the Council. (When Danforth delivered his resignation in person, Gage refused to accept it. Danforth "might absent himself," Gage held, but since he had already taken the oath, he was obliged "to give him council.") [47]

Toward evening some of the crowd went home, still unsatisfied. Others lingered about; according to John Andrews, these were primarily "the country people, being vastly more vigilant and spirited than the town." [48] The crowd drifted toward Cambridge's "Tory Row," where they paid a visit to Brigadier Brattle, whose plush estate, held in the family for four generations, extended down to the Charles River. But Brattle, the informer, had thought it best to retreat to Castle William, "the only place of safety for him in the province." [49] The crowd then went to the home of the attorney-general, Jonathan Sewall, who had accepted a post on the admiralty court. Sewall, like Brattle, had thought it wise to leave home, at least for the moment. His wife talked with members of the crowd, asking that they do no harm to her and her family. They might have listened, but Ward Chipman, a friend of Sewall, fired a gun from inside the house. The crowd proceeded to break some windows, but they inflicted no further damage. [50]

On Friday morning farmers from the outlying communities of Cambridge, Charlestown, Framingham, Waltham, Watertown, and Concord gathered on the Cambridge common; by eight o'clock the crowd was estimated at 3,000, and more were on their way. [51] The men had left their arms "at some distance behind them," but they did carry sticks. [52] They intended to make a show of strength; they did not intend to engage the British Regulars in battle.

A rumor soon spread among the crowd that British troops were headed toward Cambridge. In Boston, meanwhile, word spread that tens of thousands of men from the country were intending to invade the city. John Andrews wrote:

> Four or five expresses have come down to Charlestown and here, to acquaint us, that between Sudbury and this, above ten thousand men are in arms and are continually coming down from the country back: that their determination is to collect about forty or fifty thousand by night (which they are sure of accomplishing) when they intend to bring in about fifteen thousand by way of the Neck, and as many more over the ferry: when once got possession, to come in like locusts and rid the town of every soldier.[53]

Concern escalated to alarm. Patriot leaders from Cambridge and Boston were not ready for a confrontation of this magnitude. If soldiers came, and if farmers fetched their arms, they feared a major bloodbath.

The Cambridge committee quickly decided on a two-pronged strategy. First, they approached Lieutenant-Governor Thomas Oliver, who lived nearby. Thomas Oliver, unlike Chief Justice Peter Oliver, still maintained a modicum of credibility with the people, and he was presumed to have some influence with Governor Gage. According to Oliver,

> Early in the morning a number of the inhabitants of Charlestown called at my house to acquaint me that a large body of people from several towns in the county were on their way coming down to Cambridge; that they were afraid some bad consequences might ensue, and begged I would go out to meet them, and endeavor to prevail on them to return. In a very short time, before I could prepare myself to go, they appeared in sight. I went out to them, and asked the reasons of their appearance in that manner; they respectfully answered, they "came peaceably to inquire into their grievances, not with design to hurt any

man." I perceived they were landholders of the neighboring towns, and was thoroughly persuaded they would do no harm. I was desired to speak to them; I accordingly did, in such a manner as I thought best calculated to their minds. They thanked me for my advice, said they were no mob, but sober, orderly people, who would commit no disorders; and then proceeded on their way. I returned to my house.

Soon after they had arrived on the Common at Cambridge, a report arose that the troops were on their march from Boston; I was desired to go and intercede with his Excellency to prevent their coming. From principles of humanity to the country, from a general love of mankind, and from persuasions that they were orderly people, I readily undertook it; and is there a man on earth, who, placed in my circumstances, could have refused it? . . . [A]s I passed the people I told them, of my own accord, I would return and let them know the event of my application.[54]

The Cambridge committee also sent dispatches to Charlestown and Boston, hoping that influential patriot leaders could "appease, . . . satisfy and disperse" the crowd.[55] According to Joseph Warren:

[A] billet was brought, requesting me to take some step in order to prevent the people from coming to immediate acts of violence, as incredible numbers were in arms, and lined the roads from Sudbury to Cambridge. I summoned the committee of correspondence; but, as care had been taken to caution every man who passed the ferry from alarming Boston, I judged it best not to inform the person who warned the committee of the business they were to meet upon. They, therefore, made no great haste to get together. After waiting some time, I took as many of the members as came in my way to Charlestown, fearing that something amiss might take place. I saw the gentlemen at Charlestown, who begged us to move forward to Cambridge. On our way, we met the Lieutenant-governor Oliver. He said he was going to the general, to desire him not to march his troops out of Boston. We thought his precaution good, and proceeded to Cambridge.[56]

As Whig and Tory leaders met on the road, each with the aim of averting a confrontation, the farmers on the Cambridge common proceeded with their business. A committee opened negotiations with Joseph Lee and Samuel Danforth at Lee's home, but the people soon demanded that they speak before the full assembly. The crowd insisted the councilors resign their seats. Danforth and Lee explained they had already done so, and each offered a written declaration to that effect. The crowd then voted: Would that suffice? They decided it would.[57]

Then David Phips, sheriff of Middlesex County, was made to answer before the assembly. Phips was called to task for opening the powder house, but he pleaded that he had been under command and really had no choice. He prepared a formal statement, promising that he would "not execute any Precept that shall be sent me under the new Acts," and that he would "call in the Venires that I have sent out under the new Establishment." Would that be enough? Again the assembly voted, and they decided it would do.[58]

During these proceedings six members of the Boston committee arrived at the common. These patriot leaders—including such renowned personalities as Joseph Warren, Thomas Young, William Molineux, and William Cooper—were relieved and impressed with the demeanor of the crowd. Young wrote to Samuel Adams, who was serving as a delegate to the Continental Congress in Philadelphia: "When Dr. Warren and I arrived there Judge Danforth was addressing perhaps four thousand people in the open air; and such was the order of that great assembly that not a whisper interrupted the low voice of that feeble old man from being heard by the whole body."[59] Warren also described the scene in Cambridge to Samuel Adams: "We there saw a fine body of respectable freemen, with whom we spent the day, and were witnesses of their patience, temperance, and fortitude."[60] Edward Hill, another well-known patriot, reported to John Adams, who was also a delegate to the Continental Congress:

I cannot omit mentioning that I was present when the People assembled at Cambridge; and never saw men who appear'd so determined to pursue the measures they had plan'd—they were dress'd just as they are at work—every man appeared just as composed as if they were at a funeral—I saw many among them whom I should judge were 60 and 70 years of age.[61]

The Boston patriots, accustomed to leadership roles, could not help but join in the discussion. Cooper and Molineux took the stage and argued that Gage had a legal right to take the powder, since it belonged to the king; besides, it was old and wet. When John Bradford, also of the Boston committee, tried to interrupt, he was pushed away. After the others had finished, Bradford countered that the action was illegal since Gage had not sought the advice of the Council, as constituted under the old charter. The farmers stood and listened.[62]

Then the Boston committee suggested the assembly vote on the proposition "that they abhorred and detested all petty Mobs, Riots, Breaking Windows and destroying private Property." The people unanimously approved; in fact, they had already passed a similar proposition before the Bostonians arrived.[63] Everybody, it appears, wanted to distance themselves from the actions of the previous evening, when Sewall's windows were broken. Joseph Warren referred to that incident as the work of "some Boys and Negroes," although of course he was not there. Newspapers used the exact same phrase.[64] Undoubtedly, some of the participants from Thursday evening were present on Friday, but nobody would admit to it.

This gathering, like those at the county conventions and court closings, was highly conscious of its image. Somebody actually asked Danforth and Lee how the crowd had treated them. Lee responded that they were "the most extraordinary People that he ever saw for Sobriety and Decency."[65]

Toward noon, the heat of the day intensified. (The demonstrators had to endure "the scorching sun of the hottest day we have had this summer," Thomas Young wrote to Samuel Adams.)[66] Cooper suggested that the crowd choose a committee, which would then retire to take refreshments and "to confer about the Situation" with the Boston committee in the cool of Captain Stedman's inn; the remainder of the crowd would swelter on the common, awaiting the return of Lieutenant-Governor Oliver with news from Governor Gage. In fact, a committee had already been chosen earlier that morning, but the leaders had remained among the people. This came as a surprise to the Bostonians, who were used to operating quite differently. Historian Dirk Hoerder explains:

> [T]he stratification and deferential character of Bostonian society made them blind to the social implications of the theory of popular sovereignty. They acted as they were accustomed to at celebrations: The gentlemen drank toasts inside Faneuil Hall, and the people huzzahed outside. Now in Cambridge the action had been done by "the people," and elected spokesmen were literally overlooked by the Boston "radicals" because they did not separate from their constituents, because they did not act like the dignified and elevated "better sort." The Boston leaders, on the other hand, attempted at once physically and politically to separate from the people.[67]

Sometime after the resignations of Lee and Danforth, but before Thomas Oliver returned, customs commissioner Benjamin Hallowell, returning from Salem to Boston, rode through town in his chaise. For a time it looked like Hallowell might be able to pass though without incident, but as he was leaving Cambridge, he encountered a group of men on a narrow street. The ensuing drama added a new dimension to the day. Hallowell himself told the story of his high-speed chase with dramatic flair:

> No Insult or Affront was offered me untill I came to the Rear of them, where some people from Boston Stood, who called to me, Dam you how do you like us now, you Tory Son of a Bitch, and other language as abusive, pointing me out at the same time, to the rabble, as an Enemy to the Country. . . . [U]nder this En-

couragement more than one hundred and fifty men on horse back set out in pursuit of me, the abusive people which were many, having taken a resolution to destroy me.[68]

Just at this moment of peril, however, Hallowell received aid from a most unexpected source:

[T]he Committee of Correspondence of Boston, who had join'd the people at Cambridge, giving their opinion against the pursuit, alledging that the Shedding of one mans blood, wou'd answer no good purpose, and at the same time bring on the loss of many thousand lives, for they expected every moment the arrival of the troops from Boston; an express was sent off to Stop the Pursuers, most of them returned, 6 or 8 wou'd not be prevailed upon to go back, but continued the pursuit, overtaking of me about five miles from Boston, when one of them by the name of Bradshow, advanced before the rest, coming up to me saying that he wanted to speak to me, desiring I wou'd Stop, as I did not Comply with his request, he endeavour'd to Stop the Chaise Striking the horse over the head, trying to Catch hold of the Reins, declaring that there was five hundred men on horse back after me.

    I put on my horse, and presenting a pistol at this Bradshow, he retired at a Distance Still keeping before the Chaise, when any of them approached I presented my pistol, reserving my fire, and by this kind of defence kept myself out of their hands, the man that was before the Chaise, Cry'd out all the way as he passed, Stop the Murderer the Tory Murderer he has killed a man; This Hue and Cry occasioned a Sallying forth of the people from the Houses, which were many, others upon the Road joined in the Cry all endeavouring to Stop me.

The patriots told the story differently: Hallowell, they claimed, had fired some shots. In any case, the chase continued:

I had not been pursued more than one mile before my Chais's horse began to fail, I immediately mounted my Servants horse, leaving the Chaise with the Gentleman who came from Salem with me, the Saddle horse happened to be a fleet one, I let drop the Reins on his Neck (leaving my own house about a mile on my Right) holding a pistol in each hand, and thus ran the gantlet, and reach'd, unhurt, the Guards on Boston Neck. At one time there was not less than one hundred people Surrounding of me, all endeavoring to Seize me.

John Andrews was not a participant, but he told the tale as seen through the eyes of the patriots:

Commissioner Hallowell, coming from Salem to his house in Roxbury, pass'd by Cambridge common, where the people were collected, spoke somewhat contemptuously of them, which soon came to their ears. They immediately sent a party in pursuit of him. He saw them coming; jump'd out of his chaise; order'd his negro off the horse and got on; when he set out upon the full gallop with a pistol in each hand. One of the party, better mounted than the rest, overtook him upon the Neck, at whom he snap'd his pistol, which luckily missed fire, when he put on with full speed, and flung himself into the protection of the guard posted there.

News of the above movement of the Army, which was represented as though they were coming against them, together with the *aggravation* that Hallowell had shot a man, was carried to Cambridge, which set the people in a prodigious ferment (who before were become quite calm and compos'd) and every one retir'd to Watertown, where they had left their arms, and return'd to the Common fully equipp'd and well disposed to make a tryal of skill. They had the presence of mind to get matters in readiness to take up the bridge, to prevent their bringing the artillery to bear upon 'em, least the Combat should be too unequal.[69]

The Hallowell incident changed the tone of the day. According to a newspaper account,

A gentleman in Boston, observing the motion in the Camp, and concluding they were on the point of marching to Cambridge, from both ends of town, communicated the alarm to Dr. Roberts, then at Charlestown ferry, who having a very fleet Horse, brought the news in a few minutes to the committee, then at Dinner. The intelligence was instantly diffused, and the people whose arms were nearest sent persons to bring them.[70]

Alerted by a horseman that the redcoats were coming, patriots readied for battle—seven-and-one-half months before Paul Revere's famous ride.

The rumor, of course, proved unfounded. In fact, Thomas Oliver had visited General Gage, as promised, with the request to send no troops to Cambridge. Gage, who was composing a letter to Lord Dartmouth when Oliver arrived, wrote that the purpose of the lieutenant-governor's visit was "to beg I wou'd on no Account send any Troops there, or it wou'd prove fatal to him."[71] Gage honored the request, and he also included in his letter Oliver's respectful assessment of the demonstrators: although "worked up to a Fury," the crowd was "not a Boston Rabble but the Freeholders and Farmers of the Country."

When Oliver returned to Cambridge with positive news from Boston, he assumed the affair was over. He was wrong. Had matters been left to the committee of negotiators, he would have been let off, but the common farmers who had assembled to express their anger were not so easily palliated. Thomas Oliver's account of what happened during the afternoon of September 2 is particularly significant for the light it sheds on the relationship between the "people" and the "Committee," their supposed leaders:

On my return I went to the Committee, I told them no troops had been ordered, and from the account I had given his Excellency, none would be ordered. I was then thanked for the trouble I had taken in the affair, and was just about to leave them to their own business, when one of the Committee observed, that as I was present it might be proper to mention a matter they had to propose to me. It was, that although they had a respect for me as Lieutenant-Governor of the Province, they could wish I would resign my seat [on the Council].

I told them I took it very unkind that they should mention anything on that subject; and among other reasons I urged, that, as Lieutenant-Governor, I stood in a particular relation to the Province in general, and therefore could not hear anything upon that matter from a particular county. I was then pushed to know if I would resign when it appeared to be the sense of the Province in general; I answered, that when all the other Councillors had resigned, if it appeared to be the sense of the Province I should resign, I would submit. They [the committee] then called a vote upon the subject, and, by a very great majority, voted my reasons satisfactory. I inquired whether they had full power to act for the people, and being answered in the affirmative, I desired they would take care to acquaint them of their votes, that I should have no further application made to me on that head. I was promised by the Chairman, and a general assent, it should be so. . . .

In the afternoon I observed large companies pouring in from different parts; I then began to apprehend they would become unmanageable, and that it was expedient to go out of their way. I was just going into my carriage when a great crowd advanced, and in a short time my house was surrounded by three or four thousand people, and one quarter in arms. I went to the front door, where I was met by five persons, who acquainted me they were a Committee from the people to demand a resignation of my seat at the Board. I was shocked at their ingratitude and false dealings, and reproached them with it. They excused themselves by saying the people were dissatisfied with the vote of the Committee, and insisted on my signing a paper they had prepared for that purpose.

I found I had been ensnared, and endeavored to reason them out of such ungrateful behavior. They gave such answers, that I found it was in vain to reason longer with them; I told them my first considerations were for my honor, the next for my life that they might put me to death or destroy my property, but I would not submit. They began then to reason in their turn, urging the power of the people, and the danger of opposing them.

All this occasioned a delay, which enraged part of the multitude, who, pressing into my back yard, denounced vengeance to the foes of their liberties. The Committee endeavored to moderate them, and desired them to keep back, for they pressed up to my windows, which then were opened; I could thence hear them at a distance calling out for a determination, and, with their arms in their hands, swearing they would have my blood if I refused. The Committee appeared to be anxious for me, still I refused to sign; part of the populace growing furious, and the distress of my family who heard the threats, and supposed them just about to be executed, called up feelings which I could not suppress; and nature, ready to find new excuses, suggested a thought of the calamities I should occasion if I did not comply; I found myself giving way, and began to cast about to contrive means to come off with honor. I proposed they should call in the people to take me out by force, but they said the people were enraged, and they would not answer for the consequences. I told them I would take the risk, but they refused to do it. Reduced to this extremity, I cast my eyes over the paper, with a hurry of mind and conflict of passion which rendered me unable to remark the contents, and wrote underneath the following words: "My house at Cambridge being surrounded by four thousand people, in compliance with their commands, I sign my name, THOMAS OLIVER."

The statement Oliver signed declared that since the Massachusetts Government Act was "a manifest infringement of the Charter rights and privileges of this people," he would "solemnly renounce and resign my seat" on the Council. Oliver wanted to make it clear he was signing under pressure, but many in the assembly wanted a more forthright and total submission:

The five persons took it, carried it to the people, and I believe, used their endeavors to get it accepted. I had several messages that the people would not accept it with those additions, upon which I walked into the court-yard, and declared I would do no more, though they should put me to death. I perceived that those persons who formed the first body which came down in the morning, consisting of the landholders of the neighboring towns, used their utmost endeavors to get the paper received with my additions; and I must, in justice to them, observe, that, during the whole transaction, they had never invaded my enclosures, but still were not able to protect me from other insults which I received from those who were in arms. From this consideration I am induced to quit the country, and seek protection in the town.[72]

Oliver wished to make the distinction between the orderly morning assembly, respectable nearby landholders, and the more rowdy afternoon crowd who came from afar. Most likely, the politics of the Cambridge assembly were not that simple. Although all the participants disavowed riots and mobs, some were more radical than others in their demands and their actions—and some of the radicals came from nearby, since they had been present at Jonathan Sewall's the previous evening. Even so, an observer from Connecticut who happened to be traveling through Cambridge agreed that the mood of the crowd changed over the course of the day.

[I] mixt in with the Multitude, who were formed & standing before Lt. Gov. Oliver's House. . . . [T]here was no Tumult, but an awful stillness, Silence thro' the Lines, and among the surrounding Body of People. All was negotiated by the Committee but in the presence of the Body, the Committee communicating by the Officers Information thro' the Lines, so that all knew what was transacting. It was the after part of the Day. Gov. Oliver had a number of Gentlemen with him in his House & seemed very reluctant at the Transaction.

After some length of Waiting, he endeavored to have the people satisfied with what he had said in the Forenoon. But a weighty Spirit began to shew itself by some Gentlemen & Officers nearest, pressing thro' the Gate into the Governor's Yard with (tho' not as yet Violence yet with) Marks of Earnestness & Importunity which the Gov. and his friends saw was at length become irresistable. Thereupon the Gov. Oliver came forth abroad accompanied with a few Friends, and made and signed his Submission; which was immediately handed along the Lines & read publickly at proper Distances till the whole Body of the people were made to hear it. Upon which Satisfaction was diffused thro' the whole Body, which thereupon dissolved; the solemn Silence broken & succeeded by a chearful Murmur or general universal Voice of Joy. This was finished about sun an hour high or less.[73]

Clearly, this was no "mob," as the word was construed by conservatives. "An awful Stillness" prevailed because the demonstrators knew they were undertaking serious, and possibly treasonable, business. The need to proceed democratically was paramount. In this, the Cambridge gathering was not unique: at each of the court closings, during all the county conventions, and even during the acts of crowd intimidation directed against individuals, votes were taken at every crucial juncture. The New England town meetings, which this revolution was intended to protect, had trained people well in the art of democracy.

Lieutenant-Governor Thomas Oliver's forced resignation from the Council climaxed the Cambridge assembly. The heat broke late in the afternoon, and evening brought rain and thunder. The patriots disbanded, satisfied they had accomplished something. They had forced the man who held the second highest office in the province to submit to their will. The farmers and artisans who assembled at Cambridge had also demonstrated that the so-called leaders from Boston could not speak for the entire populace, nor, for that matter, could the elected committees. The people themselves—the assembly as a whole, as determined by democratic process—had seized the initiative and established control of this revolution-in-the-making.

And the people—not only from the areas surrounding Cambridge, but from throughout Massachusetts and even beyond provincial borders—had provided an impressive display of both popular sentiment and military mobilization. When a rumor spread that Boston had been bombarded by British fire and six men had been killed, great hordes of "Minute Men" from throughout New England and even beyond—contemporary estimates ran as high as one hundred thousand,[74] with six thousand coming from Worcester County alone[75]—headed immediately toward Boston. We have two detailed accounts of this massive outpouring of support, later to be dubbed the "Powder Alarm." The first comes from the Rev. Stephen Williams of Longmeadow:

> After we had got to the meeting house in ye afternoon—& just before ye Exercise began Mr F—— came in & informd that they had news from Boston—that the Ships in ye Harbour of Boston, & ye Army on ye Land Side were allso fireing upon ye Town so that it was like ye Town was Demolishd . . . people were put into a tumult & I closd ye prayer—& Great numbers went out . . . so many retird that it was difficult to cary on the Singing—I began my Srmon—but anon—a Signall was Given (or word Given) to the people at ye windows—so that most of the males rushd out of ye house—as if an Enemy was at ye End of Parish—So that I Soon closd my Sermn, & administerd Baptism to a child—& dismissd ye Assembly—thus we have had a disquietmt on ye Sabboth day. . . .
>
> a number of men with arms—to be ready to move in an instant if needd—ye blacksmith shop was opend—guns carrid to him to be mendd—horses to be Shod—& many Employd makeing Bullets—& a man Sent to Enfd to get powdr—in ye Evening people met again, & repaird to ye meeting house—& a number Gave in their names or listd & chose Some leader and were Getting ready to move—but while they were togather at ye meeting house—Mr J. Sykes, came again to them & informd

that ye messenger was returnd & brot tideings—that all was well, and quiet at Boston—that there had been a tumult, or Squabble at Boston—& one man Killd—but now quiet & Still—oh how have we Sind away, & misimprovd Sabboths.[76]

The other account comes from a Mr. McNeil of Litchfield, Connecticut, as told to the Reverend Ezra Stiles the following week as they rode together from Littlerest to Norwich. (A search through the Litchfield Historical Society has failed to reveal the exact identity of this "Mr. McNeil," whom Stiles said was a merchant, under age thirty, European, and "married to a rich Farmers Daughter in Litchfield.")[77] McNeil had found himself in Springfield on Tuesday, August 30, the day of the court closing there, and by Thursday evening he had made his way to Shrewsbury, "a few miles nearer Boston than Worcester." Stiles wrote in his diary:

> [McNeil] went to bed without hearing any Thing. But about midnight or perhaps one o'Clock he was suddenly waked up, somebody violently rapping up the Landlord, telling the doleful Story that the Powder was taken, six men killed, & all the people between there & Boston arming & marching down to the Relief of their Brethren at Boston; and within a qr. or half an hour he judges fifty men were collected at the Tavern tho' now deep in Night, equipping themselves & sending off Posts every Way to the neighboring Towns. They called up McNeil to tell the Story of the Springfield Affair which was News—he said he had to repeat and tell the story over & over again to New Comers till day; so he had no more Rest that night. The Men set off as fast as they were equipt.
>
> In the Morning, being fryday Sept. 2, Mr. McNeil rode forward & passed thro' the whole at the very Time of the Convulsion. He said he never saw such a Scene before—all along were armed Men rushing forward some on foot some on horseback, at every house Women & Children making Cartridges, running Bullets, making Wallets, baking Biscuit, crying & bemoaning &

at the same time animating their Husbands & Sons to fight for their Liberties, tho' not knowing whether they should ever see them again. I asked whether the Men were Cowards or disheartened or appeared to want Courage? No. Whether the tender Distresses of weeping Wives & Children softened effeminated & overcome the Men and set them Weeping to? No—nothing of this—but a firm and intrepid Ardor, hardy eager & couragious Spirit of Enterprize, a Spirit for revenging the Blood of their Brethren & rescue our Liberties, all this & an Activity corresponding with such Emotions appeared all along the whole Tract of above fourty Miles from Shrewsbury to Boston.

The Women kept on making Cartridges, & after equipping their Husbands, bro't them out to the Soldiers which in Crowds passed along & gave them out in handfuls to one and another as they were deficient, mixing Exhortation & Tears & Prayers & spiriting the Men in such an uneffeminate Manner as even would make Cowards fight. He tho't if anything the Women surpassed the Men for Eagerness & Spirit in the Defence of Liberty by Arms. For they had no Tho'ts of the Men returning but from Battle, for they all believed the Action commenced between the Kings Troops & the Provincials. The Women under this Assurance gave up their Husbands Sons &c to Battle & bid them fight courageously & manfully & behave themselves bravely for Liberty—commanding them to behave like Men & not like Cowards—to be of good Courage & play the men for our people & for the Cities of our God—& the Lord do as seemeth him good. They expected a bloody Scene, but they doubted not Success & Victory.

McNeil never saw any Thing like this in his Life:—he said, they scarcely left half a dozen Men in a Town, unless old and decrepid, and in one town the Landlord told him that himself was the only Man left.[78]

Not until McNeil was two miles from Cambridge did the truth come out: six men had not been killed, Boston had not been shelled, and the

British troops were not on the march. "The People seemed really disappointed," one man told John Adams two months later, "when the News was contradicted." [79]

This was truly an uprising of the people. With no central command, tens of thousands of men responded to the alarm. The once-radical leaders from Boston were now the moderates; the people themselves, following strict principles of participatory democracy, took over. For all its huff and bluster, however, this would remain a peaceable revolution; there would be no pitched battles unless and until the British command decided to force the issue. "It is greatly to their credit," wrote John Andrews of the Powder Alarm, "that in all the different parties that were collected, and in all their various movements, there was as much good order and decorum observ'd, as when attending church on Sundays." [80]

In Worcester County, the massive mobilization triggered by the Powder Alarm was followed in short order by an even more significant display of force. On Friday and Saturday, September 2 and 3, as they flocked toward Cambridge and Boston, Worcester patriots had merely puffed their chests. The following Tuesday, September 6, they toppled the old regime.

No riders were needed this time to announce the momentous event. In taverns and meeting houses, patriots had been readying themselves for a month. Militia units had elected new commanders, and they had stepped up the pace of their drills. Militia days, primarily social events for the previous decade, had taken on new meaning. Musket barrels were cleaned, flintlocks checked, powder and ball rolled into cartridges.

All this preparation, and the unexpected dress rehearsal provided by the Powder Alarm, would soon be put to use. If General Gage kept his word to protect the court, the patriots of Worcester County faced the strong possibility of a direct military confrontation. The lines were drawn, and the stakes were high.

Everybody knew the time and place to convene. The thirty-nine militiamen from Royalston, near the New Hampshire border, must have departed a day or two in advance in order to reach the shiretown of Worcester, thirty-five miles distant, by Tuesday morning. So too the fifty-one men from Athol. The 180 from Leicester, 200 from Westborough, and 500 from Sutton, on the other hand, probably rose before dawn and marched into town that same morning. We know these numbers from a diary kept by Ebenezer Parkman, a cautious seventy-year-old minister from Westborough. Ebenezer's son Breck, an ardent patriot, attended the event as one of the militiamen and made a special point of chronicling the particulars, which he relayed to his father the following day. In the Parkman diary, preserved at the American Antiquarian Society in Worcester, the roll call of towns is laid out neatly in three parallel columns:[81]

Worcester 260	Princeton 60	Palmer 38
Uxbridge 156	Harvard 103	Sutton 500
Westborough 200	Hubbardston 55	Westminster 120
Rutland 150	Lunenbourg 40	Oxford Troop 40
Athol 51	Western 100	N. Shrewsbury 100
Royalston 39	Winchendon 45	S. Shrewsbury 135
New Braintry 140	Southboro 35	Northboro 85
Brookfield 216	Chauxitt 200	Oxford 80
Duglass 130	Leicester 180	Oakham 50
Grafton 210	Spencer 164	Petersham 70
Holden 100	Sturbridge 150	Paxton 80
Hardwick 220	Bolton 100	Upton 100
		Templeton 120

This was a remarkable outpouring, representing practically all the adult males in many of these towns. The 4,622 militiamen, together with local onlookers, undoubtedly constituted the largest single gathering of human beings up to that point in time in Worcester County.[82] Estimated by various contemporary accounts at five to six thousand, this assemblage from the farming communities of the hinterlands rivaled the crowds of metropolitan Boston.[83]

On September 6 Reverend Parkman wrote from Westborough: "A

great company march with Staves and Fife under Capt. Maynard, to Worcester." In Springfield a week earlier, the men had also marched in a festive atmosphere "with staves and musick." There had been no need for firearms there, for the patriots had expected no resistance— but why was there no mention of firearms as the militiamen of West-borough marched toward Worcester, where they might have to battle British troops?

By the morning of September 6, there had been a sudden and sig-nificant turn of events: in the wake of the Powder Alarm, General Gage had changed his mind and decided not to send troops to Worces-ter. With militias throughout New England mobilized and ready to fight, the Boston garrison of three thousand Regulars was in no posi-tion to face off, on hostile ground, against ten times their number or more. Thomas Gage was a reasonable man, a good listener, an astute observer. He was also a loyal subject, and he was not about to instigate a war without express authorization from the Crown—and without enough forces to emerge the victor.

The patriots from Worcester, with contacts in Boston, must have had wind of Gage's decision, for on Monday, the day before the ex-pected confrontation, the American Political Society "Voted, not to bring our Fire-arms into Town the 6 Day of Sept."[84] After arming all summer, this would seem a remarkable pronouncement—unless they felt confident that Gage would not stand against them. Some of the nearby towns, like Westborough, were privy to this information and left their guns behind. Other towns, hearing the news as they ap-proached Worcester on Tuesday morning, probably hid their arms just outside of town, much as the farmers had done at Cambridge four days earlier. Some towns, however, either did not get the word or did not wish to be left without the wherewithal to defend themselves, for the Parkman diary states clearly that "a few companys had arms."[85]

By 10:00 A.M. most of the militiamen had assembled on the com-mon, adjacent to the meeting house at the south end of Main Street. Earlier that morning, local men from Worcester and probably Spencer had barricaded themselves inside the courthouse a half-mile away at the north end of town, to prevent the judges and other offi-cials from entering.[86]

Representatives from the various town committees of correspondence, meanwhile, met and formed a County Convention across the street from the courthouse at the home of Timothy Bigelow. The convention hoped to coordinate the activities of the day—no easy task, for all thirty-seven militia companies had to be consulted every time a decision was to be made. The convention quickly decided "to attend the body of the people" outside. Here in the countryside, unlike in Boston, the leaders and the people were one.

In order to insure a full voice for the people, the patriots developed a rather cumbersome political structure for the event. According to the convention's minutes, each company chose an ad hoc representative to meet with others "as a committee to wait on the judges to inform them of the resolution to stop the courts sitting, if the people concur therein." [87] These political representatives—distinct from the previously elected military commanders—would serve as links to the "body of the people." The County Convention of the committees of correspondence, not itself an elected body, could act only through consulting these representatives from the companies, who in turn had to consult with their constituents before any decisions could be finalized. Throughout the day, this bottom-heavy apparatus, although thoroughly democratic, proceeded—but slowly. The County Convention, in apparent frustration, appointed committee after committee to "inquire the occasion" for the delays.

To facilitate communications, the entire assemblage moved from the common on the southern end of town to "the green beyond Mr. Salisbury's," just to the north of Timothy Bigelow's and catercorner from the courthouse. This placed young merchant Stephen Salisbury at the hub of the action. In 1772 Salisbury had built an impressive Georgian mansion, even larger than the courthouse and rivaling the palatial abodes of John and Gardiner Chandler, which served as both his home and his store. Throughout the summer of 1774, he had profited from the increased demand for military wares and for the liquor consumed at the various meetings and conventions. Then came the Powder Alarm, and now this—nearly five thousand potential customers literally in his backyard. On September 7, Stephen wrote to his older brother Samuel, "I have been exceedingly Hurried more so than ever I was since I have been in Business." On Saturday morning, as men prepared to march toward Boston, he had taken in "£173 in Cash & fill near 5 pages in my petty worth book in Entrys for powder &c." He did another £97 of business on Monday and an all-time high of £300 on Tuesday, as thousands of militiamen clamored for their necessaries and sundries. "It was out my power to Lend all the people that wanted," he wrote. "I never had my Temper tried in Business to that degree that I had then. However I did not Show any more than I thought absolutely necessary to keep any Order." [88]

As patriots tried to organize themselves on Salisbury's green, officers of the court, locked out of their normal place of business, gathered in Daniel Heywood's tavern on Main Street near present-day Exchange, the second oldest public house in Worcester. Why there? With both the courthouse and the meeting house firmly in control of the patriots, they had to choose from among the various taverns in town. Several of the officers harbored unpleasant memories of their recent humiliation at Mary Stearns', a favorite gathering place for large groups of both Tories and patriots; William "Tory" Jones's tavern was on the southern edge of town, too far from the courthouse; the inn belonging to John Curtis, a Tory Protestor, might have been considered, but John's sons were patriots and probably among the insurgents; the public houses of Luke Brown and Asa Ward, frequent meeting grounds for the patriots, were out of the question. And so it was that three judges of the Inferior Court of Common Pleas, eighteen justices of the peace, three attorneys, and the sheriff—all holding their positions by authority of the Massachusetts Government Act—huddled inside Heywood's tavern, waiting to meet with representatives from the throngs who would determine their fates.

As at Springfield, court officials tried to get by with a statement that fell short of closing the court. A copy of this first attempt has not survived, but Parkman characterized it as "a paper . . . Signifying that they would Endeavor &c." The people, of course, wanted more than a promise of good faith. "This not satisfying," wrote Parkman, "another was drawn, & read, Promising that they would not Sit &c in that or any other Court under the new Regulation by the late act of Parliament." The second document, signed by all twenty-five officials, was entered into the minutes of the Worcester County Convention:

> GENTLEMEN:—You having desired, and even insisted upon it, that all judicial proceedings be stayed by the justices of the court appointed this day, by law, to be held at Worcester, within and for the county of Worcester, on account of the unconstitutional act of the British parliament, respecting the administration of justice in this province, which, if effected, will reduce the inhabitants thereof to mere arbitrary power; we do assure you, that we will stay all such judicial proceedings of said courts, and will not endeavor to put said act into execution.[89]

With this statement, the Inferior Court of Common Pleas and the Court of General Sessions for Worcester County were officially closed. The British had lost their authority, for ordinary citizens were effectively able to override an act of Parliament. But this alone would not satisfy the crowd: the transfer of power would have to be dramatized, plain and clear, for all to see.

By midafternoon, the stage was set. The militiamen filed onto Main Street, lining each side of the road for a quarter-mile between the courthouse and Heywood's tavern. Each company remained together, Uxbridge in front of the courthouse, Westborough next, and so on, down to Upton and Templeton outside of Heywood's tavern. The list in his diary, wrote Parkman, "except Worcester & Spencer, is the order in which the Companys Stood from the Court House and Southward."

Half with their backs to the embankment to the west of Main Street, the other half on the Mill Brook side, the militiamen waited for the officials to emerge. To climax the day, according to Parkman, "The court walked from Haywood Tavern to the Court House between the Ranks, with their Hats off; and then back," reading the statement they had signed. Since all the militiamen wanted to hear, each official had to read his submission time and again. According to one account, written by a disgruntled Tory,

At Worcester, a mob of about five thousand collected, and prevented the Court of Common Pleas from sitting, (about one
thousand of them had fire-arms,) and all drawn in two files,
compelled judges, Sheriffs, and gentlemen of the Bar, to pass
them with cap in hand, and read their disavowal of holding
Courts under the new Acts of Parliament, not less than thirty
time in their procession.[90]

Even that was not enough. Tory Protesters who were not officials
of the court were rounded up and forced to walk the gauntlet as well,
reading the recantations they had submitted two weeks before. There
could no longer be any doubt who held power in Worcester County.

Under circumstances such as these, not even the most strident Tory
dared resist. Two judges of the Court of Common Pleas, Thomas
Steel and Joseph Wilder, meekly submitted. (The third judge present,
staunch patriot Artemas Ward, read the statement willingly, while
Chief Justice Timothy Ruggles was still hiding behind British lines in
Boston.) Timothy Paine, one of the justices of the peace and by now a
veteran recanter, was forced once again to take off his hat and make
his way through the ranks. High Sheriff Gardiner Chandler required
an extra guard of four men to insure that he would not be handled too
roughly by the crowd.[91] Ten years later, an exiled John Chandler, once
the most powerful man in Worcester, would complain to the British
government:

> [I]n September, A.D. 1774 a mob of several thousands of Armed
> People drawn from the neighboring Towns assembled at
> Worcester for the purpose of Stopping the Courts of Justice
> then to be held there which having accomplished they seized
> your memorialist who in order to save himself from immediate
> death was obliged to renounce the aforesaid Protest and Sub-
> scribe to a very Treasonable League and Covenant.[92]

Their political business accomplished, most of the militiamen went
home at the end of the day. Stephen Salisbury's business had been ac-

complished as well. On Wednesday he wrote to his brother Samuel that, with the convention adjourned, "my Hurry has now Subsided." He also proclaimed that he had in his possession more than one thousand pounds in loose cash, a sum that seemed to make him a bit anxious.[93]

A few of the most active patriots stayed on, still meeting as the Worcester County Convention. The following day, somewhat anticlimatically, someone had the idea to force yet another recantation from the justices who had addressed Governor Gage on June 21 with unkind words about the patriots. Although eight of the eleven justices had already been forced to walk through the crowd the day before, the victorious patriots seized the opportunity to play their hand yet one more time. When all was said and done, six local Tories, wondering whether this sort of treatment would ever end, fled to Stone House Hill across the town line in Holden, where they prepared to defend themselves if attacked.[94]

If the emphasis on humiliation seems extreme, it nevertheless served well as an alternative to violence. Although thousands of angry men had assembled to assert their collective will, there is no indication that any harm was inflicted to person or property. (Had there been any, the Tories most certainly would have complained about it to British officials.) At the close of the day, the convention had requested "the officers of each company of the people assembled, to keep good order; enjoin it on their men not to do the least damage to any person's property; but to march quietly home."[95] It appears that this request was heeded. "I don't understand that there was any Disorder," wrote the conservative Ebenezer Parkman. "Tis said the people behaved with Silence Decency & in good order."

The patriots could claim victory in every respect. Governor Gage and his Regulars had stayed away. No blood had been shed. The Inferior Court of Common Pleas and the Court of General Sessions of the Peace had been shut down, and with them the last vestiges of British control over Worcester County. The courts would never again meet under authority of the Crown, nor would any official appointed by the British Government exercise any power in Worcester County.

Notwithstanding the ubiquitous character of the Massachusetts Revolution of 1774, the dramatic court-closing in Worcester can be seen as its defining moment. When Gage failed to show up as threatened, it became clear to patriots throughout the colony that he would offer no further resistance. In Concord, Plymouth, and the rest of the county seats, patriots would close the courts in subsequent weeks without fear of interference by the British army. Their revolution had prevailed, at least in its initial phase.

5

CONSOLIDATION

As of September 6, 1774, the Worcester County Convention held undisputed political power in the county. But, having toppled the old regime, the convention faced a troubling question: How would the people now govern themselves? In the absence of established authority, radicals as well as conservatives feared what they called a "state of nature," in which both people and property were left unprotected. With the old structure gone, a new one was needed in short order—but this would have to proceed in a democratic and orderly fashion. Worcester patriots felt confident that the fundamental issue of a new government would soon be addressed at the provincial level, but they had to figure some way to make do in the interim.

On September 7, before it adjourned, the County Convention determined the minimal machinery that would get them through "till the rising of the Provincial Congress, proposed to sit at Concord, on the second Tuesday of October next." So the justices of the peace who had held office before the Act took effect were pressed back into service—under new management, of course. (Timothy Ruggles, John Murray, and James Putnam were specifically excluded.) They were to hear no civil cases, however, and were to act only "as single justices," meaning that they could not come together as a court. The coroners, sheriffs, and probate judge would also continue in office under the authority of the 1691 charter, not the Massachusetts Government Act. It was the bare minimum, but at least there would be some protection against looting or any other opportunistic behavior in the month before a more permanent solution could be arranged.

At first glance, the return to office of some deposed justices would seem to indicate that this was not much of a revolution after all.[1] Quite the reverse is true. That the County Convention appointed certain individuals to fill minor offices for a month is not nearly so significant as its presumptive assertion of authority. The main issue here is that they took it upon themselves to make any appointments at all. In the absence of the legally constituted government it had just removed, the Worcester County Convention had proclaimed itself in charge, right down to their resolution "to put the laws in execution respecting pedlars and chapmen."

The most significant authority assumed by the County Convention concerned the militias. Officers who had not already done so were called upon to resign their commissions, and the towns were told to choose their successors. (Often, if they were patriots, the old officers would be returned to duty.) The militias were instructed in how to train ("Voted, That the Norfolk exercise be adopted") and how to ready themselves for major battles—by procuring "one or more field pieces, mounted and fitted for use; and also a sufficient quantity of ammunition for the same," and by having officers "appoint a suitable number of men, out of their respective companies, to manage said field pieces."

If government was meant to protect life and property, as the people of Massachusetts assumed in that day and age, this was no time to go without. First the Worcester County Convention—and soon the Provincial Congress—stepped up to fill the void as patriots prepared for a British attack. The people of Massachusetts would soon have to protect the gains they had just achieved.

British authorities were not about to let one of their colonies slip from their grasp without putting up a fight. Governor Gage, perhaps better than most, understood the implications of the Massachusetts Revolution of 1774: there could be no final conclusion without military confrontation. After the court closures at Great Barrington, Springfield, and Worcester, after Gage's failure to prevent the Salem town meeting, after Thomas Oliver's resignation at Cambridge and the intimidation of all "mandamus counsellors" outside of Boston, and after the immense outpouring of popular support during the Powder Alarm, there was no disputing patriot control over rural Massachusetts.

Gage was worried: If the rebels should engage in a military offensive, how could a garrison of three thousand soldiers hold out against a force several times their number?

On September 5, in the immediate wake of the Powder Alarm, Gage prepared to defend Boston by fortifying its only entrance by land, "the Neck." John Andrews reported:

> The alarm caus'd by the movement of the country has induc'd the Governor to order a number of field pieces up to the neck guard, and this morning has got a number of workmen there, to build blockhouses and otherways repair the fortification. It was reported that he was going to cut a canal across and break off the communication with the country other than by a bridge; in consequence of which the Select men waited upon him. He assur'd them he had no intention to break ground, but was only about securing the entrance into the Town, that the inhabitants as well as the soldiers may not be expos'd to inroads from the country.[2]

For Governor Gage, "the country" had become an ominous threat, but for the selectment of Boston, the threat came from the British army, not the outlying farmers who kept the townspeople supplied with food. Bostonians were fearful that Gage would reduce "this Metropolis . . . to the state of a Garrison"; they complained that "the Guards posted in that Quarter, in assaulting and forceably detaining several Persons, who were peaceably passing in and out of the Town, may discourage the Market People from coming in with their Provisions as usual, & oblige the Inhabitants to abandon the Town."[3]

In his letters to William Barrell over the next several days, John

Andrews gave a running account of Gage's efforts at fortification and the response of local patriots:

September 6th. . . . The townspeople are in general very uneasy and dissatisfied with the Governor's fortifying the entrance; so much so, they cant get any one workman to assist 'em. They've got an engineer from New York, who is trying what he can do with a number of carpenters and masons out of the army. They talk of sending to New York for a number of mechanics to affect it: It is my opinion, if they are wise, they wont come. . . .

September 8th. . . . Yesterday, between one and two o'clock P.M., the General, with a large parade of attendants, took a survey of the skirts of the town; more particularly that part opposite the country shore. 'Tis suppos'd they intend to erect Batteries there to prevent any incursions of the country people from that quarter, having effectually secur'd the Neck by the disposition of the field pieces; and their caution extends so far as to have a guard patrole Roxbury streets at all hours of the night, as well as another posted at Charlestown ferry every night, after the evening gun fires. . . .

September 9th. . . . [N]otwistanding the six field pieces planted at ye Neck, they have brought twelve cannon from the Castle, some nine and some four pounders, which they have dispos'd about the entrance of the town. And this is not the only proof of their fear; for I am well inform'd that they keep so many and such strict guards of nights, that the soldiers don't get but one undisturb'd night's sleep out of four.

September 10th. They have drawn off the whole of the troops from Salem, and the Board of Commissioners, with the Governor's family and furniture, are all arriv'd here, not thinking themselves secure in a town surrounded by the country as that is. . . .

September 12th. . . . The General has set about two hundred soldiers to work upon the fortifications this morning. . . . Many of the inhabitants are *serious* about leaving the town, as they are in general apprehensive that when the Governor has sufficiently fortified it, *military Law* will be declar'd, and no one suffer'd to go out but by his permission, notwithstanding what he may have said to the contrary. There is no knowing, Bill, what may take place with us. For my own part, I endeavor to make myself as easy as I can; but if they should come to disarming the inhabitants, the matter is settled with the town at once; for *blood* and *carnage* must inevitably ensue—which God forbid! should ever take place.[4]

Andrews also told of a cat-and-mouse game concerning a stash of cannons and ammunition. On September 8 General Gage received intelligence that patriots across the river in Charlestown had buried some "ammunition, such as shot, &ca., belonging to the battery there." That afternoon he sent an officer to examine the premises, and once the officer had confirmed the intelligence, Gage prepared to seize the cache, just as he had done a week earlier at the Quarry Hill powder house. This time, however, he would come up empty:

The inhabitants, suspecting what would take place, provided a number of teams, such as carry ship timbers, and slung all the guns belonging to the battery, and carried up country, together with the reposit of shot, &ca. About midnight another *formidable* expedition was set on foot. The boats from all the Men of War were man'd with soldiers, with orders to dismantle the fort and bring off all the Ordnance, Stores, &ca.: but I imagine their chagrin was as great as their disappointment.[5]

Undeterred, Gage pursued the matter further. Three days later he sent out "a number of officers and soldiers . . . who were employ'd . . . in traversing the streets and by-ways, and tampering with the children, to get out of them where the cannon were hid." The British continued to search for two more days, when "an officer prevail'd on a negro at Charlestown to inform 'em where the cannon were lodg'd; which being known there, they mustered about three thousand, and with teems carried 'em about ten or a dozen miles further up. Several among 'em were eight and forty pounders, which weigh'd between two and three ton apiece." [6]

This quest to seize weapons would continue for many months; in the end, it would lead to actual combat. More often than not, the patriots prevailed. In addition to hiding their own caches outside Boston, they managed to make off with some artillery from within British lines. On September 16, Andrews wrote to Barrell:

> Ever since ye cannon were taken away from Charlestown, the General has order'd a double guard to ye new and old gun houses, where ye brass field pieces belonging to our militia are lodg'd: notwithstanding which, the vigilance and temerity of our people has entirely disconcerted him, for We'n'sday evening, or rather night, they took these from the Old house (by opening the side of the house) and carried away through Frank Johonnot's Garden. Upon which he gave it in orders the next day to the officer on guard to remove those from the New house (which stands directly opposite the encampment of the 4th Regiment and in the middle of the street near the large Elm tree), sometime the next night into the camp; and to place a guard at each end, or rather at both doors, till then. At the fixed hour the Officer went with a number of Mattrosses to execute his orders, but behold, the guns were gone! He swore the *Devil* must have help'd them to get 'em away. However, they went to work, and brought off the carriages, harness, utensils, &ca., which they reposited in the Camp. Its amazing to me how our people manag'd to carry off the guns, as they weigh near seven hundred weight apiece; more especially that they should do it, and not alarm the guards. [7]

This was no longer just a political conflict; at issue were weapons, not votes or petitions. The Massachusetts revolution was taking on a military dimension. Although no battles had yet been fought, events were driven by the struggle over armaments and fortification as the combatants jockeyed for starting position, if and when war broke out.

The patriots, by hoarding weaponry, demonstrated their willingness to fight. Thomas Gage understood this, and he tried to make the authorities in London understand as well. With remarkable clarity, he wrote to Lord Dartmouth:

> [N]othing less than the Conquest of almost all the New England Provinces will procure Obedience to the late Acts of Parliament for regulating the Government of the Massachusetts Bay. . . . The Country People are exercising in Arms in this Province, Connecticut, and Rhode Island, and getting Magazines of Arms and Ammunition in the Country, and such Artillery, as they can procure good and bad. They threaten to attack the Troops in Boston, and are very angry at a Work throwing up at the Entrance of the Town. . . .
>
> Had the Measures for regulating this Government been adopted seven Years ago, they would have been easier executed, but the executive Parts of Government have gradually been growing weaker from about that Period, and the People more lawless and seditious. . . . [M]y first Object was to give it Force, in which I hoped to have made some Progress, when the Arrival of the late Acts overset the whole, and the Flame blazed out in all Parts at once beyond the Conception of every Body.[8]

This was it in a nutshell: The Massachusetts Government Act had instigated a revolution which could not be contained except by military force. But if the British decided to attack, the rebels would be sure to respond. Was there any way out but war?

Outside Boston, where the "Country People" had seized control, all opposition to the patriots ceased. "Not a Tory but hides his head," Abigail Adams wrote to her husband John, who was attending the Continental Congress in Philadelphia.[9] Earlier in the summer, once-powerful men like John Chandler of Worcester and Israel Williams of Hatfield might have hoped to put up an argument on behalf of the Crown; after the court closures, they dared not try. All "government men" faced limited options: to submit (which generally involved some sort of public humiliation) or to flee. On September 9, Andrews wrote:

> The present temper of the People throughout the Province is such, that they wont suffer a *tory* to remain any where among 'em without making an ample recantation of his principles; and those who presume to be so obstinate as not to comply, are oblig'd to take up their residence in this city of refuge.[10]

Men who once ruled were forced to grovel. "The church parson thought they were comeing after him, and run up garret they say, an other jumpt out of his window and hid among the corn whilst a third crept under his bord fence, and told his Beads," wrote Abigail Adams from Braintree on September 14.[11] Colonel Elisha Jones, the sixty-five-year-old patriarch of Weston—proud father of fourteen sons and one daughter—was ritualistically humiliated by 300 men who "made his Mightiness walk through their Ranks with his Hat off and express his Sorrow for past Offences, and promise not to be Guilty of the like for the future."[12]

The greatest humiliations were bestowed on those who had once exercised the greatest power, men like the "river god" Israel Williams. One week after the closing of the Hampshire County court, when told that a large crowd from a neighboring town was on its way in search of Williams and other friends of government, the Hatfield constable, instead of trying to protect his townsmen, agreed that the "corrupt vicious crew" of Tories "deserved to be Delt with in Severity."[13] Williams was subjected to frequent harassment in the succeeding months, culminating in one of the most notorious mob actions of the revolution:

> [Williams] was taken from his house by the mob in the night, carried several miles, put into a room with a fire, the chimney at the top, and doors of the room being closed, and kept there for many hours in the smoke, till his life was in danger, then carried home, after being forced to sign what they ordered.[14]

Concord physician Joseph Lee was taken to task for a grievous sin: While hundreds of his neighbors gathered on the common the night of September 1 and prepared to march into Cambridge, Lee set forth to warn councilor Joseph Lee (no relation) that a crowd was on its way. According to local folklore, Concord's Joseph Lee "was seen in the morning fording the river above the South Bridge in great haste, with his long stockings down to his heels." [15] When word got around about Lee's treachery, he was forced to repent. The wording of his apology was excessive and flamboyant, certainly not authored by Lee himself:

> Whereas I, Joseph Lee, of Concord, Physician, on the Evening of the 1st ult, did rashly and without Consideration, make a private and precipitate journey from Concord to Cambridge, to inform judge Lee, that the Country was assembling to come down . . . that he & others concern'd might prepare themselves for the Event, and with an avowed Intention to deceive the People; by which the Parties assembling might have been exposed to the brutal Rage of the Soldiery, who had timely Notice to have waylaid the Roads and fired on them while unarmed and Defenceless in the dark.
>
> By which imprudent Conduct, I might have prevented the salutary Designs of my Countrymen, whose innocent intentions were only to request certain Gentlemen, sworn into Office on the new system of Government, to resign their Offices, in order to prevent the Operation of that (so much detested) Act of the British Parliament for regulating the Civil Government of the Massachusetts Bay: By all of which I have justly drawn upon me the displeasure of my Country.
>
> When I cooly reflect on my own imprudence, it fills my Mind with the deepest Anxiety.
>
> I deprecate the resentment of my injured Country, humbly confess my Errors, and implore the Forgiveness of a generous and free People. Solemnly declaring that for the future, never to convey any intelligence to any of the Court Party, whether directly or indirectly, by which the designs of the People may be

frustrated in opposing the barbarous Policy, of an arbitrary, wicked and corrupt Administration.

Joseph Lee [16]

There was more repenting and recanting going on in Massachusetts in the late summer of 1774 than at any time since the Salem witch trials, and perhaps more than our nation has ever experienced since— the McCarthyism of the 1950s notwithstanding. [17]

The county of Essex met on September 6, the same day as Worcester. There was no shortage of radicals here (Essex included the old capital of Salem, which had dramatically defied Governor Gage two weeks earlier), but rather than force judges to run the gauntlet, Essex patriots granted them permission to continue in office by virtue of their original appointments *before* the Massachusetts Government Act. This was an innovative and decidedly nonviolent method of staging a revolution: by a twist of logic. The convention resolved

> that the judges, justices, and other civil officers in this county, appointed agreeably to the charter and the laws of the province, are the only civil officers in the county whom we may lawfully obey; that authority whatever, can remove these officers, except that which is constituted pursuant to the charter and those laws; that it is the duty of these officers to continue in the execution of their respective trusts, as if the aforementioned act of parliament had never been made; and, that while they thus continue, untainted by any official conduct in conformity to that act, we will vigorously support them therein, to the utmost of our power, indemnify them in their persons and property, and to their lawful doings yield a ready obedience. [18]

Lest this approach seem too moderate, the convention also proclaimed "that all civil officers in the province, as well as private persons, who shall dare to conduct in conformity to the aforementioned act . . . are unfit for civil society; their lands ought not to be tilled by the labor of any American, nor their families supplied with clothing or food." They closed their convention by declaring, in effect, their willingness to go to war:

> [T]hough we are deeply anxious to restore and preserve harmony with our brethren in Great Britain; yet, if the despotism and violence of our enemies should finally reduce us to the sad necessity, we, undaunted, are ready to appeal to the last resort of states; and will, in support of our rights, encounter even death, "sensible that he can never die too soon, who lays down his life in support of the laws and liberties of his country."[19]

The patriots of Suffolk County also convened on September 6, meeting first in Dedham and then adjourning to Milton on September 9. With the British army stationed in Boston, the political hub of the county, patriots did not control Suffolk to the extent they controlled other counties. They could not forcibly close the courts, but they could and did express their outrage in what would become the only document of the Massachusetts Revolution of 1774 to achieve any significant notice in the annals of history. The Suffolk Resolves, as they came to be called, opened with an ostentatious display of rhetoric:

> Whereas, the power, but not the justice; the vengeance, but not the wisdom of Great Britain, which of old persecuted, scourged, and exiled our fugitive parents from their native shores, now pursues us, their guiltless children, with unrelenting severity: and whereas this, then savage and uncultivated desert, was purchased by the toil and treasure, or acquired by the valor and blood of those, our venerable progenitors, who bequeathed to us the dear bought inheritance, who consigned it to our care and protection; the most sacred obligations are upon us to transmit the glorious purchase, unfettered by power, unclogged with shackles, to our innocent and beloved offspring.[20]

And so it went. The verbiage was clearly the work of educated Boston Whigs, not their country cousins who were actually driving this revolution forward. Eventually, after more excessive prose, delegates to the Suffolk County convention addressed the business of the day:

- They opposed both the Massachusetts Government Act and the Boston Port Bill, stating that "no obedience is due from this province, to either or any part of the acts above mentioned; but that they should be rejected as the attempts of a wicked administration to enslave America."

- Although they did not have the power to close the courts, they recommended that "no regard ought to be paid to them by the people of this county," and that officers of the court or jurors who refused to serve would receive their support.

- They recommended that taxes not be paid to the officers of the established government "until the civil government of the province is placed upon a constitutional basis."

- They demanded resignations from all "mandamus counsellors"; those who failed to comply by September 20 would "be considered by this county as obstinate and incorrigible enemies to this colony."

- They opposed the fortification of the Boston Neck and appointed a committee to carry their protest to Governor Gage.

- They objected to the Quebec Act, claiming that the legalization of the Catholic Church in Canada was "dangerous in an extreme degree, to the protestant religion, and to the civil liberties of all America."

- They recommended "to take away all commissions from the officers of the militia," and that new officers be elected by the people.

- They advocated yet another nonconsumption agreement against "British merchandize and manufactures."

- Like the other conventions, they endorsed a convening of a Provincial Congress in October.

- They promised to "pay all due respect" to the Continental Congress sitting in Philadelphia, and to submit to their decisions.

- Finally, as was characteristic of all the county conventions, they opposed "all routs, riots, or licentious attacks upon the property of any persons whatsoever." They held that "in a contest so important, in a cause so solemn, our conduct shall be such as to merit the approbation of the wise, and the admiration of the brave and free of every age and of every country." [21]

The Suffolk Resolves, hardly the first of the protests, presented the Massachusetts Revolution of 1774 to a wider audience. Since the Boston Whigs were well-connected to delegates of the Continental Congress, including their own Samuel and John Adams, they dispatched Paul Revere to Philadelphia with a copy of the Suffolk Resolves. Revere arrived on September 16; the following day, the Massachusetts delegates read the Resolves and asked the Continental Congress to endorse them. Congress praised the people of Massachusetts for their opposition to "wicked ministerial measures" and voted unanimously "that they most thoroughly approved the wisdom and fortitude . . . expressed in the resolutions determined upon at a meeting of the delegates for the county of Suffolk, on Tuesday, the 6th instant." [22] John Adams wrote in his diary on September 17: "This was one of the happiest Days of my Life. In Congress We had generous, noble Sentiments, and manly Eloquence. This Day convinced me that America will support Massachusetts or perish with her." [23]

On September 13, one week following the county conventions in

Worcester, Essex, and Suffolk, patriots in Middlesex County met at Concord, where the Inferior Court of Common Pleas and the Court of General Sessions of the Peace had been scheduled to convene. On September 9, three judges of the Inferior Court of Common Pleas—Samuel Danforth, Joseph Lee, and James Russell, who had all been embroiled in controversy because of their appointments as "mandamus counsellors"—had decided to avoid another confrontation by postponing the Court of Common Pleas until October. If this was a tactical effort to deflect resistance, it failed. The patriots still showed up in force to deal with the Court of General Sessions of the Peace.

When ten judges and justices of the General Sessions court tried to convene on Tuesday morning, they were confronted by "a great Number of Freeholders and others" who blocked the door to the courthouse. The judges proposed a compromise: they would open the court but conduct no business. The patriots told the men of the court they would take the matter under consideration, and while the convention deliberated on the town common, the judges and justices retreated to Ephraim Jones's inn and waited—through the morning, past midday, and into the late afternoon. At last, "after the Setting of the Sun," the "Body of the People" gave their reply: there would be no compromise. The court would not sit on any terms.[24]

Patriots did not stop there. Incensed with the devious effort to postpone the Inferior Court of Common Pleas, they called to task two deputy sheriffs who had posted the official notice. The deputies were forced to beg forgiveness from the people and promise never to transact any business under authority of the Act. One deputy resigned his post.

Three more counties were scheduled to convene their courts in September: Cumberland (in the future state of Maine), Bristol, and Barnstable. In each county, patriots held a convention on the day of the court session. The Cumberland convention followed the lead of Essex by allowing the courts to sit under the old charter if they chose to do so. (The island county of Dukes and the Maine county of York would also take this approach later in the fall, although the courts never did hold fall sessions in Dukes.) As in Essex, however, patriots stated emphatically that they were opposing, not sanctioning, the Massachusetts Government Act. In fact, they were presumptively declaring the Act illegal by insisting that the government continue "as if the aforementioned act had never been invented." People who supported the Act, according to the Cumberland convention, "should be considered as malignant enemies to our charter rights, unfit for civil society, and undeserving of the least regard or favor from their fellow countrymen." This was more than mere rhetoric. The convention gave teeth to the words by holding that tax collectors should not "pay one farthing more into the province treasury, until the government of the province is placed on a constitutional foundation, or until the Provincial Congress shall order otherwise." [25]

The Bristol convention, meeting in Taunton on September 28 and 29, declared that the courts were to be "interrupted for a season," and court records indicate that no session was held during the fall of 1774. The patriots of Bristol, acting with the knowledge that the Suffolk Resolves had already been endorsed by the Continental Congress, declared that "it is unnecessary for us to be more particular, as we most cheerfully adopt their measures and resolutions." They did add, however, that "considering the complexion of the times it is absolutely necessary that every Town and inhabitants of same be furnished with arms and ammunition." [26]

In the town of Barnstable on September 27, "a great number of people" gathered at the courthouse door, while thirteen judges and other justices for the Inferior Court of Common Pleas and the Court of General Sessions of the Peace, displaced from their normal quarters, huddled together "at the House of Mr. Crocker, Innholder in this Town." The convention of patriots drafted a letter to the court officials in which they "humbly" requested that the justices "desist from all business in said courts, and from holding any sessions thereof, till the minds of the Continental, or of a Provincial Congress, be obtained." The justices replied that "the court was about to sit in the same constitutional way as we have always done," and that "not one of the said justices . . . incline[d]" to support the Massachusetts Government Act. They promised they would "do all that is in our power in a *constitutional way,* to prevent said act from taking place"—if only they were allowed to convene their courts.

The delegates were not convinced. They noted that two of the justices had signed an address supporting the late Governor Hutchinson, another two had voted against sending delegates to the Continental Congress, and yet another had sold East India Company tea. The people needed "some better assurance" from the justices; "barely saying they did not incline" to support the Act was not enough. They rejected the justices' plea and asked for a straight yes-or-no answer: Would the officials try to convene the court? Rather than confront an angry crowd, the justices caved in. They were made to sign the usual "solemn declaration, that they would not accept any commission, in consequence of the late acts of the British parliament, or do any business, in their respective offices, in conformity thereto." Having submitted, they were spared the added humiliation of reading their declarations in public.[27]

In the town of Plymouth, delegates from the Plymouth County committees of correspondence met at the county courthouse on September 26 and 27 in preparation for the court session slated for the following week.[28] Their resolutions closely paralleled those of counties that had met before them, but of more importance was their ability to mobilize for the day of the court opening. On October 4, according to a letter to Gage from two of the deposed justices, a crowd estimated at two to four thousand men, "stiling themselves the body of the people, took possession of the court-house and the avenues leading to it, and prevented the courts of General Sessions of the peace and court of common pleas from sitting or proceeding to business."[29] The patriots started by sending a committee to the justices, asking them to comply with the convention's opposition to the Massachusetts Government Act. The justices replied

> that we do not now, nor will, at any Time hereafter, hold or exercise our Commissions in any other Way than what is prescribed by our Charter and well-known Constitution; and that we will not in any Way countenance, aid or support the Execution of the

late Acts of Parliament for altering the Charter and Government of the Province.

In some counties this would have sufficed, for the justices had proclaimed the Act null and void—but the patriots of Plymouth wanted
more. They told the justices that "we think it inexpedient for the
Courts to set at present," to which the justices obediently replied,
"We will not open, set, act or do, or adjourn either of said Courts, 'till
the Determination of the Continental Congress is known." [30] Faced
with a crowd that could have done them great harm, these officers of
the court pledged their willingness to submit to the congress sitting in
Philadelphia, unsanctioned by law and arguably illegal.

Even that was not enough. As in Worcester, some ardent patriots
noted that eight of the nineteen justices had signed addresses to
Hutchinson and Gage. These Tories had been asked to repent, and
they did. This was all well and good, the patriots told the elite of Plymouth County, but what about your military commissions? On the
evening of October 4, those Tories who held offices in the militia
were asked to resign. The officers tried to bide for time, but to no
avail. The next morning, the crowd came after them again, demanding their signatures on resignation papers. Under the circumstances,
their options were limited. "[O]ur refusal wou'd only further enrage
and exasperate the people and draw their vengeance upon us," two of
the officers wrote to Gage. "[W]e were induced to sign the paper, the
whole body of the people being then advancing to enforce our Compliance." [31]

The victorious crowd understandably wanted to celebrate, as John
Andrews related to William Barrell:

Yesterday met at Plymouth, the body of that county, to the number of four thousand, when they proceeded to make all the ad-
dressors and protestors there make a publick recantation. After
which, they attempted to remove a Rock (the one on which their
fore-fathers first landed, when they came to this country) which
lay buried in a wharfe five feet deep up into the center of the

town, near the court house. The way being up hill, they found it impracticable, as after they had dug it up, they found it to weigh ten tons at least.[32]

By the first week of October, patriots in seven of the nine contiguous mainland counties of Massachusetts (not counting the small island counties of Dukes and Nantucket or the sparsely populated Maine counties of York, Cumberland, and Lincoln) had forced the courts to close: Berkshire, Hampshire, Worcester, Middlesex, Bristol, Barnstable, and Plymouth. The patriots of Essex had tried to avoid confrontation by permitting the court to sit under the old charter, but their accompanying rhetoric left no doubt that they were still acting in direct defiance of British authority. Only in Suffolk County, which included Boston with its British garrison, did patriots fail to exercise complete control—and yet it was the Suffolk Resolves which put the local revolution on the political map in the rest of the colonies. The cumulative effect of these local actions was profound: the court system of Massachusetts had been dismantled, and with it, the everyday functioning of government.

On September 20 and 21, the Worcester County Convention met again, timed to coincide with the scheduled meeting of the Superior Court in Worcester. To nobody's surprise, Governor Gage dared not convene the highest court in the province right in the heartland of resistance. After perfunctorily (and unnecessarily) telling the sheriff to "adjourn the superior court appointed by law to be held this day," the Worcester convention got down to the main business at hand: filling the governmental void.[33]

First came the matter of debts, so important to struggling farmers. As with the conventions in other counties, the delegates called upon

every inhabitant of this county to pay his just debts, as soon as possible, without any dispute or litigation, and if any disputes concerning debts or trespasses should arise, which cannot be settled by the parties, we recommend it to them to submit all such cases to arbitration; and if the parties, or either of them, shall re-

fuse to do so, they ought to be considered as co-operating with
the enemies of the country.

The farmers of Worcester County did not wish to imprison their
neighbors who could not pay their bills. Now that they were in control, they told the justices of the peace to "liberate any persons confined in jail for debt, who are entitled to such liberation by the laws of
the province."

In preparation for the defense of the revolution, convention delegates proceeded to reorganize the militia into seven new regiments.
There was absolutely no precedent allowing the convention, unsanctioned by law, to take this measure, but they did it anyway. They also
set dates for the election of new officers and repeated their call for
each town to arm itself "with one or more field pieces, mounted and
fitted for use." (Ironically, while the patriots were arming themselves,
they called upon Governor Gage "to desist from any further hostile
preparations" and dismantle the fortification of the Boston Neck—
but the patriots, in the heat of the moment, were not in a position to
appreciate the irony.)

Less dramatically, the convention appointed a standing committee
to correspond with the various towns, to call conventions in the future, and "to prepare matter to lay before this body at their several
meetings." This seemed like a small and logical move, but its implications were enormous. They had, in effect, established the beginnings
of an administrative machinery. They also demonstrated their intention to continue their meetings. With the collapse of the British-
supported regime, this convention would be called upon to perform
some of the normal functions of government.

In the long run, however, the County Convention was no substitute for an enduring government. It was basically a political party, not
an elected body officially sanctioned by the people. The representative branch of the Massachusetts General Court had always been the
House—and that body had been summoned by Governor Gage to
convene at Salem on October 5. Legally, it was the House, not the
County Convention, that was entitled to speak for the people.

But if representatives from the towns attended the House session, they would be sanctioning the Massachusetts Government Act, sitting side-by-side with a military governor and his councilors. This could not be. The towns wanted to elect representatives, but there was no existing representative body they could accept.

The solution was to convene the Provincial Congress. Back in August, delegates to the four-county meeting had set a tentative date: the second Tuesday in October. As the county conventions met to deal with their courts, they all endorsed the idea. So delegates to the Worcester Convention of September 20 and 21 proposed to transform the elections scheduled for the October 5 General Court into elections for the Provincial Congress. They would vote for their representatives as prescribed by law; then, if the House were forced to meet under the provisions of the new Act rather than the 1691 charter, the representatives would be instructed to "immediately repair to the town of Concord, and there join in a provincial congress, with such other members as are or may be chosen for that purpose, to act and determine on such measures as they shall judge to be proper to extricate this colony out of the present unhappy circumstances." [34] Since representatives attending the Provincial Congress would be duly elected by the people, that body would in effect usurp the powers of the old General Court.

This did not sit well with Governor Gage. Any elected body, he reasoned, was likely to add force to the opposition. On September 12 he had warned Dartmouth that the rebels "talk of fixing a Plan of Government of their own." On September 25 he reported that they had summoned the old Council to Salem; their idea was presumably to meet under the 1691 charter, a direct challenge to the Massachusetts Government Act. The governor's councilors, meanwhile, "dare not attend at Salem, unless escorted there, and back again by a large Force, which as Affairs are circumstanced will answer no End." Understanding he would lose a political showdown at Salem, and unwilling to undertake a military showdown which he might lose as well, Gage had no choice but to bow out. On September 28, because of "the present disorder'd, and unhappy State of the Province," the governor of Massachusetts issued a proclamation canceling the elections for the October 5 session of the General Court. [35]

The people of Massachusetts ignored Gage's proclamation and staged their elections anyway. Some towns instructed their representatives to go to Salem on Wednesday, October 5; if the General Court was not convened under authority of the old charter, they were to move on to Concord and join the new Provincial Congress the following week. Other towns, concerned that electing representatives to the General Court might be construed as supporting the Act, decided to send their representatives straight to the Provincial Congress at Concord. The town of Worcester elected two representatives: Timothy Bigelow was to attend the Provincial Congress, while Joshua Bigelow was told first to go to Salem for the General Court and then, if and when that body failed to convene, to join his cousin in Concord.

On October 4, 1774, the citizens of Worcester, in their instructions to Timothy Bigelow, issued what amounted to a declaration of independence—twenty-one months before Thomas Jefferson's document would be signed by the Continental Congress in Philadelphia:

If all infractions of our rights, by acts of the British Parliament, be not redressed, and we restored to the full enjoyment of all our privileges, contained in the charter of this province, issued by their late majesties, King William and Queen Mary, *to a punctillo*, before the day of your meeting [October 5, the very next day], then, and in that case, you are to consider the people of this province absolved, on their part, from the obligation therein contained, and to all intents and purposes reduced to a state of nature; and you are to exert yourself in devising ways and means to raise from the dissolution of the old constitution, as from the ashes of the Phenix, a new form, wherein all officers shall be dependent on the suffrages of the people for their existence as such, whatever unfavorable constructions our enemies may put upon such procedure. The exigency of our public affairs leaves us no other alternative from a state of anarchy or slavery.[36]

On Wednesday morning, October 5, ninety men who had been elected by their towns met in the courthouse at Salem. There they awaited the attendance of Governor Gage, who obviously had no intention of showing up, having already dissolved this fledgling General Court. Even so, the men waited patiently from dawn till dusk, proving they were willing to meet under the law—the Charter, of course, not the Act—before convening themselves into a body without legal sanction.

The next day, their formal obligations fulfilled, the representatives resolved themselves into a Provincial Congress. No governor had sworn them in, and no official body had granted them any sort of legal authority, but in their minds that did not matter, for they received their authority straight from the people. The towns they represented had asked them "to take into consideration the dangerous and alarming situation of public affairs in this province," and "to consult and determine on such measures" as might resolve the crisis.[37]

The first business of the Congress on Thursday, October 6, was to choose a chairman (John Hancock) and a clerk (Benjamin Lincoln). Members then adjourned until the following Tuesday—the second Tuesday of October, the date which revolutionaries throughout Massachusetts had anticipated since the last week in August, when delegates from four counties had thrown their support behind Worcester's suggestion for a Provincial Congress.

At 10:00 on the morning of October 11, the ninety representatives to the aborted General Court at Salem joined with some 200 other delegates at the courthouse in Concord, where they reconvened the Provincial Congress. (The following week they would move to Cambridge, which was closer to Boston and possessed an infrastructure better able to accommodate so many outsiders.) Altogether, 209 of the 260 towns and districts of Massachusetts sent delegates—a far greater participation than the General Court had ever inspired. Only the smallest and most distant communities failed to attend.[38]

The most serious business of the Provincial Congress concerned procuring arms, raising money to pay for them, and establishing governmental and military structures to coordinate their revolution. If the patriots hoped to remain in control of Massachusetts, they would have to reconstruct some semblance of governmental authority and prepare for a possible counterrevolution staged by British Regulars.

On October 20 the Congress appointed a committee "to consider what is necessary to be now done for the defence and safety of the province." [39] Meeting behind closed doors to preserve military secrecy, the body of the whole spent several days discussing and debating the findings of the committee. On October 24 the Congress appointed another committee to determine "the most proper time for this province to provide a stock of powder, ordnance, and ordnance stores"; later the same day, the committee issued its report— *"Now was the proper time."* [40]

On October 26, after a week of deliberating on military matters, the Congress authorized the procurement of various armaments:

16 field pieces, 3 pounders, with carriages, irons, &c.; wheels for ditto, irons, sponges, ladles, &c., @ £30	£480 0 0
4 ditto, 6 pounders, with ditto, @ £38	£152 0 0
Carriages, irons, &c., for 12 battering cannon, @ £30	£360 0 0
4 mortars, and appurtenances, viz: 2 8-inch and 2 13-inch, @ £20	£80 0 0
20 tons grape and round shot, from 3 to 24 lb., @ £15	£300 0 0
10 tons bomb-shells, @ £20	£200 0 0
5 tons lead balls, @ £33	£165 0 0
1,000 barrels of powder, @ £8	£8,000 0 0
5,000 arms and bayonets, @ £2	£10,000 0 0
And 75,000 flints	£100 0 0
Contingent charges	£1,000 0 0
In the whole	£20,837 0 0 [41]

How would the newly-formed Congress come up with money to pay for all this? Since this Congress enjoyed no legal sanction, it was hardly in the position to collect taxes—yet without money, it could do nothing. On October 14, the Provincial Congress had "advised" the towns to withhold any payments to the official receiver-general (tax collector) of Massachusetts, Harrison Gray. On October 28, two days after approving the shopping list of armaments, it appointed a receiver-general of its own, Henry Gardner. It "recommended" that the sheriffs, constables, and collectors of the towns and districts pay whatever sums they had in their possession to Gardner instead of Gray; it "earnestly recommended" that they continue to collect funds according to the old warrants; it "strongly recommended" that the inhabitants honor their tax obligations and pay the collectors, who would turn the money over to the new receiver-general.[42]

During its first session, the Provincial Congress devoted much of its attention to the reorganization of the militia. On October 26, in addition to authorizing the procurement of armaments, it established a Committee of Safety with power to "alarm, muster, and cause to be assembled" the militia. The Committee of Safety was also empowered to appoint new militia commanders, while the men in each company were encouraged to elect new officers if they had not already done so. Companies were encouraged "to hold themselves in readiness, on the shortest notice from the said committee of safety, to march to the place of rendezvous." Since the "lives, liberties, and properties of the inhabitants of this province" depended on "their knowledge and skill in the art military, and in their being properly and effectually armed and equipped," the Congress recommended that all men arm themselves and drill with the militia. If arms were lacking, it recommended that the selectmen of the towns "take effectual care, without delay, to provide the same."[43]

The Provincial Congress adjourned on October 29, with plans to reconvene on November 23. In the interim, the Committee of Safety was instructed to sit in Cambridge, where it could keep an eye on the movement of British troops. The Congress also appointed seven leading figures, including John Hancock, James Warren, Elbridge Gerry, and Joseph Hawley, to meet during the recess. These two standing committees were the beginnings of an executive wing of the embryonic government.

The most convincing witness to the power of the Massachusetts Revolution of 1774 was Thomas Gage, the man in charge of putting it down. In his letters to Lord Dartmouth that fall, Gage chronicled the activities of his opponents, referring often to the proceedings of the Provincial Congress.

On October 3, two days before rebel representatives were slated to meet illegally in the rogue General Court at Salem, Gage wrote: "I don't find that the Spirit abates any where, for it is kept up with great Industry. . . . I don't suppose People were ever more possessed with Zeal and Enthusiasm." The rebels were not only disobeying his edicts but refusing his money. Boston carpenters, he complained, would not accept any contracts to build barracks for his soldiers, and even workers from New York declined the job due to patriot pressure and propaganda. "This Refusal of all Assistance has thrown us into Difficulties," he wrote, "but I hope to get through them, and to be able to put the Troops under Cover, tho' not so comfortably as I cou'd wish." In the end Gage was forced to have the soldiers themselves perform most of the work.[44]

On October 17, after the Provincial Congress had met for a week at Concord, Gage recorded some very disturbing rumors:

> There are various Reports spread abroad of the Motions made at the Provincial Congress, whilst at Concord, some, it's said, moved to attack the Troops in Boston immediately, other to value the Estates in the Town, in order to pay the Proprietors the Loss they might sustain, and to set the Town on Fire.[45]

Fueled by fear, these rumors must have spread like wildfire among the Loyalists huddled in Boston. Gage offered no comment in his letter to Dartmouth; we can only conjecture whether or not he gave them any credence.

On October 30 Gage gave a most alarming state-of-the-province report:

> Nobody here or at home could have conceived, that the Acts made for the Massachusett's Bay, could have created such a Ferment throughout the Continent, and united the whole in one

common Cause, or that the Country People could have been raised to such a pitch of Phrenzy. . . . If Force is to be used at length, it must be a considerable one, and Foreign Troops must be hired, for to begin with Small Numbers will encourage Resistance and not terrify; and will in the End cost more Blood and Treasure. An Army of Such a Service should be large enough to make considerable Detachments to disarm and take in the Counties. . . .

Many of their Leaders I apprehend mean to bully and terrify, and others to push Matters to extremity, puffed up by Hopes of Assistance from the whole Continent, and the Certainty of the immediate Aid of the four New-England Provinces, which they flatter themselves are alone sufficient to withstand all the Force of Great Britain. The People are told that the present Acts only lead to others which are to divide their Lands into Lordships, and tax them at so much Pr Acre. . . .

I am concerned that Affairs are gone to so great a Length that Great Britain cannot yield without giving up all her Authority over this Country, unless some Submission is Shewn on the part of the Colonies which I have tried at here tho' hitherto without Effect. And Affairs are at such a Pitch thro' a general union of the whole, that I am obliged to use more caution than could otherwise be necessary, least all the Continent should unite in hostile Proceedings against us.[46]

Much in this assessment was accurate. Angry and fearful, the rebels had placed the most powerful man in Massachusetts in a terrible bind: he could not yield without giving up authority, yet he was forced to "use more caution" in order to avoid a war. Thomas Gage, the commander-in-chief of the king's forces in Massachusetts, dared not call on his troops to disband the Provincial Congress, which was seizing authority before his very eyes. On November 2 he wrote helplessly, "I shall not be surprised, as the Provincial Congress seems to proceed higher and higher in their Determinations, if Persons should be Authorized by them to grant Commissions and Assume every Power of a legal Government, for their Edicts are implicitely obeyed throughout the Country." [47]

What rankled Gage the most was the rebels' attempt to collect taxes. Immediately following the Congress's appointment of a rebel receiver-general, Gage had Gray, the official receiver-general, issue a public notice warning local tax collectors against paying money to his new competitor, "notwithstanding any Advice they have received to the contrary, from any Bodies of Men, who cannot legally controul them, however numerous or respectable they may be." [48]

Fearing that the pleas and threats of his receiver-general might go unheeded, Gage followed with a proclamation of his own, which he placed in the newspapers and distributed as a broadside:

PROVINCE of MASSACHUSETTS BAY
By the GOVERNOR
A PROCLAMATION

WHEREAS a Number of Persons unlawfully assembled at Cambridge, in the month of October last, calling themselves a *Provincial Congress,* did in the most open and daring Terms, assume to themselves the Powers and Authority of Government, independent of, and repugnant to his Majesty's Government legally and constitutionally established within this Province, and tending utterly to subvert the same; and did amongst other unlawful Proceedings, take upon themselves to Resolve and direct, a new and unconstitutional Regulation of the Militia, in high Derogation of his Majesty's royal Prerogative; and also to elect and appoint Henry Gardner Esq. of Stow, to be Receiver General, in the room of HARRISON GRAY Esq., then and still legally holding and executing that Office; and also to order and direct the Monies granted to his Majesty to be paid into the Hands of the said Henry Gardner, and not to the said Harrison Gray Esqr., and further, earnestly to recommend to the Inhabitants of the province to *oblige* and *compel* the several Constables and collectors to comply with and execute the said Directions of the Law: all which Proceedings have a most dangerous Tendency to ensnare his Majesty's Subjects, the Inhabitants of this Province, and draw them into Perjuries, Riots, Sedition, Treason, and Rebellion.

For the Prevention of which Evils, and the calamitous Consequences thereof;

I have thought it my Duty to issue this Proclamation, hereby earnestly exhorting, and, in His Majesty's Name strictly prohibiting all his liege Subjects within this Province, from complying, in any Degree, with the said Requisitions, Recommendations, Directions or resolves of the aforesaid unlawful assembly, as they regard his Majesty's highest Displeasure, and wou'd avoid the Pains and Penalties of the Law. And I do hereby charge and command all justices of the Peace, Sheriffs, Constables, Collectors and other Officers, in their several Departments, to be vigilant and faithful in the Execution and Discharge of their Duty in their respective Offices, agreeable to the well known established Laws of the Land; and, to the utmost of their Power, by all lawful Ways and Means, to discountenance, discourage and prevent a Compliance with such dangerous Resolves of the above-mentioned, or any other unlawful Assembly whatever.

GIVEN at Boston this 10th Day of November in the Fifteenth year of the Reign of his Majesty, George the Third, by the Grace of God of Great Britain, France and Ireland, King Defender of the Faith, &c. Annoque Domini 1774.

THOs. GAGE

By His Excellency's Command,

Tho. FLUCKER, Secretary

GOD Save The KING [49]

For all its pomp and circumstance, Gage's edict had no perceptible impact. Like the "Proclamation Encouraging Piety and Virtue" he had delivered in July, these strong words were delivered by a governor who had lost his power to command.

Governor Gage would not be able to rule his subjects unless Commander-in-Chief Gage proved capable of conquering them. This he knew, and he repeated it often to Dartmouth. The problem, of course, was that Gage did not possess sufficient force to subdue the province of Massachusetts. The British garrison in Boston included slightly more than three thousand soldiers; at one time that had seemed plenty—there were about as many soldiers in Boston as there were adult male civilians—but after tens of thousands of rebels under arms had demonstrated their willingness to fight, a mere three grand did not appear very imposing. On November 2 Gage told Lord Dartmouth it would take "an Army Twenty Thousand strong" to take back the countryside.[50] On the same day he wrote to Viscount Barrington, the British secretary of war:

> If you think ten Thousand Men sufficient, send Twenty, if one Million is thought enough, give two; you will save both Blood and Treasure in the End. A large Force will terrify, and engage many to join you, a middling one will encourage Resistance, and gain no Friends.[51]

But Gage had already received all the troops he would get, at least for the near future. He possessed scarcely enough military might to defend Boston, let alone try to conquer a hostile province with 300,000 people.

Governor Gage commanded so little authority that he was scared to convene his own Council, even under the protection of British troops. On December 15, he wrote to Dartmouth, almost pathetically: "Taking any Step by their Advice would add no weight to the Authority of Government, but rather be an Argument for Disobedience; for that Reason I have avoided the Assembling of them in Council as much as possible."[52] Intimidated by the patriots, Thomas Gage— once the mightiest man in North America—hesitated to meet with his few remaining councilors, the best friends he had in Massachusetts, even under the watch of his own army.

The old government had shriveled, and a new government was beginning to emerge "from the ashes of the Phenix," as the people of

Worcester had suggested. The Revolution of 1774 was a success: all traces of British authority had vanished from Massachusetts, save for the military garrison in Boston. "Government has now devolved upon the people," wrote the disgruntled Jonathan Judd, Jr., a conservative shopkeeper from Hampshire County, "and they seem to be for using it." [53]

PART 3

AFTERMATH

6

BATTLE LINES

On September 25, 1774, Governor Gage wrote to Secretary of War Barrington: "Affairs here are worse than even in the Time of the Stamp-Act. I don't mean in Boston, but throughout the Country." [1] Three weeks later, during the opening session of the Provincial Congress, John Pitt informed Samuel Adams, who was still in Philadelphia at the Continental Congress, that the delegates from Boston were "by far the most moderate Men." [2] The radical thrust of this revolution no longer emanated from the Boston Committee of Correspondence; it came from the rural communities which had just put an end to British authority across the Massachusetts countryside.

This gave cause for concern—not only for Governor Gage, but for the established patriot leadership of Boston, who seemed taken aback by the sudden radicalism of their rural compatriots. Early in September, heartened by their victories in Great Barrington, Salem, Springfield, Cambridge, and Worcester, many from the countryside pushed a more revolutionary agenda than anyone in Boston had ever contemplated: instead of basing their opposition to the Massachusetts Government Act on the existing 1691 charter, they advocated a return to the original charter of 1621, under which the people had elected their own governor, and the representatives in the General Court, not Parliament, had exercised exclusive jurisdiction in the colony. Thomas

Young, in a letter to Samuel Adams, explained the sentiments of the country radicals: "They say we can never be easy in the condition we have been in for years past." The people were tired of being "held in one eternal political jangle" and living under a political system in which "a party is so easily made of the most powerful men in every County and even town against the common People."[3] They had no desire to continue under a system of patronage which favored the elite. The town of Leicester, in Worcester County, argued vociferously against returning to the status quo: "Charters have been bubbles—empty shadows, without any certain stability or security." Men who had stood tall in the face of British authority would not be satisfied with "patching up" the 1691 charter.[4]

"[A]lmost all in the western counties," Joseph Warren wrote to Samuel Adams, "are for taking up the old Form of Government, according to the First Charter. It is exceedingly disagreeable to them to think of being obligated to contend with their Rulers, quarrel for their rights every year or two."[5] But Warren and the Boston leaders were hesitant to endorse such a radical stance: "The resumption of the old charter of this colony is much talked of; but I think should be handled very gently and cautiously . . . lest we should be thought of as aiming at more than the colonies are willing to contend."[6] On September 12 Warren asked Adams for advice on how to respond, and on September 24 Adams replied that the "safest" approach was simply to reconvene the General Court, minus the governor, in order to give the appearance of not abolishing the legal government. "You know there is a charm in the word 'constitutional,' " he concluded.[7]

The following day, clearly troubled by the matter, Adams wrote to Warren again:

> I have been assured, in private conversations with individuals, that, if you should be driven to the necessity of acting in the defence of your lives or liberty, you would be justified by their constituents, and openly supported by all means in their power; but whether they will ever be prevailed upon to think it necessary for you to set up another form of government, I very much question.[8]

In their desire not to alienate potential allies, the Boston leadership tried to slow down the dizzying pace of a rebellion they had once hoped to foster. This was not without precedent: in the wake of the Stamp Act riots in 1765, these same men had redirected the energies of more radical street mobs.[9] But they faced a much harder task when they tried to rein in the country folk in 1774.[10] Bostonians who were used to exerting more than their share of influence on provincial politics now had to contend with the fact that 58 percent of the delegates to the Provincial Congress came from the agricultural counties of Worcester, Hampshire, and Middlesex, where rebels had been particularly insistent on deposing British officials.[11] These men would not necessarily stick to the party line, as delineated by the Boston leadership. Having successfully unseated British authority, rural rebels were in no mood to cede to a handful of town moderates.

Rural discontent with Boston leadership was not new. In 1769 and 1770 patriots from Worcester complained bitterly about rumors that Boston merchants were undermining the very nonimportation agreement which they themselves had promoted.[12] When the tax on tea triggered a new round of nonimportation, the Worcester town meeting charged once again that "the mercantile part of this Province" was violating the agreement, and that urban merchants, by raising prices, were placing self-interest above patriotism and practicing "an extortion that is sufficient to put them to the blush."[13] Now, when the Continental Congress endorsed a sweeping nonimportation boycott on October 20, country radicals succeeded in getting the Provincial Congress to pass a strongly worded prohibition against the sale of *all* goods imported from British territories (a previous agreement pertained only to goods imported after December 1).

The old agreements lacked enforcement procedures, but this one would not. Committees of inspection were to possess the authority to "take a full inventory of all goods, wares, and merchandize," to seize any contraband, and to "publish the names of such refractory merchants, traders, or purchasers, that they may meet with the merits of enemies to their country."[14] In the debates within the Provincial Congress, according to James Lovell of Boston, rural delegates expressed "anger and resentment" over "mercantile chicanery." "The country knows what it can do in inland places," Lovell wrote, "and seems determined to let England know that in the present struggle, commerce has lost all the temptations of a bait to catch the American farmer." [15]

John Andrews described a remarkable incident in which unnamed country radicals dictated policy to the Boston Committee of Correspondence concerning affairs within Boston itself. In September, when Governor Gage tried to build barracks for the soldiers, "the country people" insisted that nobody supply the British with materials or labor.

[They] sent committees to the severall contractors to let them know if they supply'd any further they would incur the resentment of the *whole* country; and at the same time signified to our committee of correspondence that they did not think it eligible for the workmen here to go on with building barracks or preparing houses for the reception of the troops, as we might possibly, by persisting, not only incur blame from our sister colonies, but essentially affect the union now subsisting between town and country; which circumstance caus'd the Committee to get together Saturday P.M., when they pass'd a vote, that it was not prudent for ye workmen to go on with ye frames, &ca., nor in any shape to contribute towards the accommodation of the soldiery, as they might themselves give offence to their country brethren.[16]

When Gage complained about the boycott to the Boston committee, Andrews reported, local patriots admitted that they personally favored building barracks—"They conceiv'd it much more for the benefit of the town (if the Soldiery must be here) to have them kept together, rather than to be *scatter'd* over the town, as in *that* case it would be a very difficult matter to keep them in order." But regardless of their own views, Boston committee members were no longer in a position to call the shots. "They reply'd it was not in their power to influence *the country*, and it lay principally with *them* whether the workmen should proceed or not."

Andrews also chronicled a sudden transformation of the image of the common farmer. At one time these country folk had been dismissed as backward, of no particular significance politically—but suddenly they assumed a reputation of mythological proportions. Andrews related two stories:

> When the 59th Regiment came from Salem, and were drawn up on each side of the *Neck*, a remarkable tall countryman, near eight feet high, struted between 'em, at the head of his waggon, looking *very* sly and contemptuously on one side and t'other; which attracted the notice of the whole regiment.—Ay, ay, says he, you don't know what *boys* we have got in the country. I am near nine feet high, and one of the smallest among 'em—which caused much merriment to the spectators, as well as surprise to the soldiers. . . .
>
> It's common for the Soldiers to fire at a target fix'd in the stream at the bottom of the common. A countryman stood by a few days ago, and laugh'd very heartily at a whole regiment's firing, and not one being able to hit it. The officer observ'd him, and ask'd why he laugh'd? Perhaps you'll be affronted if I tell you, reply'd the countryman. No, he would not, he said. Why then, says he, I laugh to see how awkward they fire. Why, I'll be bound I hit it ten times running. Ah! will you, reply'd the officer; come try: Soldiers, go and bring five of the best guns, and load 'em for this honest man. Why, you need not bring so many: let me have any one that comes to hand, reply'd the other, but I chuse to load myself. He accordingly loaded, and ask'd the officer where he should fire? He reply'd, to the right—when he pull'd tricker, and drove the ball as near the right as possible. The officer was amaz'd—and said he could not do it again, as that was only by chance. He loaded again. Where shall I fire? *To the left*—when he perform'd as well as before. Come! Once more, says the officer.—He prepar'd the third time.—Where shall I fire now?—*In the Center.*—He took aim, and the ball went as exact in the middle as possible. The officers as well as soldiers

star'd, and tho't the Devil was in the man. Why, says the countryman, I'll tell you *now*. I have got a *boy* at home that will toss up
an apple and shoot out at the seeds as its coming down.[17]

While John Andrews chuckled, Thomas Gage grimaced. On October 5, Andrews wrote:

> The Dispositions of the people in the Country are in general so
> restless, that they are continually sending Committees down
> upon one errand or other—which has caus'd the Governor to
> say, that he can do very well with the Boston Selectmen, but the
> damn'd country committees plague his soul out, as they are very
> obstinate and hard to be satisfied.[18]

But on October 29, after hearing of the radical agenda put forward
during the first session of the Provincial Congress, Andrews himself
expressed concern rather than amusement over these country revolutionaries:

> Our provincial congress have adjourn'd themselves for three
> weeks. Had much rather they were dissolv'd—as they are prin-
> cipally compos'd of spirited, obstinate countrymen, who have
> *very* little patience to boast of. Am therefore much afraid they
> will adopt measures that may impede the adjustment of our dif-
> ferences—as the more prudent among 'em bear but a small pro-
> portion. They have follow'd the example of the Continental
> congress and kept all their debates and transactions to them-
> selves. All we can learn is, that they have several times agitated
> the matter about requesting the inhabitants of this town to leave
> it: which is as absurd as it is impracticable. Several times since
> their sitting it is likewise been reported, that they were about es-
> tablishing a standing army to be compos'd of fifteen thousand
> men: a scheme not only ridiculous, but fraught with a degree of
> madness at this juncture.[19]

Andrews, like Gage and the Boston leadership, had reason to be worried by such programs. If the Provincial Congress did move to establish a standing army of fifteen thousand men, and if they did manage to evacuate the city, they were likely to start a war by attacking the outnumbered British troops in Boston. "The Country is very uneasy, long they cannot be restrained," wrote Benjamin Church. "They urge us and threaten to compel us to desert the Town. They swear the Troops shall not continue unmolested." [20] James Lovell wrote that the country people "press us to leave town in the strongest manner. . . . [I]t is become a downright task for the warmest patriots of our town and county to confine the spirit of the other counties." Lovell feared that "the provincial congress, with all their efforts to confine the inland spirits solely to the defensive, will surely fail" unless the British ministry made some concessions. Otherwise, the enraged country folk might undertake "a capital winter stroke." [21]

The prospect of war scared Bostonians like John Andrews, James Lovell, and Benjamin Church. Their homes and businesses might well be laid to waste. Andrews and Lovell believed in the patriot's cause, but like many others, they began to soften their support when radicals threatened to nudge the revolution toward armed conflict. Andrews began to speak more fondly of Governor Gage, who was attempting to avoid a confrontation. Church became a spy for the British.

Factions were emerging—and as usual, these could broadly be categorized as hawks and doves. Samuel Adams and the Boston Committee of Correspondence have typically been portrayed as hawks who drove the rebellion relentlessly to its logical conclusion. These men had played a pivotal role in the spread of republican ideology in 1772 and 1773, but during August and September of 1774, it was the farmers and artisans from the countryside who propelled the revolution forward by overthrowing the established order. Many of these country patriots wanted to go even further by driving the British army from Boston and revamping the Massachusetts government to reflect the will of the people. These "obstinate countrymen"—farmers who were "nine feet tall" and could "shoot the seeds out of an apple"—superceded the Boston leadership as the vanguard of the first American Revolution.

At least for the moment, however, the hawks did not prevail. Country radicals failed in their efforts to take control of the Provincial Congress in the fall of 1774. When the field shifted from the courthouses and town commons of rural communities to the halls of deliberative chambers, the people who had initiated this uprising began to lose control of it. Their voices would still resonate for more than a decade, but the most striking feature of this revolution—the making of all decisions by direct participants in public actions—started to atrophy with the meeting of the Provincial Congress.

Before dissolving the First Provincial Congress in early December, members chose five delegates to send to the Second Continental Congress: John Hancock, John Adams, Samuel Adams, Thomas Cushing, and Robert Treat Paine. Hancock, the wealthiest and most prominent of all Massachusetts patriots, was chairman of the Provincial Congress; the other four had already served in the First Continental Congress. By selecting these men, and by choosing other moderates to serve on key committees, members of the Provincial Congress reconfirmed the old revolutionary leadership. Representatives from the hinterlands, who tended to be more radical, might have constituted the majority of the Congress, but they did not run the show. Historian L. Kinvin Wroth has calculated that more than two-thirds of the men (twenty-three out of thirty-four) who served on key committees or held multiple assignments in the First Provincial Congress came from Boston or other "major trading towns" of the East, even though these towns accounted for only twenty percent of the delegates.[22]

Several factors helped moderate leaders maintain control.[23] Not only did they have standing, education, and plenty of political experience, but they also had an argument that was difficult to refute: if the revolution were to succeed, it could not proceed too fast. People in other colonies, and cautious patriots (such as John Andrews) within Massachusetts, did not wish to precipitate a war, nor were they ready to form a new government. When men from Worcester and other communities that had overthrown British rule spoke of creating a new government, they ran the risk of scaring off their less radical allies.

Sensing a rift within the insurgency, some Loyalists found the nerve to fight back. In an open letter dated December 22, Brigadier Timothy Ruggles contended that people were becoming disillusioned by the "banditti whose cruelties surpass those of savages." The rebels had achieved their early victories "before it was known that independency was the object in contemplation," and now it was time for people "who have not yet been guilty of an overt act of rebellion" to declare themselves for government and against lawlessness. To this end, Ruggles circulated his own "Association," in direct reponse to the revolutionary Association which had been endorsed by the Continental Congress and was then circulating throughout the country. The signers of Ruggles's Association pledged:

> 1st. That we will upon all occasions, with our Lives, and Fortunes, stand by and assist each other, in the defence of Life, Liberty, and Property, whenever the same shall be attacked, or endangered by any Bodies of Men, riotously assembled, upon any pretence, or under any authority, not warranted by the Laws of the Land.
>
> 2dly. That we will upon all occasions, mutually support each other in the free exercise, and enjoyment of our undoubted right to Liberty, in eating, drinking, buying, selling, communing, and acting what, with whom, and as we please, consistent with the Laws of God, and the King.
>
> 3dly. That we will not acknowledge, or submit, to the pretended authority, of any Congresses, Committees of Correspondence, or other unconstitutional Assemblies of Men; but will at the risque of our Lives, if need be oppose the forceable exercise of all such authority.
>
> 4thly. That we will to the utmost of our Power, promote, encourage, and when called to it, enforce obedience to the rightfull Authority of our most Gracious Sovereign King George the third, and of his Laws.
>
> 5thly. That when the Person or Property of any one of us

shall be invaded or threatened by any Committees, mobs, or unlawful Assemblies, the others of us will upon notice received
forthwith repair, properly armed, to the Person on whom, or
place where such invasion or threatening shall be, and will to the
utmost of our Power, defend such Person and his Property, and
if need be, will oppose and repel force with force.

6thly. That if any one of us shall unjustly and unlawfully be
injured in his Person or Property, by any such Assemblies as
before-mentioned, the others of us will unitedly demand, and if
in our Power compel the Offenders, if known, to make full repa-
ration and satisfaction for such Injury; and if all other Means of
Security fail, we will have recourse to the natural law of Retalia-
tion.[24]

The Association circulated by the Brigadier was the most publicized,
but others also gained currency within Loyalist circles. We have no indication that these declarations made any favorable impression on
moderates, nor did they produce much of an impact in rural Massachusetts, where any sane man would still be foolish to flaunt his defiance of the revolution in such a public manner. Even Governor Gage,
who had "taken Pains to promote" the Associations, admitted they
were playing to a limited audience: "I confess that I expect the Associ-
ators will be composed only of former Protesters and Addressers." [25]

The real threat to the Massachusetts revolution came not from a
handful of disgruntled Tories but from the king's Regulars, who had
turned Boston into a garrison town. These men, although seriously
outnumbered, were well armed and trained. They might any day be
dispatched into the countryside to seize rebel arms.

On December 13 Gage made his first move, described and explained by John Andrews:

This morning the Welch fusileers, together with a detachment
from another regiment, form'd a body of 400 men, and equip'd
with knapsacks &ca., march out of town as far as the punch
bowl in Brooklyne, when they return'd again. What this ma-
noeuvre can be for, I cant imagine, other than to give the men an

airing, or with a view to make frequent feints of the kind in order to familiarize the people to it, whereby in [the] future they may make an irruption into the country without creating any suspicion of their design, or possibly to make the Soldiers acquainted with the different roads near town.[26]

Again, on December 21, Andrews reported that "two or three Regiments continue to go out of town every day, sometimes to Cambridge, and at other times towards Dedham."[27] Although Gage's intent might well have been to disguise some future invasion, the political impact of these minor maneuvers worked against him: if ever he hoped to drive a wedge between moderates and radicals, parading his troops outside the town limits was not the way to do it. These gestures, with their threatening implications, only served to promote solidarity among the radical and moderate patriots, who could find common ground behind the issue of self-defense.

Although neither side developed concrete plans to stage an attack, both acted as if armed conflict were imminent. For both, access to arms and ammunition was paramount. Even if the rebels had more men to put on the battlefield, the British ministry reasoned, they would not be able to resist a counterrevolution without weapons and powder. British officials consequently issued an order to stop the importation of arms and ammunition into North America, while they simultaneously prepared to secure the stocks already there.

Sixty miles north of Boston, Fort William and Mary, which guarded the New Hampshire port of Portsmouth, housed a significant military cache. Early in December, Paul Revere and a number of fellow artisans, meeting clandestinely at the Green Dragon Tavern in Boston to coordinate the gathering of intelligence, surmised (incorrectly) that British ships spotted in the Atlantic were headed toward Portsmouth to secure Fort William and Mary, which was protected at the time by only six soldiers. On December 13 Revere rode on frozen roads to Portsmouth, where he warned local patriots that British ships were on their way to take the arms, ammunition, and powder stored at the fort back to Boston.

The following morning four hundred rebels stormed Fort William and Mary, overwhelmed the guards, and took off with one hundred barrels of gunpowder; the day after that an even larger crowd seized all the muskets they could find and sixteen cannons. By the time British ships from Boston arrived at Portsmouth to take back the fort, all guns and powder had been hidden deep in the patriot-controlled interior.[28]

The British lost more than armaments in the attack upon Fort William and Mary: here was proof that their authority had dissipated. Six weeks later General Gage complained to Secretary of State Dartmouth that "the Magistrates have not Support Sufficient to enable them to apprehend any of the People concerned in the Attack of Fort William and Mary, or keep them safe in Jail after Commitment." [29]

Politically as well as militarily, Commander-in-Chief Gage was under considerable pressure to come up with some sort of victory in the field, but with travel and transport difficult in winter, he made no offensive moves during December or January. The rebels used this time to gather supplies, train the militia, and organize communications. On February 24, 1775, Gage's intelligence network reported on the state of rebel preparedness:

Committee of safety appointed by the Congress consisting of Hancock, Warren, Church, Heath and Gearey, these are to observe the motions of the Army, and if they attempt to penetrate into the Country, imedietly to communicate the intelligence to Colo. Ward, Colo. Bigelow, and Colo. Henshaw, who live in or near the Towns of Worcester, and Leicester. Colo. Warren of Plymough and Colo. Lee of Marblehead, they are to send express's round the Country to collect the Minute Men who are to oppose the troops. These Minute Men amount to about 15,000 and are the picked Men of the whole body of Militia, and all properly armed.

There are in the Country thirty-eight Field pieces and Nineteen Companies of Artillery most of which are at Worcester, a few at Concord, and a few at Watertown.

There whole Magazine of Powder consisting of between Ninety and an Hundred Barrells is at Concord.

There are eight Field pieces in an old Store or Barn, near the landing place at Salem, they are to be removed in a few days, the Seizure of them would greatly disconcert their schemes.

Colo. Lee, Colo. Orme, Mr. Devons, Mr. Chever, Mr. Watson, and Moses Gill, are appointed a Committee of supply, who are to purchase all military stores, to be deposited at Concord and Worcester.[30]

Where should Gage make his first strike? To go after the storehouse of powder in Concord or the artillery in Worcester would undoubtedly trigger another mass mobilization of patriot forces, this time more organized and threatening than the Powder Alarm. The coastal town of Salem, however, seemed viable: not only could it be reached by British ships, but it was farther from the heartland of the province, where radical patriots held sway. The rebels must also have known that their weapons stored at Salem were more vulnerable, since they were planning to hide them somewhere else.

Gage chose to strike immediately at Salem, before the rebels had time to evacuate their arms. On Sunday, February 26, he dispatched Colonel Alexander Leslie and 240 troops first by boat to Marblehead, then overland toward Salem. In this surprise offensive, the British made two strategic mistakes: they marched on a Sunday, when the inhabitants of Salem were already gathered in church, and they chose a route to town which was guarded by a drawbridge. William Gavett, a Salem resident, recalled the incident in great detail:

Colonel David Mason had received tidings of the approach of the British troops and ran into the North Church . . . during service in the afternoon, and cried out, at the top of his voice, "The British reg'lars are coming after the guns and are now near Malloon's Mills." One David Boyce, a Quaker who lived near the church, was instantly out with his team to assist in carrying the guns out of the reach of the troops. . . .

The northern leaf of the draw was hoisted when the troops approached the bridge, which prevented them from going any

further. Their commander, Col. Leslie, . . . then remarked to
Capt. Felt, or in his hearing, that he should be obliged to fire
upon the people on the northern side of the bridge if they did
not lower the leaf. Captain Felt told him if the troops did fire
they would all be dead men, or words to that effect. It was understood afterwards that if the troops fired upon the people, Felt
intended to grapple with Col. Leslie and jump into the river, for,
he said, "I would willingly be drowned myself to be the death of
one Englishman." . . .

The people soon began scuttling two gondolas which lay on
the western side of the bridge, and the troops also got into them
to prevent it. One Joseph Whicher, the foreman in Col.
Sprague's distillery, was at work scuttling the colonel's gondola,
and the soldiers ordered him to desist, and threatened to stab
him with their bayonets if he did not—whereupon he opened
his breast and dared them to strike. They pricked his breast so as
to draw blood. . . .

It was a very cold day, and the soldiers were without over-
coats, and shivered excessively and shewed signs of being cold.
Many of the inhabitants climbed upon the leaf of the draw and
blackguarded the troops. Among them was a man who cried out
as loud as possible, "Soldiers, red-jackets, lobster-coats, cowards, damnation to your government!" . . .

Colonel Leslie . . . said, "I will get over this bridge before I
return to Boston, if I stay here till next autumn. . . . By God! I
will not be defeated"; to which Captain Felt replied, "You must
acknowledge you have already been baffled."

In the course of the debate between Colonel Leslie and the inhabitants, the colonel remarked that he was upon the King's
Highway and would not be prevented passing over the bridge.

Old Mr. James Barr, an Englishman and a man of much
nerve, then replied to him: "It is *not* the King's Highway; it is a
road built by the owners of the lots on the other side, and no
king, country or town has anything to do with it." . . .

Then the colonel asked Captain Felt if he had any authority to order the leaf of the draw to be lowered, and Captain Felt replied there was no authority in the case, but there might be some influence. Colonel Leslie then promised, if they would allow him to pass over the bridge, he would march but fifty rods and return immediately, without troubling or disturbing anything. Captain Felt was at first unwilling to allow the troops to pass over on any terms, but at length consented, and requested to have the leaf lowered down. The troops then passed over and marched the distance agreed upon without violating their pledge, then wheeled and marched back again, and continued their march through North Street, in the direction of Marblehead.

A nurse named Sarah Tarrant, in one of the houses near the termination of their route, in Northfields, placed herself at the open window and called out to them: "Go home and tell your master he has sent you on a fool's errand and broken the peace of our Sabbath. What," said she, "do you think we were born in the woods, to be frightened by owls?" One of the soldiers pointed his musket at her, and she exclaimed, "Fire if you have the courage, but I doubt it." [31]

The next time the British marched outside of Boston in search of arms—on April 19, 1775—they would go in greater numbers and in the dead of night. Having learned from their mistakes at Salem, they would avoid the Sabbath and choose a route that did not have a drawbridge.

The Worcester patriots, firmly in control in their town and county, continued to drill on the common and stockpile not only guns and powder but provisions, in case they were called to go off to war. During the winter months they dealt also with another troubling concern: the Provincial Congress had so far failed to act decisively on the matter of a new government. In the absence of a government that enjoyed any sort of legal sanction, how could the rule of law prevail? When and how would they legitimize the civil authority they had seized?

During the first week in January, two months earlier than was customary, Worcester patriots called a town meeting to choose their representative and to implement the recommendations of the Continental Congress and the Provincial Congress. The minutes of the meeting refer frequently to these higher bodies, which appeared to lend some sort of authority to the array of extralegal institutions local patriots were creating. The Continental Congress had called for an "Association" throughout the colonies, to be enforced by "committees of inspection." The Worcester town meeting acted accordingly and appointed twelve men to serve on the committee of inspection; ten of these, as well as the moderator for the town meeting, were members of the American Political Society. (The other two were Nathan Perry, the former moderator who was now a confirmed patriot, and David Bigelow, Timothy's brother.) The meeting also took a crucial step toward establishing the legitimacy of the Provincial Congress by ordering Worcester's tax collectors to pay "all the Province monies now in their hands" to Henry Gardner, the new receiver-general. Finally, it repeated its request that the Provincial Congress get on with the business of setting up a new government on a more formal footing. The Provincial Congress, it suggested, should ask the Continental Congress "what measures are the most proper for this Province to adopt respecting civil Government, which at this day we are deprived of." [32]

At the County Convention that met on January 26 and 27, delegates spent most of the time addressing another issue relating to civil authority: what to do about people who were selling liquor without a license. Under the old governmental structure, liquor licenses were granted and drink laws were enforced by the Court of General Sessions of the Peace in each county—but now the courts were closed. In the absence of supervision, there was a sudden increase in "the misbehavior of innholders, retailers, and persons selling liquors without a license." Not only did this create "a tendency to corrupt the morals of the people," but it also demonstrated that "the law of the province" was not being enforced. Although the County Convention did not actually issue new licenses, it did advise "the committees of correspondence, inspection, and selectmen in every town" to treat violators of the old drink laws in much the same manner as they treated Tories: they would be held up to "public view, and treated not only with neglect but contempt, as enemies of the public as well as of private good, until they reform." [33]

The Worcester County Convention, like the Worcester town meeting, looked to higher bodies to give them some sense of legitimacy— even though the Provincial and Continental Congresses, like the County Convention itself, were at least extralegal, and arguably illegal. The County Convention "strongly recommended" to the committees of inspection "to see that all traders keep strictly to the rules laid down by the Continental and Provincial Congress." It dared not call the dictates of the Congresses "laws," but it did call them "rules."

And rules were to be obeyed—even under threat of force. During September and October most county conventions had decried riots, disorder, and the use of violence. Now, the Worcester County Convention modified the usual proclamation: it resolved to suppress "all acts of violence, except so much as is necessary to carry the resolves of the Continental and Provincial Congress into execution." The policies of the de facto government were to be enforced by whatever means necessary. [34]

Once local Tories had been defeated, the patriots of Worcester began to show signs of division. Back in August and September they had come together to close the court and force councilors to resign, and even now they were united in opposition to the British administration. But they were not of one opinion as to how to proceed. When the County Convention urged a ban on Tory newspapers, a "Freeholder in the county of Worcester" argued against it; there was "so little force" in the Tory position, he maintained, that patriots should "read all they can" so as "to confirm them in their opposition." [35] Many thought that patriots, while they held the upper hand, should attack the outnumbered British troops in Boston; others felt such a move would be premature and ill advised. Perhaps the most ticklish question was whether or not to create a new government. To do so would be to declare independence, and some were unwilling to go that far.

These issues were debated informally in taverns and more formally by the American Political Society. As men talked and argued, tempers flared. On December 5, the American Political Society tried to settle a feud between two of its members. This was only the beginning: "an unhappy Difference Subsisting in this Town" eventually led to irreconcilable factions within their own organization. By the spring of 1775, this voluntary association had outlived its usefulness, and within a year it would disband.[36]

The revolution in Worcester County was in limbo. During the last week in March, when patriots tried to convene their next County Convention, attendance was so poor that they decided to publish a note in the *Massachusetts Spy:*

> As a number of towns in this county have not been publickly represented in this Convention, it is therefore recommended that the attendance of one or more members of the several towns therein, be given at their future meetings; and that they do not depart without leave when assembled, until an adjournment or dissolution thereof.[37]

Radical patriots found it difficult to wait for the rest of the colonies, the rest of the province, and the rest of their neighbors to recognize the obvious implications of the Revolution of 1774. Men like Timothy Bigelow and Ephraim Doolittle, who focused their energies on military preparation, chafed to get on with the fighting before internal dissension destroyed the patriot forces. On March 1, Bigelow wrote to William Henshaw of Leicester with some alarming news concerning Thomas Wheeler, a founding member and past chairman of the American Political Society:

> Col. Tho. Wheeler waited upon me this day and said that he had something to tell me that would surprise me as accordingly it did very much, viz. that he was determined from this time forward to withdraw all his aid and assistance from the common cause, and that he was determined not to have any further concern in the Militia, he was now fully convinced was wrong, &c. I thought it my duty to let you know that there was no dependence on the man that was undeservingly raised to be your Col.[38]

On March 21, Doolittle wrote a revealing letter to John Hancock, president of the Provincial Congress:

> [W]e are in a most Lamentable Scituation for want of a Sanction of Government on our Establishments our Tory Enemies using all their Secret machinations to divide us and Break us to pieces; ad to this the Dificulties that arise by ambitious men who are Indeavouring to Break our Companys to pieces in order to get Promotion for as there is no Establishment but what a Rises in the Breasts of Individuals, we are Continually Breaking to Peaces and a Number of Companys in my Regiment are now in such Circumstances and I fear if we are not soon Called to action we shall be Like a Rope of Sand and have no more Strength.[39]

From the outside, patriots appeared as motivated as ever. As Dr. Robert Honyman traveled through the Massachusetts countryside in late March 1775, he wrote in his diary: "The People all the way I travelled . . . are furious in the cause of liberty."[40] But insiders told a different story. Patriots needed to refocus on their common enemy. They needed a war to pull them back together.

During the early months of 1775, the split between moderates and radicals continued at the provincial level. Although the internal workings of the second Provincial Congress, which convened on February 1, were kept secret, reliable British intelligence revealed many differences within the chambers of the Congress.[41] The result was gridlock. At the end of the third week of the session, James Warren complained to Samuel Adams that the Congress was "dwindling into a School of debate and Criticism rather than . . . a great Assembly to resolve and act."[42]

While representatives had little trouble agreeing on some propositions—"In consideration of the coldness of the season, and that the Congress sit in a house without fire, *Resolved,* That all those members who incline thereto may sit with their hats on while in Congress"—they found no common ground on the matter of electing a new governor. If they did elect a governor, some reasoned, they could transform their Provincial Congress into a General Court and proceed with the business of government under the laws of the 1691 charter, but since the idea of an alternative government headed by a new governor might alienate potential allies, the proposal failed to carry.[43] In reality, the Provincial Congress performed many governmental functions— it passed rules which people were expected to obey, intervened in election disputes, collected taxes and authorized expenditures, and organized and supported the militia—but the representatives were not yet ready to admit it to the world.

On February 9 the Provincial Congress empowered five members of the eleven-man Committee of Safety to call out the militia any time they perceived an attempt to implement the Massachusetts Government Act by force.[44] While most delegates thought this measure necessary for the defense of the revolution, some feared that the judgment of five men, possibly mistaken, could instigate a war that patriots would probably lose. Joseph Hawley wrote to a fellow moderate, Thomas Cushing:

> When once the blow is struck it must be followed, and we must conquer, or all is lost forever. If we are not supported, perseveringly supported, by divers other colonies, can we expect any thing else, than, in a short time, to fall a prey to our enemies? . . .
>
> [I]f we, by order of our committee of safety, should begin the attack, and so bring on hostilities before the general express consent of the colonies that hostilities are altogether unavoidable, . . . I conceive that there will be infinite hazard that the other governments will say, that we have unnecessarily and madly plunged into war, and therefore, must get out of the scrape as we can, and we shall have no other aid from them. . . .
>
> I know your concern will be, that if we proceed in this deliberate way, the spirit of our people will evaporate and be lost. But let me assure you, that there in no danger of that. If I can make any judgment, all the danger is, on the other hand, that our people will rashly and headily rush into hostilities before they can be

upheld and supported: they will consequently fail of success . . .
and the good cause will be lost forever.[45]

This was a difficult argument to counter, yet it led nowhere: the
other colonies were not likely to pledge their full support unless or
until the British actually attacked. Indeed, the current stalemate would
not be broken unless one side or the other mounted a military offensive. Joseph Hawley could only hope that the Committee of Safety
would exercise sound judgment and not order some action that might
be construed as offensive.

For the next six weeks the power granted to the Committee of
Safety continued to rankle moderates. When representatives reconvened on March 22 after a monthlong recess, they revisited the matter.
On March 30, after British troops marched through the countryside
with no particular objective, the Provincial Congress finally spelled
out the conditions under which the Committee of Safety would call
out the militia: if 500 British troops went on the march outside of
Boston "with Artillery and Baggage," they would sound the alarm.[46]
According to General Gage's spies, this matter triggered "several
grand debates" which would continue over the next three weeks, right
up to April 19.[47]

Few seemed to doubt the inevitability of a British attack, and with
good reason. General Gage faced considerable pressure to mount an
offensive from his officers, who began to call him an "Old Woman"
because he did not act more aggressively.[48] He also faced rebuke from
London for his failure to take back the colony he had lost to "a tumultuous Rabble, without any Appearance of general Concert, or without any Head to advise, or Leader to conduct."[49] It was simply not
acceptable for the governor of Massachusetts, who doubled as the
commander-in-chief of the forces in North America, to leave the entire countryside in the hands of the rebels while he and his troops secluded themselves in Boston. He would have to figure out some way
to break the stalemate.

But Gage was closer to the ground than officials back in London,
and he realized he did not have the manpower to retake—and hold—

Massachusetts. Many of his men had died of illness over the winter; others were discontent and on the verge of mutiny.[50] He needed reinforcements.

On January 27, Lord Dartmouth wrote to Gage that help was on the way: 700 marines, three infantry regiments, one regiment of light dragoons, and financial support for the existing forces in Boston. "It is hoped . . . that this large Reinforcement to your Army will enable you to take a more active & determined part," he wrote. "The King's Dignity, & the Honor and Safety of the Empire, require, that . . . Force should be repelled by Force." Dartmouth also urged Gage to mobilize Loyalists who were willing to fight, making particular reference to Timothy Ruggles. Although he left the details of the matter to Gage's "Judgement and Discretion," Dartmouth did make two suggestions: arrest the leaders of the Provincial Congress and declare martial law. This letter, aggressive in tone, instructed Gage in no uncertain terms that it was time to make his move.[51]

Although Gage did not receive Dartmouth's letter until April 14, patriots got wind of the reinforcements on April 2. They also learned that Parliament had declared Massachusetts to be in a state of rebellion, that it had asked the king to uphold British authority at any cost, and that Lord Chatham's final plea to remove the troops from Boston had been soundly defeated. In the eyes of the patriots, Parliament was essentially declaring war.[52]

In the Provincial Congress, "the late very alarming intelligence from Great Britain" dramatically altered the political landscape.[53] Issues on the radical agenda—a standing army and the evacuation of Boston—could no longer be pushed aside. According to one of General Gage's informers, "the people without doors are clamorous for an immediate commencement of hostilities but the moderate thinking people within wish to ward off that period till hostilities shall commence on the part of Government which would prevent their being censured for their rashness by the other Colonies." Delegates from seaports like Boston remained hesitant, fearful that their towns would be burned once war broke out, but "several members" from inland communities were "positively required by their Constituents to urge the immediate raising of an army." Again, the West was leading the way, the East dragging behind. "Upon the whole a spirit of irresolution appears throughout all their transactions," the spy's report concluded.[54]

On April 5 the Provincial Congress adopted fifty-three "articles, rules, and regulations for the army, that may be raised for the defence and security of our lives, liberties, and estates." These rules covered much ground: they required all officers and soldiers to "diligently frequent divine service and sermon," they laid out strict standards of discipline, and they limited punishment in noncapital offenses to no more than "thirty-nine stripes for any one offence."[55] But the rules were still hypothetical—as of yet, there was no such army.

Three days later, however, the "committee on the state of the province" submitted a sweeping resolution:

> *Resolved,* That the present dangerous and alarming situation of our public affairs, renders it necessary for this colony to make preparations for their security and defence, by raising and establishing an army, and that delegates be appointed forthwith to repair to Connecticut, Rhode Island and New-Hampshire, informing them that we are contemplating upon, and are determined to take effectual measures for that purpose; and for the more effective security of the New England colonies and the continent, to request them to co-operate with us, by furnishing their respective quotas for general defence.[56]

If the hawks managed to carry this resolution in the body of the whole, they would get a standing army—not only in Massachusetts but in all of New England. Despite their fears, moderates found it politically inexpedient to oppose the measure. They pushed for a recess to consult their constituents, but they dared not appear too unpatriotic by standing in the way of the committee's recommendation. Ninety-six of the 103 members present voted to establish an army.[57]

Heated debates continued the following week as delegates started to work out the details of what a standing army would entail. On April 15, the final day of the session, Gage's spy reported that "there was great division [among] members of the Congress and great irresolu-

tion shewn in the Course of their debates this week." [58] Two of the key
players, according to the spy, were Joseph Henshaw of Leicester and
"Mr. Biggelow" of Worcester.[59]

One of the problems, it seems, was a paucity of funds. How could
the Congress support an army when Henry Gardner, the receiver-
general, had received less than one-quarter of the previous year's
taxes? With or without adequate funds, however, members voted to
begin the process. On April 13, they directed the Committee of Safety
"to engage a suitable number of persons, and form six companies of
the train for the artillery already provided by this colony." The following day, the Congress opened applications for field officers, cap-
tains, and subaltern officers.[60]

With conflict imminent, people in droves fled Boston, now little
more than a military outpost. Most members of the Boston Committee of Correspondence left the night they heard rumors of Dartmouth's orders. James Warren wrote on April 7, "The Inhabitants of
Boston are on the move." [61] On April 10, a Boston newspaper reported
that "a number of Families are moving themselves and their most
valuable Effects from this Town into the Country, in Consequence of
the late Advices from England," [62] and the following day John Andrews noted "the streets and Neck lin'd with waggons carrying off the
effects of the inhabitants . . . imagining to themselves that they shall
be liable to every evil that can be enumerated, if they tarry in town." [63]
On April 14, the Provincial Congress recommended that donations
intended for relief of the poor in Boston be used to help evacuate the
city.[64] Nobody wanted to be in the path of competing armies when
open hostilities commenced.

On April 15, the Congress declared a recess until May 10, but it
made contingency plans "considering the great uncertainty of the
present times, and that important unforeseen events may take place,
from whence it may be absolutely necessary that this Congress should
meet sooner than the day abovesaid." In fact, the Congress foresaw
the "unforeseen events" quite accurately when it authorized its members from Charlestown, Cambridge, Brookline, Roxbury, and Dorch-
ester (the communities rimming Boston) to reconvene the body "in

case they should judge it necessary." [65] If and when the British went on the march, congressional delegates would rush back to work.

The question now was not *whether* the British would strike, but *when* and *where*. Concord and Worcester, where the rebels stored their military wares and extra provisions, were the most likely prospects. Governor Gage dispatched a number of spies to explore the possibilities.[66] One of these, twenty-two-year-old John Howe, kept a detailed journal which he later summarized:

> On the 5th of April, 1775, General Gage called on me to go as a spy to Worcester to examine the roads, bridges and fording places, and to see which was the best route to Worcester to take an army to destroy the military stores deposited there. Accordingly Col. Smith and myself dressed ourselves as countrymen with gray coats, leather breeches, and blue mixed stockings, with silk flagg handkerchiefs round our necks, with a small bundle tied up in a homespun checked handkerchief in one hand, and a walking stick in the other. Thus equiped we set out like countrymen to find work.[67]

When the spies stopped for breakfast at a tavern in Watertown, a woman who waited on their table recognized Smith as a British officer. His disguise revealed, Smith returned to Boston, while Howe continued with the mission. Posing as a gunsmith seeking employment, Howe gathered information on the state of the roads and the disposition of the people. At one point along the road he noted "the largest tree I ever saw" and asked a local man what kind it was. Howe recorded the response:

> He said buttonwood, and further said that the people were going to cut it down to stop the regulars from crossing with their cannon. I asked him how they would know when the regulars were coming in time enough to cut the tree down. He said they had men all the time at Cambridge and Charlestown looking out. This tree would completely blockade the road should they do it.

All along the way Howe encountered fierce patriotism. Secluded during daylight hours by local Tories, he traveled mostly at night and in the snow. When he arrived in Worcester on April 8, his Tory guide showed him "the place where the military stores were deposited." This would be the British target, but to get there the troops would have to travel roads that were "very hilly and bad" and face a hostile and armed populace.

On his way back toward Boston, Howe veered toward the north on a route that took him through Concord. Here, too, local Tories showed him where the patriots were hiding their "flour, arms and ammunition"—and here too he discovered that people were preparing to fight.

Upon his return to Boston on April 12, Howe shared the results of his mission with Gage and his officers:

> The general said, "John, we have examined your journal; you are well deserving the name of a good soldier and a lucky and expert spy. How large an army will it take to go to Worcester and destroy the stores and return safe?" By answering that question I must stand or fall, but I was determined to give my opinion in full, turn as it would. I said, if they should march 10,000 regulars and a train of artillery to Worcester, which is forty-eight miles from this place, the roads very crooked, stony and hilly, the inhabitants generally determined to be free or die, that not one of them would get back alive. . . . The general asked me what I thought of destroying the stores at Concord, only eighteen miles. I stated that I thought 500 mounted men might go to Concord in the night and destroy the stores and return safe; but to go with 1000 foot to destroy the stores the country would be alarmed; that the greater part of them would get killed or taken.

Howe's advice seemed sound. Back in September 1774, General Gage had thought better of sending his troops to face the hotbed of patriots in Worcester; now, reinforcements or no, he thought better of it again. Gage decided to make his move on Concord instead.

7

THE END OF REVOLUTION

On the morning of April 19, 1775, the British staged their first major counter-revolutionary attack. During the preceding night 700 soldiers had left Boston and headed toward the military stores at Concord. Their route took them through Lexington, where at dawn they encountered a small company of minutemen who had hastily assembled on the common. The British fired, killing eight and wounding ten more, then proceeded to Concord, only to find that the magazine had been emptied. On their march back to Boston, the Regulars were forced to run the gauntlet of rebel fire. Hiding behind trees and stone walls, farmers-turned-marksmen picked off 273 men who had been sent from the other side of the Atlantic to shore up the fading British presence in Massachusetts.

News of the British attack on Lexington and Concord raced across the countryside. William Lincoln, Worcester's early nineteenth-century historian, recorded the story as it was passed down from those who were there:

> Before noon, on the 19th of April, an express came to the town, shouting, as he passed through the street at full speed, "to arms! to arms! the war is begun!" His white horse, bloody with spurring, and dripping with sweat, fell exhausted by the church.

Another was instantly procured, and the tidings went on. The passage of the messenger of war, mounted on his white steed, and gathering the population to battle, made vivid impression on memory. The tradition of his appearance is preserved in many of our villages.

The bell rang out the alarm, cannon were fired, and messengers sent to every part of the town to collect the soldiery. As the news spread, the implements of husbandry were thrown by in the field, and the citizens left their homes with no longer delay than to seize their arms. In a short time the minute men were paraded on the green, under Capt. Timothy Bigelow: after fervent prayer by the Rev. Mr. Maccarty, they took up the line of march. They were soon followed by as many of the train bands as could be gathered, under Capt. Benjamin Flagg. On that day, 110 men marched from the town of Worcester for Concord.[1]

And so it went from town to town. Patriots, it was said, answered the call to arms without hesitation. This was their moment, and through the years it has become our moment too. Even today, this is how most Americans envision the Revolutionary War.

In September 1774, and again in April 1775, the country folk of Massachusetts were nearly unanimous in their enthusiastic support for the rebellion against an oppressive regime. In the years that followed, however, both unanimity and enthusiasm would falter. This would be a long and protracted war, and by the time it was over, the democratic ideals and processes which had propelled the first American Revolution would be severely challenged.

Worcester, like so many other towns, gave willingly at first but begrudgingly later on. Minutemen from Worcester had come upon the scene too late for action on April 19, but the majority stayed around as the new army congealed on the outskirts of Boston. When Timothy Bigelow was promoted to major, Jonas Hubbard took his place as captain of the company from Worcester. On April 24, Hubbard's company had fifty-nine men; on August 1, a roll call listed sixty-two.[2] During the summer of 1775 a significant number of local patriots were willing to bring their revolutionary fervor to the battlefield.

The war itself was slow to develop. After the dramatic opening, the two sides settled down behind their respective lines: the British within Boston, the Americans laying siege from the outside. With the Americans more numerous but the British better equipped and trained, neither side possessed the strength to dislodge the other. On June 17 the British attacked at Breed's Hill at a cost of over one thousand casualties; after this "Battle of Bunker Hill," they dared not strike again.

The men from Worcester and other towns throughout New England who held the British at bay saw little action during the summer of 1775. Farmers accustomed to constant hard labor did not take well to inactivity, nor did they readily submit to following orders when they saw no clear reason for doing so. On June 12, the Provincial Congress appointed a committee of seven, including Joseph Hawley, "to inquire into the reason of the present want of discipline in the Massachusetts army." [3] On July 8, because of "the difficulties and troubles which have and daily are arising in our camps, by reason of divers evil-minded persons selling spirituous liquors," the Congress required that any sale of liquor to the troops receive the prior approval of a commanding officer. [4]

In late August and early September, exactly one year after the closing of the courts, the American high command recruited over one thousand men to undertake a dangerous but potentially historic mission: an assault on the city of Quebec, the poorly guarded British outpost in Canada. Colonel Benedict Arnold commanded the mission, and Major Timothy Bigelow served immediately under him. (Bigelow had been sent into Canada in 1760 as a private during the French and Indian War.) Jonas Hubbard was placed in charge of a company that included about a dozen soldiers from Worcester. [5]

The Quebec expedition, chronicled in the diary of Worcester surveyor John Pierce, was a disaster. [6] As they struggled through the Maine wilderness, soldiers were reduced to eating their dogs. Once they arrived on the outskirts of the city, according to Pierce, they debated whether they had sufficient resources to stage the assault:

Last night we had a General Review and to Day they are taking their Names to see how many will Scale the walls and how many will not &.C. amongst our men there is Great Searchings of heart with respect to Scaleing of walls and what the event will be God only Knows—Its not my opinion to Scale nor the opinions of my Capt [Jonas Hubbard] nor Lt. that's well Known and its not the opinion of Majr Bigelo neither.[7]

The men from Worcester, that hotbed of patriotism, lined up on the side of caution—or cowardice, as others would accuse. They did not wish to risk their lives in a battle they thought they could not win. Only two of Hubbard's company voluntarily "signed to Scale the walls of Quebeck."

But eager voices prevailed. On New Year's Eve, just hours before many terms of enlistment were about to expire, the Americans prepared to attack. Timothy Bigelow and Jonas Hubbard and the rest of the men from Worcester joined in, even though most thought better of it. Their misgivings proved well-founded. Hubbard and two of his townsmen were mortally wounded.[8] Hundreds of men were captured, including Timothy Bigelow; those who did not die or escape remained prisoners-of-war for more than half a year.[9]

Despite the tragedy at Quebec, patriots from Worcester continued to put their bodies on the line. During the summer of 1776, when the British undertook their first major offensive in New York, the September town meeting decided not to consider any important issues because of "the great number of the free men of this Town being absent for the Defence of this and the other american states."[10] Again in 1777, when soldiers were needed to take on General Burgoyne's large force near Bennington, Vermont, and Saratoga, New York, seventy-two men signed up. Half of these either had been members of the American Political Society or had the same surnames as members, in many cases their sons.[11] (Earlier, 45 percent of the members of the American Political Society had answered the alarm on April 19, 1775, and another 20 percent had the same surnames as men who answered the alarm.[12])

With time, however, most of those who had been most active in the early stages of the Revolution left the fighting to others. Increasingly,

Worcester found it difficult to meet its quotas for new recruits. Like the rest of the province and the other rebellious colonies, it resorted to a draft—and a draftee was allowed to hire a substitute, if he could afford one. Money replaced patriotism as the motivation to join the army. In July 1776, March 1777, and November 1777, the town approved extra taxes to pay the bounties of the men it hired to meet its quotas.[13] By September 1779, Worcester was borrowing money for bounties, and the following month it voted "to choose a Committee to hire the money necessary for the raising this towns quota of Soldiers for this Service on the faith & Credit of the town." Seven local men lent the town £2,515 in inflated currency, plus interest, to hire thirteen soldiers.[14]

There were now three classes of patriots: those who paid money in order to escape military service, those who were too poor to pay and who therefore had to serve, and those who made money on this arrangement by charging interest. The system wasn't exactly equitable, but it seemed the only way to field an army.

By 1780 this method of procuring soldiers to fight in defense of liberty was itself breaking down. Since wartime inflation had rendered currency virtually meaningless, and since few potential recruits were willing to sign up for a bounty that would quickly lose its value, the Worcester town meeting of June 23 resolved to pay the soldiers it hired with produce and grain instead of soft cash.

By the end of 1780, Worcester experienced a sort of taxpayers' revolt. Hard-pressed due to wartime scarcities, many citizens could no longer afford to pay the taxes required to hire other men to fight. After five bitter meetings (December 25, January 22, January 29, February 5, and February 9) in which votes were taken and retaken, resolutions passed and then rescinded, Worcester switched to a system called "classing." The town was divided into a number of different classes balanced according to wealth, and each class had to figure out some way of producing one soldier.[15]

Whether through the regular system of drafting or by classing, the net result was the same: poor men did the fighting toward the end of the war, while others stayed home—including the most vocal patriots. Of the twenty-one men who enlisted in the army early in 1781 to fulfill the town's quota, not one had been a member of the American Political Society, nor had any answered the initial call to Concord. These were not the men who started this war, but they were the ones who ended it. Of the ten with known occupations, seven were farmers, two were shoemakers, and one a butcher. At least two were African American.[16] They were either too poor to vote or they did not come from Worcester, for not a single one appears on the list of town voters for 1779.[17]

Worcester, like other towns, had difficulty in meeting its quotas not only for men but for provisions and supplies. The Continental Army depended on communities like Worcester for blankets and shirts, shoes and stockings, horses and cattle—but how much could common farmers afford to give, and for how long? On March 3, 1778, with tensions running high around fiscal issues, the selectmen and town treasurer were accused of financial mismanagement. Sixteen soldiers had not been paid, an investigative committee charged, while town officials refused to disclose how much money they held in their hands from the collection of fines. The town voted down this section of the committee report, but it did accept the charge that "the Selectmen Engrossed to them selves the Business of Transporting . . . Salt from Boston & have Charged Such Sums Per Bus as must amount to nearly 130 Dollars above the original Cost. . . . [The] salt was distributed to a part of the Inhabitants of the Town in very unequal and undue Proportions."[18]

A small matter to us, but large at the time, since salt was essential for meat storage. At the next election all seven selectmen and the town treasurer were replaced. The committee that made the charges included Joshua Bigelow and three other members of the now-defunct American Political Society; the officials they displaced included such seasoned patriots as David Bigelow (Joshua's cousin and Timothy's brother), William Young, Nathan Perry, and Benjamin Flagg.[19] The Revolution in Worcester no longer proceeded with a unified front.

Everyone came together, however, when it came to complaining about high taxes. Nobody recorded a dissent on November 15, 1779, when the selectmen were instructed to petition the Assembly "to obtain relief from the excess of the last tax" and to request lower taxes in the future, nor on July 9, 1781, when townspeople stated that "for Several years last past your petitioners have been called upon by Government for larger Sums of money & greater numbers of Soldiers than their just proportion."[20] The citizens of Worcester still tried to take the moral high ground, even though they now enjoyed taxation *with* representation, but complaints about high taxes did not have the same revolutionary ring as the desperate struggle against disenfranchisement. Political life in small-town Massachusetts was drifting back toward normalcy.

After the commencement of armed conflict, the Provincial Congress was still troubled by its outlaw status. Although it had taken on many of the legislative and executive functions of government (even to the point of supporting a "lunatic" at public expense),[21] it had no clear authorization by a constitution or any official body to act in a governmental capacity.

Many of the more radical members, meanwhile, voiced concerns over the centralization of governmental powers. During the Revolution of 1774 the people had exercised direct control over all decision making. Before 1774, when patronage prevailed, too much power had been assumed by the elite; now, radicals in the western counties tried to prevent any backsliding toward the old order. These revolutionaries believed strongly that no one man, nor any group of men, should ever be granted too much power, and on April 29, 1775, they convinced the Provincial Congress to draft a number of rules to prevent domination of its meetings by individual delegates.[22] On May 18 the Congress recommended that the towns not choose military officers as representatives. On May 25 the Worcester town meeting instructed its representative:

> You are therefore in all Grants of the Publick money to be especially Carefull that no more is given to any person for his services than an adequate pay for the same, & that no person be allowed to live in luxury and idleness or become oppulently rich at the publick expense. There is nothing in a well ordered Government that requires it; and in whatever Community it is al-

lowed they are raising such another tribe of Tyrants to destroy themselves as we are now justly fighting against.

It was the centralization of power that lay at the root of the problems with Great Britain: "a Corrupt Despotick ministry with a wink or a nod rules both King and Parlimint with such absolute sway that they are but a meer nose of Wax turned and moulded any, and every way to answer Despotick purposes." By contrast, Worcester insisted that "we have such a form of Government Established as that every officer in it be dependant upon the Suffrages of the people for their place & pay." [23]

With moderates hesitant to usurp the powers of government for fear of scaring away allies in other colonies, and with radicals reticent to relinquish power to any new governmental authority, the Provincial Congress continued to shy away from admitting that it had in fact become the government of Revolutionary Massachusetts. Even after Lexington and Concord, it self-consciously used the term "recommend" (sometimes proceeded by "strongly") instead of such words as "require" or "prohibit."

But this charade could not go on forever. On May 16, 1775, the Provincial Congress sent a letter to the Continental Congress requesting "your most explicit advice, respecting the taking up and exercising the powers of civil government, which we think absolutely necessary for the salvation of our country." [24] On June 20 the Provincial Congress received an answer: the towns were to choose representatives who would convene as the Assembly, choose their own Council, and proceed to "exercise the powers of government"— without the third component of the General Court, the governor. [25]

The Provincial Congress responded immediately by requesting the towns to hold new elections, and the towns quickly returned the same men (or others of the same persuasion) to office. On July 19, 1775, the Provincial Congress dissolved itself. On July 20, the new General Court instructed that all the "resolves, doings, and transactions" of the Provincial Congress be "confirmed and established, as lawful and valid." [26]

Finally, it was official: Massachusetts had a new government. But it was a government sanctioned by only a handful of delegates from other colonies, meeting in faraway Philadelphia. The Continental Congress had done no more than affirm the charter of 1691, instituted under the reign of William and Mary—and for radical Massachusetts patriots, this would not suffice. Only the people of Massachusetts had the authority to form their own government.

Throughout most of the Revolutionary War, as the rebel army fought off the British, many of the men who had shut down the system in 1774 battled politically to form a government firmly rooted on "the Suffrages of the people." The most outspoken proponents of a more progressive governmental structure were the western farmers from Berkshire County. In December 1775, many Berkshire patriots, at a convention in Stockbridge, voted not to recognize the General Court as the valid government of Massachusetts. As in the summer of 1774, they were concerned with the judges and justices of the courts: the new judges were appointed by the Council, which was dominated by moderates. Some of the men the Council selected to serve in Berkshire County had held appointive offices under the British, some were very wealthy, and one was a former Tory. Four of the new justices who currently served as members of the General Court were essentially appointing themselves into office. This was precisely the pattern of multiple officeholding that the radical revolutionaries had struggled to change. Rather than submit to the judges and justices appointed by the Council, they kept the courts closed.[27]

Not all citizens of Berkshire agreed with radical opposition to the new government. Six towns from the southern end of the county condemned the Stockbridge convention for its attempt "to dissolve all Government, and introduce dissension, anarchy, and confusion among the people."[28] Again, all patriots were not of one mind about how to proceed.

On December 25, radicals from Pittsfield, in a petition to the General Court, argued "that every Town may retain the previlege of nominating their Justice of the peace and every County their Judges. . . . If the right of nominating to office is not invested in the people we are indifferent who assumes it whether any particular persons on this or on the other side of the water." Rather than submit to officials who had not been elected, they preferred to continue without any government at all. "Since the Suspension of Government," they boasted, "we have lived in great love peace and good order for more than 16 Months." They insisted on continuing that way: "Upon the foregoing premises and on account of obnoxious persons being appointed to rule us. The Court of this County of Quarter Sessions etc. is ordered to desist from any future Sessions." These people possessed no legal authority to "order" the courts to close—but they did have the power, and the judges and justices meekly obeyed. Recalling the events of the summer of 1774, officials who had been appointed by the Council dared not force the issue.[29]

In May 1776, after continuing complaints from Berkshire, Hampshire, and Worcester counties, the General Court sharply reduced the fees paid to judges and justices. This might have appeased some, but it was not nearly enough for the radicals from Pittsfield, who once again argued their case:

> But if Commissions should be Recalled, and the Kings Name struck out of them, if the Fee Table be reduced never so low, and multitudes of other things be done to still the people all is to us as Nothing whilst the foundation is unfixed and the Corner stone of Government unlaid. We have heard much of Governments being founded in Compact. What Compact has been formed as the foundation of Government in this province?[30]

On September 17, 1776, the General Court asked the towns whether the current government should try to compose a new constitution. The responses were mixed: many gave their assent, but a significant number voiced reservations.[31] Some of those objecting felt that only a convention of delegates chosen specifically for the purpose, not the existing legislature, had the authority to draft a new constitution. Several towns in Worcester County expressed concern that the General Court, with a preponderance of members from the more populous eastern towns, would codify this "unequal representation" within the new document.[32] Nearly all the towns demanded they be given the opportunity to approve or reject any proposed constitution.

In May 1777 the General Court approved a resolution intended to bypass the need for a special constitutional convention: the towns, at their next annual meetings, should specifically empower their representatives "to form such a Constitution of Government, as they shall judge best calculated to promote the Happiness of this State."[33] The General Court of 1778 then proceeded to draft a new constitution—but it was overwhelmingly rejected. While some opponents thought the constitution too radical and others too conservative, most agreed on two central criticisms: it did not contain a bill of rights, and it had been written by the legislature, not by a constitutional convention. Several western towns took issue with the appointment of civil officers by the governor and Senate, and with the indefinite terms of judges and justices. Lenox, in Berkshire County, offered an eloquent critique of the £60 property requirements for the franchise:

> All men were born equally free and independent, having certain natural & inherent, & unalienable Rights, among which are the enjoying & defending Life and Liberty & acquiring, possessing & protecting Property. . . . We conceive this article declares Honest Poverty a Crime for which a large Number of the true & faithful Subjects of the State, who perhaps have fought & bled in their Countrys Cause are deprived of the above mentioned Rights (which is Tyranny) for how can a Man be said to be free & independent, enjoying & defending Life and Liberty & protecting Property, when he has not a voice allowed him in the choice of the most important Officers in the Legislature, which can make laws to bind him and appoint Judges to try him in all cases as well of Life & Liberty as of Property.[34]

Radicals in Berkshire County continued to insist that the courts remain closed until the people of Massachusetts had written and approved their own constitution. On August 12, 1778, a Berkshire County Convention voted 545 to 329 to oppose the opening of the

Sessions Court and 660 to 161 to keep the Court of Common Pleas closed. (People were more concerned with civil suits against debtors in the Court of Common Pleas.) [35] Two weeks later, in a petition to the General Court, the Berkshire convention defended itself against charges that they were "a Mobbish, Ungovernable refractory, licentious and dissolute People." With obvious pride, they recalled that they were "the first County that put a Stop to Courts" back in 1774, and that they "were soon followed by many others, Nay in effect by the whole State." Now, they wanted the courts to remain closed "rather than to have Law dealt out by piece meal as it is this Day, without any Foundation to support it." They had said as much before, but this time they upped the ante: if no moves were made toward a constitutional convention, they might secede from the state: "there are other States, which have Constitutions who will We doubt not, as bad as we are, gladly receive us." [36]

When the "Berkshire Constitutionalists" (as they came to be called) tried to get patriots from Worcester and Hampshire counties to support their position, they provoked a rather bitter response from their once-radical comrades in the town of Worcester:

> We cannot agree with you, Gentlemen, with respect to the non-admission of the Courts of Quarter Sessions and Common Pleas, untill the formation and acceptance of a new Constitution. . . . The reason given for stoping the Courts of Quarter Sessions and Common Pleas, will be equally conclusive for stoping the Superior Courts, the consequence of which will be, that, untill the formation and acceptance and establishment of a new Constitution which will require time and ought not to be done in a hurry without due consideration all treasons and misprisions of treasons, murders and felons of what kind soever, committed in your County, cannot be tried; for the Laws make it necessary that these Crimes shall be tried in the same County they were Committed. Every member of Society must dread the consequence of suffering such offences to pass with impunity; our Lives, liberties and Estates would become insecure, and we

should soon be in a situation worse than that of a State of nature. . . .

The idea of Committees forming County Conventions, and these County Conventions advising State Conventions to act in opposition to, or in conformity with the General Court, the supreme authority of the State, seems to us at present to involve in it the greatest absurdity and to be intirely inconsistent with the best and most established maxims of government. . . .

When the talons of Slavery were about to fasten upon us, . . . it was necessary for the people to bestir themselves and invent some method to prevent the fatal catastrophe; the Committees of the several towns in each County did then assemble together and form County Conventions, which were at that time very favourable, and tended greatly to the Salvation of America. But when we had repelled the fatal blow, . . . and agreeable to the recommendation of the Continental Congress, assumed the forms and execution of legislative, and executive government, the reason and necessity of the Convention ceased. At this day, it appears to us they can do no good, but may be productive of great and lasting mischief. . . .

We in this County, and we will venture to say those of other counties in this State, that have had the experience, are perfectly satisfied, and well pleased, that the laws are once more regularly executed. We feel the good effects of it. We cannot be deprived of our personal liberty and property, by the capricious and arbital decision of a body of men who are guided by no rule.[37]

For Daniel Bigelow (Timothy's brother) and the other members of the Worcester Committee of Correspondence, Inspection and Safety, the time for revolution had passed. Extralegal actions, at one time permissible, were no longer so. Former rebels were now spewing conservative arguments in defense of the status quo.

But for the Berkshire Constitutionalists, the Revolution was still in process. When on May 4, 1779, the Superior Court tried to meet in Great Barrington for the first time in five years, the judges found the

courthouse packed with people who demanded they not conduct any
business. The angry crowd was smaller this time—only about 300
people, compared with 1,500 for the original court closing on August
16, 1774—but the judges decided not to force the issue. The court remained closed.[38]

But how long could this last?

Finally, in June 1779, the General Court issued a call for a constitutional convention on September 1. The convention met three times
over the next six months, and on March 2, 1780, it sent drafts of the
new constitution to the towns for their approval. The ratification
process was a bit unwieldy: each town was to vote on each article separately, writing amendments if need be. But there was no way of
sending the amended articles on to the other towns, so in the end the
votes were tallied as simple "yeas" and "nays."

The document itself was more conservative than ardent revolutionaries would have preferred: the governor (not the towns) appointed most officials, with the approval of the Council; judges held
office on good behavior; justices of the peace served renewable terms
of seven years; property requirements for the right to vote were
steeper than ever; the Senate, which served both as the upper house of
the legislature and the governor's Council, was apportioned according to property ownership, not population.[39] Even so, the towns in
Berkshire County gave their overwhelming approval to the new constitution, which did contain a Bill of Rights and some provisions
against plural officeholding.

However conservative, the Massachusetts Constitution of 1780
was a social compact, prepared by the people's delegates and approved by the people themselves. After six years of living beyond the
law, the radicals in Berkshire—the first to have closed the courts—
called an official end to the internal revolution in Massachusetts.

But the need for revolution did not end with the Massachusetts Con-
stitution of 1780, nor with the British surrender the following year.
The war had led to hard times, and there were more hard times ahead.
Gone were the days when the people marched proudly "with staves

and musick." There were no grand celebrations at the close of the war, no public welcoming of the poor men and boys who straggled home after the fighting was over.

Timothy Bigelow, Worcester's closest approximation of a war hero, returned a defeated man. He tried to resume his trade as a blacksmith, but others had taken up most of his business. Years later, the people of Worcester would celebrate his alleged heroism: "He fought more like tiger than a man," it was said.[40] At Yorktown, "Old Col. Tim was everywhere all the time, and you would thought if you had been there, that there was nobody else in the struggle but Col. Bigelow and his regiment." [41]

The military records tell a different story. In 1779 Bigelow was "reported sick at Ridgefield." In 1780 he was "reported absent at Fishkill." On January 1, 1781—nine months before Yorktown—he was "reported deranged," meaning stripped of his position as an officer.[42] On March 15, 1781, the *Massachusetts Spy* reported on "the investigation of the Conduct of Col. BIGELOW, on the 31st of December, 1775, in the attack on the city of Quebeck, in consequences of aspersions against his conduct, on that day, by Col. Lamb." [43] (John Lamb, who, according to one of the participants, "had nearly one half of his face carried away by a grape or canister shot" at Quebec, probably did not appreciate Bigelow's reticence to engage in the assault.)[44] Although Bigelow was acquitted, his reputation had been tainted. Eighty years later Worcester would build a monument to Timothy Bigelow, but at the time of his return nobody seems to have bestowed any accolades on the blacksmith who went to war.

Instead of celebrating, the people of rural Massachusetts grumbled. It had been a long and grueling war, which wreaked havoc on the economy. Although British soldiers never did venture into the hinterlands of Massachusetts after their one brief march to Concord on April 19, 1775, the burden of supporting the war fell heavily on a people who had little to spare—and everybody seemed convinced they had borne more than their fair share. Lowering taxes superceded the fight against British authority as the cause of the day. According to historian Robert A. Feer,

Sometime between 1779 and 1786, almost every town in Massachusetts petitioned the state legislature for a tax abatement or some other remedial legislation. Each town paraded some condition, supposedly unique to itself, which merited special consideration. . . . Chelsea was having trouble collecting its taxes because a third of the town was salt marsh and the ocean was eating away the upland. Marblehead deserved better treatment because fully one half of the town was made up of widows and fatherless children. . . . Uxbridge was in difficult straits because of the expense of settling a new minister. . . . Several Berkshire towns were each convinced that its location was by far the worst in the Commonwealth.[45]

Worcester residents made several such complaints. In July 1781, it told the Assembly House and Senate that its quotas for soldiers and provisions were set too high.[46] In January 1782, sixty-two citizens petitioned to hold a special meeting in response to an excise tax on such "luxuries" as "Wine, Rum &c. and on Wheel carriages." Liquor was "absolutely necessary," the town protested, "for the Farmer whose Fatigue is almost unsupportable in hay Time & harvest and other Seasons of the year—and for the New Beginners in bringing forward new Townships where they have nothing to drink but water and perhaps are exposed to more Hardships than any other persons."[47] That May, the town voted to send delegates to a county convention "to Take under Consideration Sum matter of grevance that we think we Labour under," and the following month it elucidated these grievances: lifetime pensions to officers, high salaries to members of the General Court, the meeting of the General Court in faraway Boston, poor bookkeeping by the treasurer, inefficient operation of the courts, large land grants in Maine.[48] The central theme was clear: Ordinary farmers, already burdened, found it troublesome enough to feed their own livestock; they had no desire to feed officials at the public trough.

With taxes higher than ever to pay for the war debt, farmers labored under a disproportionate share of the burden. Two-thirds of the state tax assessment was based on ownership of land, leaving wealthy merchants and professionals off the hook while requiring tillers of the soil to pay with money they did not have. The government demanded payment in specie, as did the merchants to whom many farmers were indebted.

Traditionally, farmers had been allowed to pay off many of their debts with goods or labor, but now many creditors would not be satisfied with anything less than hard cash. Indebted farmers were the weakest link in what historian David Szatmary has labeled the "chain of debt" following the Revolutionary War.[49] Cut off from the lucrative trade with the British West Indies, American importers found it difficult to pay off their trading partners across the seas, who were demanding specie. The importers put the squeeze on inland retailers, who in turn tried to squeeze specie out of their customers, the farmers.

When payment was not forthcoming, importers sued retailers, and retailers sued farmers. By examining court records, Szatmary calculated that between 1784 and 1786, suits for the collection of debts involved 31.4 percent of the adult males in Hampshire County and 32.8 percent in Worcester County. Prominent merchants such as Springfield's John Worthington, the former "river god" and councilor, initiated many of these suits. "In every case involving a known retailer," Szatmary notes, "the debtor earned his livelihood through farming and usually owed country shopkeepers less than twenty pounds for a few British imports."[50]

When a farmer failed to pay his debts or his taxes, the court could seize his property (sometimes land, but more often livestock) for sale at public auction. "The constables are daily venduing our property both real and personal, our land after it is appraised by the best judges under oath is sold for about one-third of the value of it, our cattle about one-half the value," complained the citizens of Greenwich, in Hampshire County. William Whiting, a sympathetic judge from Berkshire County, reported that "Great numbers of farmers have been constantly stripped of whatever little stocks they possessed, and those often sold at public auction for a mere trifling."[51]

This wasn't the way the Revolution was supposed to turn out. Some farmers had actually fared well during the war, benefiting from increased wartime markets. Other men had suffered, either physically or financially, by wartime hardships. Either way, the end of the war was not expected to bring on hard times, but it did. Farmers found themselves overextended, while soldiers who had fought for freedom found they had nothing to show for their efforts. In the fall of 1785, John Reed, from western Middlesex County, wrote:

> How often have we been told what Good days we Should have if our independence was made Sure—are these the Good Days that were Expected—is there not Something a miss . . . has not many been oppressed a Hundred to one more then ever they had been by Brittan Before.[52]

Maybe the Revolution was not dead after all. What if the farmers, once again fearful that they might be forced into tenancy, decided to band together and overthrow the oppressive regime, just as they had done back in 1774?

In August 1786, exactly twelve years after they had closed the British-controlled courts, plain farmers throughout the hinterlands of Massachusetts started to organize for a repeat performance. They met in taverns and they called for county conventions, just as they had done in 1774. On August 17, forty-one of the fifty towns in Worcester County sent delegates to a convention in Leicester, and five days later fifty of the sixty towns in Hampshire County sent delegates to a meeting in Hadley.[53] Farmers in the counties of Middlesex, Berkshire, and Bristol also staged conventions, and the grievances listed at these meetings bore a striking resemblance to the earlier complaints against the Massachusetts Government Act in 1774: the courts were out of control, the upper body of the legislature was not representative, government officials should be paid directly by the people.[54]

Following a script which had worked once before, the radicals then tried to close the courts. The Court of Common Pleas for Hampshire County was slated to meet in Northampton on August 29, one day shy of the twelfth anniversary of the court closure in nearby Springfield. Again, "a large Concourse of People" marched under fife and drum to the courthouse, and again the judges retreated to a nearby tavern, tried to negotiate with the insurgents, and agreed in the end to adjourn the court without conducting any business. One week later the script was repeated in Worcester, followed by Concord in Middlesex County, Taunton in Bristol County, and Great Barrington in Berkshire County, the site of the original court closure in 1774. The crowds were smaller this time, numbering in the hundreds instead of the thousands, but they sufficed to intimidate the judges. In Great Barrington the sheriff called forth the militia to defend the court, but the loyalties of the militiamen were suspect: whose side would they support? When the judges asked for a head count, 150 to 200 of the militiamen lined up in their favor, while 700 to 800 stated they were willing to side with the insurgents. Democracy prevailed at least for the day, and the judges agreed to step aside.[55]

"Shays' Rebellion," as it came to be called, was consciously conceived as a sequel to the Revolution of 1774.[56] Plain folk fearful of losing their modest properties tried to recreate the scenario which had played out in their favor once before. They met in conventions, marched with martial music to the courts, and forced the judges to conduct no business. So far, so good. But the rest of the scenario played out differently. As before, access to arms and ammunition was critical, and when the insurgents went after the armories this time, they faced an opposition which was more local, and more powerful, than hired foreign soldiers huddled up in Boston.

In 1774 the overwhelming majority of the inhabitants of rural Massachusetts had supported the insurgents, making any opposition futile. This time, a majority of the country people might have been sympathetic, but that majority was far from overwhelming. Many of the prominent revolutionaries from Massachusetts—men like Samuel Adams and Artemas Ward—lined up firmly on the side of the government. When the weak national government failed to raise an army to suppress the rebels, there were plenty of rich people in Boston eager to hire an army of their own, and enough young Americans

willing to serve for pay. Many merchants who had bought their way
out of service during the Revolutionary War signed up to fight this
time on behalf of a cause that was truly their own.[57]

During the late fall of 1786 the insurgents continued to keep the
county courts from meeting, and in January 1787 they made their big
move: a raid on the Springfield armory. Because of a lapse in communication, they failed to coordinate their attack and suffered a major
setback. Pursued by the merchants' army, the rebels retreated through
the winter snow. At Petersham they were surprised by their foes and
forced to scatter. Some took refuge in Vermont, but within a month
guerrilla bands were making raids on the homes of prominent retailers and army officers in western Massachusetts.

Back in 1774, similar methods of intimidation forced the few de-
fenders of the status quo to flee for their safety to Boston, but this time
the intimidation achieved no lasting results. By June 1787 these last
isolated raids had ceased. The second time around, rebellious farmers
were unable to replicate the dramatic success of the Revolution of
1774.

The key difference between the successful Revolution of 1774 and
the unsuccessful Revolution of 1786 was the lack of unanimity in the
sequel. A revolution characterized by majoritarian democracy, with
its multifarious intimidations and humiliations, works well when up-
ward of 90 percent of the people stand behind it, but when the populace is more evenly divided, the enforcement of the will of the
majority tends to inspire resistance. Historian Kenneth J. Moynihan
has found that the Worcester town meeting decided in favor of the
county conventions during Shays' Rebellion by a slim but consistent
majority of 54 to 46 percent.[58] A minority as sizable as this might be
defeated, but it will not be overwhelmed—and sometimes, with help
from outside, the minority can actually prevail, as it did in 1786.

We have no record of where Timothy Bigelow stood with respect
to the uprising of 1786, but we do know that he was no longer a prominent local leader. Upon returning from the war he had been forced to
borrow from the Salisbury brothers, who continued to prosper.[59] On
February 15, 1790, while terminally ill, Bigelow chose to be impris-

oned for debt rather than sell off his property. On March 31 he died. The record book for the Worcester County jail reads:

> Timothy Bigelow, Worcester, Esquire.
> Time of commitment, February 15, 1790, by Execution.
> By authority of Levi Lincoln, Esq.
> Description: Six Feet, Dark Complexion.
> Discharged April 1, 1790, by Death.[60]

Timothy Paine, the former councilor who had been on the wrong side of the 1774 Revolution, found himself aligned with the victors this time around. Paine was chosen as Worcester's representative to the General Court from 1788 through 1790, and he was almost elected to the first national Congress.[61] On April 7, 1790, the day Timothy Bigelow's one-line obituary ran in the *Massachusetts Spy,* the patriot printer Isaiah Thomas reported that Paine and Artemas Ward, the first commander-in-chief of the Continental Army, had polled an equal number of votes for state senator in the town of Worcester.[62] Like Springfield's John Worthington, Paine's wealth and talent proved more important in the long run than his political orientation.[63] Two of Timothy Paine's sons, Nathaniel and William, were among the creditors taking debtors to court in 1786—even though William was still in exile.[64] (William returned to Salem the following year, and in 1793 he moved back to Worcester when he inherited his father's formidable estate.)

Clark Chandler, son of the exiled John Chandler, had already moved back to Worcester, where he operated the store established by his father on the corner of Front and Main. The former town clerk who had been forced to dip his hand in ink reaped his revenge in a very practical manner: in the year before the uprising of 1786, Chandler dragged fifteen debtors into court.[65]

Despite its radically democratic impulses, the first American Revolution stopped far short of social transformation. In some respects, Massachusetts towns were less progressive at the end of the war than they had been in the late summer of 1774. Factions without marked ideological differences jockeyed for power. Class distinctions had been accentuated by a war that called upon the poor to fight while others stayed home. The new state government, more so than the pre-revolutionary charter of 1691, favored those who owned property over those who did not. In 1774 farmers only *feared* that debts might lead to foreclosures; by 1786 many faced the immediate loss of land or livestock through litigation. When these farmers tried to close the courts, as they had done twelve years earlier, they failed.

The success or failure of a revolution, however, can not be determined solely by the extent of subsequent regression. Although the French Revolution led in the end to Napoleon Bonaparte, and the Russian Revolution to Joseph Stalin, each of these revolutions deposed a repressive regime and initiated progressive, if temporary, reforms. The Massachusetts Revolution of 1774, like many others, achieved its greatest victories early on.

The first American Revolution succeeded on many counts. In toppling the old order, it resolved several of the contradictions inherent in colonial democracy. It ended the system of royal patronage. It removed monarchical restraints on the people's will. Although few in 1774 advocated an outright break with Britain, the overthrow of the established government led inevitably to war, and war to independence. The rebellion in rural Massachusetts led directly to the establishment of home rule throughout the colonies.

The Revolution of 1774 can be seen as the crowning achievement of communal self-government in colonial New England. More than ever before, people assumed collective responsibility for the fate of their communities. Those who served as hog reeves or fence reeves in 1760 came together in 1774 to terminate British authority.

These colonial New Englanders, well versed in the enforcement of community norms, acted as a body to stifle royalist dissent. Insurgents applied social pressure and intimidation to achieve their ends, practicing a crude but effective form of democracy to enforce the will of the majority. Even so, they were more political and less destructive than a mere "mob," as they never tired of proclaiming. These responsible revolutionaries practiced remarkable restraint, proving themselves masters in the application of force without violence.

Above all, the revolutionaries of 1774 pioneered the concept of participatory democracy, with all decisions made by popular consent. Half a century before the so-called Jacksonian Revolution, they demonstrated that ordinary citizens, without shedding blood, could seize control of their government. While more learned patriots expounded on Lockean principles, these country folk acted according to those principles by declaring their social contract with the established government null and void. Although the consequences were frightening and potentially disastrous, the townfolk of Massachusetts were the first American colonists to follow revolutionary rhetoric to its logical conclusion.

All authority derives from the people, they proclaimed, as they deposed British officials. As much as any revolutionaries in history, they applied this statement reflexively upon themselves. They abrogated no authority as they went about their business; they pledged allegiance to no charismatic leaders. In all their committees and conventions, the will of the people was the only master they served. Democratic to its core, this first American Revolution set a standard for direct political participation that has not been bettered since.

EPILOGUE: WHY THE STORY HAS NOT BEEN TOLD

Typically, a revolution lives on in memory. Not so with this one. How strange that "Shays' Rebellion," which failed, has received so much scholarly attention, while the 1774 overthrow of the government, which succeeded, has been so neglected. This oversight gives cause to wonder: how can an event with such monumental consequences have been overlooked?

The reasons—and there are several, thoroughly interrelated—all lie in the grammar of popular historical narratives.

The telling of history cries out for individual protagonists. If an isolated hero or leader doesn't emerge naturally, we try to invent one.[1] In this case, however, none could even be conjured. There was no one person, nor even a small group, who could have made the Revolution of 1774 any more or less than it was. This revolution was conducted by and for the participants, giving it both power and legitimacy.

The anonymous character of the revolution was hardly an accident. The numerous committees, appointed to perform specified and circumscribed tasks, were never empowered to make final decisions or take decisive actions; they always had to report back to the people. When Timothy Paine and Thomas Oliver were forced to resign, radical crowds overruled the moderate, ad hoc representatives. At the closing of the courts in Worcester, runners were dispatched to poll the various militia units in order to insure that all actions received the endorsement of the entire assembly. With all actions taken by "the body of the people," there were could be no tales of individual heroism so pervasive in popular history.

The success of these revolutionaries in establishing a truly democratic movement has helped insure their anonymity. Nathan Baldwin, Joseph Henshaw, Ephraim Doolittle—these are not household names. In 1861 the Daughters of the American Revolution from Worcester (now headquartered in the former house of the Tory, Timothy Paine) built a monument in honor of Timothy Bigelow, and the local chapter took on his name. But his fame, such as it is, did not spread far, and not much is really known about him. He left no diary, no memoir, and only a handful of letters. We have his vital statistics, his military record, the minutes of various meetings, some mortgage records, and a few words from local folklore—that is all.[2]

Without entrenched leaders, there could be no chain of command. The people of each locality, although communicating with each other through their committees of correspondence, received no orders from a central authority. They did develop some shared motifs—most notably, forcing officials to recant while passing through the ranks, hats in hand—but the local groups operated without any coordinating body to plot a strategy or plan the various confrontations.

The Massachusetts Revolution of 1774 was not only decentralized but thoroughly ubiquitous. Both temporally and geographically, it lacked concrete definition. It simply erupted, everywhere and whenever. It has been as confusing, perhaps, to students of history as it was to Governor Gage, who had no idea how to respond.

Again, the very strength of this revolution contributed to its obscurity. A ubiquitous uprising might be harder to contain than a tidy one, but it is also more difficult to perceive. In 1774, nineteen of every twenty people in Massachusetts lived outside of Boston, yet all print information flowed through urban channels. Most court closures were given but brief play in the papers, nor were they much discussed by prolific revolutionary writers like John and Samuel Adams, who were not present at any of the uprisings.

Partly because source material is so skewed, a sort of urban chauvinism has left its mark on the telling of the American Revolution. This has led to a serious misreading of the historical process. The standard textbook narrative goes something like this: To punish Bostonians for the Tea Party, the British government passed the Coercive Acts, known in America as the Intolerable Acts. The most important of these, the Boston Port Act, was meant to isolate Boston by shutting off all commerce, but it had the reverse effect: people outside of town responded by coming to the aid of their beleaguered compatriots. The American Revolution thereby sounds a philanthropic note: Colonists outside of Boston acted from the goodness of their hearts.

But it was the Massachusetts Government Act, not the Boston Port Act, which led common people throughout the colony to take decisive action. Politically disempowered and fearful of economic ruin, the patriots of rural Massachusetts risked their all not just to help their neighbors but to help themselves. The other colonies, understanding that Massachusetts was already in a state of rebellion, felt compelled to take sides. If Britain could disenfranchise the people of Massachusetts, none of the colonies was safe.

Losing their franchise—the power of their vote—was the catalyst that drove ordinary people to rebel. This does not conform neatly to some notions of "revolution." The Massachusetts farmers who overthrew British rule were not poor peasants exploited by greedy landlords but freeholders scared of losing their modest holdings. People do not have to be reduced to great depths of poverty before they rebel. The common farmers of Massachusetts staged a preemptive revolution: they resisted oppression before, not after, being driven into tenancy.

The "middle-class" nature of the Revolution of 1774 has put us off the scent.[3] So has the absence of bloodshed. When the British staged their counterrevolutionary attack on Lexington and Concord, people lost their lives. That was the beginning of what became known as the Revolutionary War, but the actual revolution which triggered this military offensive succeeded without a body count. Unfortunately, the telling of history often requires one.

At Lexington, professional British soldiers fired at a handful of local farmers. This act of violence, allegedly perpetrated by the enemy, gave the Americans the moral high ground and helped mobilize support.[4] The story has been repeated so often that it has effectively muffled the revolution of the preceding year. Leaderless, ubiquitous, and bloodless, the first transfer of political authority from the British to the Americans has not been able to compete. It was not lacking as a revolution; it has only lacked an audience to comprehend and appreciate it.

In January 1775, Lord Dartmouth found it difficult to believe that Governor Gage had lost out to "a tumultuous Rabble, without any Appearance of general Concert, or without any Head to advise, or Leader to conduct."[5] Dartmouth failed to comprehend the power of the people to act in their own behalf, and even today, the revelation that ordinary people, "without any Head to advise," toppled the British-controlled government in Massachusetts engenders blank, incredulous stares.

In truth, there should be nothing so startling about the Revolution of 1774. It was simply a matter of people seizing control of their own political destiny. Surely, we need not look incredulously at that.

NOTES

Introduction

1. James R. Trumbull, *History of Northampton, Massachusetts, from its Settlement in 1654* (Northampton: Press of Gazette Printing Co., 1902), 348.
2. For Oliver's resignation, see chapter 4, note 72; for Paine's resignation, see chapter 3, notes 39–46.
3. Abigail to John Adams, September 14, 1774, L. H. Butterfield, ed., *Adams Family Correspondence* (Cambridge: Belknap Press, 1963), 1: 152.
4. Gage to Lord Dartmouth, September 2, 1774, Clarence E. Carter, ed., *Correspondence of General Thomas Gage* (New Haven: Yale University Press, 1931), 1: 370.

1 People and Place

1. Evarts B. Greene and Virginia D. Harrington, *American Population before the Federal Census of 1790* (Gloucester, MA: Peter Smith, 1966), 17, 22.
2. Franklin P. Rice, ed., *Worcester Town Records from 1753 to 1783* (Worcester: Worcester Society of Antiquity, 1882), 139, 149; William Lincoln, *History of Worcester, Massachusetts, from its Earliest Settlement to September, 1836* (Worcester: Charles Hersey, 1862), 67–8.
3. Mason A. Green, *Springfield, 1636–1886: History of Town and City* (Springfield: C. A. Nichols & Co., 1888) 266; Gregory H. Nobles, *Divisions Throughout the Whole: Politics and Society in Hampshire County, Massachusetts, 1740–1775* (Cambridge: Cambridge University Press, 1983), 82.
4. *Willard's History of Greenfield* (Greenfield, MA: Kneeland and Eastman, 1838), 42–8.
5. Dirk Hoerder, *Crowd Action in Revolutionary Massachusetts, 1765–1780* (New York: Academic Press, 1977), 52–3; *Boston Gazette*, February 25, 1771.
6. Hoerder, *Crowd Action*, 52–3, 250–1; Rice, *Worcester Town Records*, 218, 319–321;

George A. Billias, "Pox and Politics in Marblehead," *Essex Institute Historical Collections* 92 (1956): 43–58; Gerald H. Clarfield, "Salem's Great Inoculation Controversy," *Essex Institue Historical Collections* 106 (1970): 277–296.

7. Jackson Turner Main, *The Social Structure of Revolutionary America* (Princeton: Princeton University Press, 1965), 22–3. Early statistics listing the number of "artisans" give a misleading impression, since many, and perhaps most, artisans at the time still engaged in some farming. A man who worked on shoes was listed in the records as a shoemaker, even if he continued to work a farm.

8. Compilation of the 1771 tax list for the town of Amherst, from *The History of the Town of Amherst, Massachusetts* (Amherst: Carpenter & Morehouse, 1896, 1771), 1: 74; compilation of the 1771 tax list for the town of Worcester, from Kevin J. MacWade, *Worcester County, 1750–1774: A Study of a Provincial Patronage Elite* (Boston University: Ph.D. thesis, 1973), 14.

9. See Michael Zuckerman, *Peaceable Kingdoms: New England Towns in the Eighteenth Century* (New York: Alfred A. Knopf, 1970).

10. David W. Conroy, *In Public Houses: Drink and the Revolution of Authority in Colonial Massachusetts* (Chapel Hill: University of North Carolina Press, 1995), 147–9. Conroy found "one public house for every 200–250 inhabitants," but adult males accounted for only about one-fifth to one-sixth of the population. [Robert E. Brown, *Middle-Class Democracy and the Revolution in Massachusetts, 1691–1780* (Ithaca: Cornell University Press, 1955), 52.]

11. Conroy, *In Public Houses,* 153–4; Lee N. Newcomer, *The Embattled Farmers: A Massachusetts Countryside in the American Revolution* (New York: King's Crown Press, 1953), 113.

12. Conroy, *In Public Houses,* 241–3.

13. Robert E. Brown, *Middle-Class Democracy,* 21–37, 48–51, 78–99. The controversial issue of the franchise in colonial Massachusetts is discussed in Michael Zuckerman, "The Social Context of Democracy in Massachusetts," *William and Mary Quarterly,* Third Series, 25 (1968): 523–544; Kenneth A. Lockridge and Alan Kreider, "The Evolution of Massachusetts Town Government, 1640–1740," *William and Mary Quarterly,* Third Series, 23 (1966): 549–574; James A. Henretta, "Economic Development and Social Structure in Colonial Boston," *William and Mary Quarterly,* Third Series, 22 (1965): 75–92; Jack R. Pole, "Historians and the Problem of Early American Democracy," *American Historical Review* 67 (April 1962): 626–646; Richard Buel, Jr., "Democracy and the American Revolution: A Frame of Reference," *William and Mary Quarterly,* Third Series, 21 (1964): 165–190.

14. Nobles, *Divisions Throughout the Whole,* 114–115.

15. E. Francis Brown, *Joseph Hawley, Colonial Radical* (New York: Columbia University Press, 1931), 44.

16. See Pole, "Historians and the Problem of Early American Democracy."

17. For discussions of the "river gods" and the ways in which they wielded power, see Nobles, *Divisions Throughout the Whole,* 20–35, and Robert J. Taylor, *Western Massachusetts in the Revolution* (Providence, RI: Brown University Press, 1954), 11–33.

18. Hannah married a Williams; Lucretia married John Murray, the most powerful man in

Rutland; Elizabeth married James Putnam, the prominent lawyer who trained John Adams and who later became attorney-general (Eleanor Putnam, daughter to James and Elizabeth, went on to marry her cousin Rufus, a son of John Chandler IV); Katharine married Levi Willard, from a leading family of Lancaster. The Willards of Lancaster were not unlike the Chandlers of Worcester, producing eight justices of the peace. [MacWade, *Worcester County Elite*, 29–30.]

19. MacWade, *Worcester County Elite*, 29–31, 79. The genealogy of the Chandler clan is traced in Charles Nutt, *History of Worcester and Its People* (New York: Lewis Historical Publishing Co., 1919), 74–9. The other prominent families were the Wards of Shrewsbury and the Willards and Wilders of Lancaster. These families were connected in many instances by marriage.

20. Lorenzo Sabine, *Biographical Sketches of Loyalists of the American Revolution* (Port Washington, NY: Kennikat Press, 1966; originally published in 1864), 2: 116.

21. MacWade, *Worcester County Elite*, 8.

22. John L. Brooke, *The Heart of the Commonwealth: Society and Political Culture in Worcester County, Massachusetts, 1713–1861* (Amherst: University of Massachusetts Press, 1989), 41; Burton W. Potter, "Colonel John Murray and his Family," Worcester Society of Antiquity, *Proceedings*, 24 (1908): 19. James Stark, in his biographical sketches of Loyalists, chose to interpret this clear indication of influence rather generously: "On election day his home was open to his friends and good cheer dispensed free to all from his store." [James H. Stark, *The Loyalists of Massachusetts and the Other Side of the American Revolution* (Boston: James H. Stark, 1910), 376.]

23. L. H. Butterfield, ed., *Diary and Autobiography of John Adams* (Cambridge: Harvard University Press, 1961), 1: 83. Lorenzo Sabine, the mid–nineteenth century historian who had many kind words to say about men of Ruggles's stature, and who admired Ruggles for "his shrewdness, his sagacity, his military hardihood and bravery," stated bluntly that the Brigadier "was a wit and a misanthrope; and a man of rude manners and rude speech." [Sabine, *Loyalists of the American Revolution*, 2: 245.]

24. Worcester Probate Registry, 14: 292–3. I am indebted to Thomas Doughton for this reference.

25. MacWade, *Worcester County Elite*, 175–6; Main, *Social Structure of Revolutionary America*, 22.

26. MacWade, *Worcester County Elite*, 56–8; Sabine, *Loyalists of the American Revolution*, 1: 303; Stark, *Loyalists of Massachusetts*, 389. Estimates of the estates of Loyalists, Donald E. Johnson observes, have to be treated with some care due to inflated currencies and the vested interests of the Loyalists who filed their claims with the British government hoping for compensation. [Donald E. Johnson, *Worcester in the War for Independence* (Clark University: PhD. Thesis, 1953), 117.] According to the early twentieth-century historian Charles Nutt, Chandler's estate was worth a whopping £147,559. [Nutt, *History of Worcester*, 77.] When the exiled John Chandler submitted claims to the British government totaling only £17,000, he was dubbed "the honest Refugee." [Sabine, *Loyalists of the American Revolution*, 1: 304.] John Murray complained that because of Chandler's modest claim, he received less compensation than other men who had inflated their claims and who would have gladly "eaten in Chandler's kitchen" back in Worcester.

[E. Alfred Jones, *The Loyalists of Massachusetts: Their Memorials, Petitions and Claims* (Baltimore: Genealogical Publishing Company), 217.] A complete list of his actual holdings can be found in Andrew M. Davis, *The Confiscation of John Chandler's Estate* (Boston: Houghton, Mifflin and Company, 1903).

27. Pole, "Historians and the Problem of Early American Democracy," 640. Cockades, worn on hats, signified social standing, as, of course, did wigs.

28. Brooke, *Heart of the Commonwealth*, 125; MacWade, *Worcester County Elite*, 86. Ironically, the town had incurred its fines by failing to send a representative to the General Court. Apparently, until Ruggles showed up, no local inhabitant possessed the time and resources to undertake the task.

29. MacWade, *Worcester County Elite*, 86–7.

30. John Adams to Abigail Adams, June 30, 1774, in Butterfield, *Adams Family Correspondence*, 1: 116.

2 Division

1. Kenneth Lockridge, "Land, Population, and the Evolution of New England Society," *Past and Present* 39 (1968): 62–80. Several local studies support this picture: Edward M. Cook, Jr., "Social Behavior and Changing Values in Dedham, Massachusetts, 1700–1775," *William and Mary Quarterly*, Third Series, 27 (1970): 546–580; Kenneth Lockridge, *A New England Town: The First Hundred Years, Dedham, Massachusetts, 1636–1736* (New York: Norton, 1970); Philip Greven, *Four Generations: Population, Land, and Family in Colonial Andover, Massachusetts* (Ithaca: Cornell University Press, 1970); Robert A. Gross, *The Minutemen and Their World* (New York: Hill and Wang, 1976).

2. Lockridge, "Land, Population, and Evolution of New England Society," 73.

3. Betty Hobbs Pruitt, "Self-Sufficiency and the Agricultural Economy of Eighteenth Century Massachusetts," *William and Mary Quarterly*, Third Series, 41 (1984): 339.

4. Nobles, *Divisions Throughout the Whole*, 227. See also Douglas L. Jones, "The Strolling Poor: Transiency in Eighteenth Century Massachusetts," *Journal of Social History* 8 (1975): 28–54.

5. Compiled from the "Worcester Warnings" listed in Nutt, *History of Worcester*, 38–40.

6. Rice, *Worcester Town Records*, 192.

7. Lockridge, "Land, Population, and Evolution of New England Society," 72–3.

8. Benjamin W. Labaree, *Colonial Massachusetts: A History* (Millwood, NY: KTO Press, 1979), 153. For treatments of local economies based on account books rather than cash, see Andrew H. Baker and Holly V. Izard, "New England Farmers and the Marketplace, 1780–1865: A Case Study," *Agricultural History* 65 (Summer 1991): 29–52; Susan Geib, *Changing Works: Agriculture and Society in Brookfield, Massachusetts, 1785–1820* (Boston University: Ph.D. thesis, 1981); Fred Anderson, *A People's Army: Massachusetts Soldiers and Society in the Seven Years' War* (Chapel Hill: University of North Carolina Press, 1984), 28–32.

9. MacWade, *Worcester County Elite*, 84; Richard L. Bushman, "Massachusetts Farmers and the Revolution," *Society, Freedom, and Conscience: The American Revolution in Virginia, Massachusetts, and New York* (New York: W. W. Norton, 1976), 119.

10. See Cook, "Social Behavior and Changing Values in Dedham," 573.
11. Brooke, *Heart of the Commonwealth*, 140.
12. Nobles, *Divisions Throughout the Whole*, 201. In some backcountry areas, significant numbers of creditors came from neighboring communities; classes took on a regional definition. Many of the merchants and gentry who took Berkshire County farmers to court, for instance, came from the Hudson Valley and Connecticut. [Theodore M. Hammett, *The Revolutionary Ideology in its Social Context: Berkshire County, Massachusetts, 1725–1785* (Brandeis University: Ph.D. Thesis, 1976), 91–2.]
13. See Epilogue, note 3.
14. Main, *Social Structure of Revolutionary America*, 22, 41–3.
15. Cited from the General Records, Town of Leicester, in MacWade, *Worcester County Elite*, 93–4.
16. Taylor, *Western Massachusetts in the Revolution*, 55.
17. *Boston Evening-Post*, July 6, 1767. See also *Boston Evening-Post*, January 5, 1767.
18. *Boston Evening-Post*, July 13, 1767.
19. Rice, *Worcester Town Records*, 129.
20. For the complete declaration, see Jack P. Greene, ed., *Colonies to Nation, 1763–1789: A Documentary History of the American Revolution* (New York: W. W. Norton, 1975), 63–5; Edmund S. and Helen M. Morgan, *The Stamp Act Crisis: Prologue to Revolution* (Chapel Hill: University of North Carolina Press, 1953), 105–107.
21. Thomas McKean to John Adams, August 20, 1813, *The Works of John Adams*, Charles Francis Adams, ed. (Boston: Little, Brown, and Co., 1856), 10: 60–61. We must be wary of McKean's claim that it was Ruggles who backed down; as one of the contestants, McKean could hardly have said otherwise.
22. John Adams, *Diary and Autobiography*, 1: 295.
23. MacWade, *Worcester County Elite*, 105.
24. Robert E. Brown noted that twenty of the blacklisted representatives failed to be reelected [*Middle-Class Democracy*, 228], but Richard D. Brown observes that three of these came from towns which sent no representatives at all the following year. Some allowance must also be made, according to Richard D. Brown, for normal turnover, which he estimates would account for "perhaps six to ten of the listed representatives." [Richard D. Brown, *Revolutionary Politics in Massachusetts: The Boston Committee of Correspondence and the Towns, 1772–1774* (Cambridge: Harvard University Press, 1970), 26–7.] Even so, the blacklisting seems to have had some impact, since only twelve of the thirty-two men listed were returned to office.
25. Francis G. Walett, "The Massachusetts Council, 1766–1774: The Transformation of a Conservative Institution," *William and Mary Quarterly*, Third Series, 6 (1949): 605–627; Lawrence H. Gipson, *The Coming of the Revolution, 1763–1775* (New York: Harper and Brothers, 1954), 163–164; MacWade, *Worcester County Elite*, 106.
26. Charles Martyn, *The Life of Artemas Ward* (New York: Artemas Ward, 1921), 33–6; MacWade, *Worcester County Elite*, 112–113.
27. John Adams, *Diary and Autobiography*, 3: 265–270.
28. Rice, *Worcester Town Records*, 138–140. These instructions were reprinted in Lincoln, *History of Worcester*, 66–7.
29. *Boston Gazette*, February 29, 1768.

30. *Pennsylvania Gazette,* May 15, 1766; Lee N. Newcomer, *The Embattled Farmers: A Massachusetts Countryside in the American Revolution* (New York: Columbia University Press, 1953), 25.

31. Johnson, *Worcester in the War for Independence,* 15–23. For the Worcester nonimportation agreement, see Nutt, *History of Worcester,* 521–522; Lincoln, *History of Worcester,* 69–70.

32. The circular letter is reprinted in Greene, *Colonies to Nation,* 134–136, and Harry A. Cushing, ed., *The Writings of Samuel Adams* (New York: G. P. Putnam's Sons, 1904), 1: 184–188.

33. Hillsborough's reply is also reprinted in Greene, *Colonies to Nation,* 143.

34. A complete list of those who voted for and against rescinding, as well as those who were absent, was published in the *Boston Gazette,* July 11, 1768.

35. Hammett, *Revolutionary Ideology in Berkshire County,* 312; Newcomer, *Embattled Farmers,* 26–7.

36. MacWade, *Worcester County Elite,* 128.

37. *Boston Gazette,* July 6, 1772.

38. For an excellent discussion of the issues surrounding judicial tenure in the colonies, see Bernard Bailyn, *Pamphlets of the American Revolution, 1750–1776* (Cambridge: Belknap Press, 1965), 1: 249–255.

39. Richard D. Brown, *Revolutionary Politics in Massachusetts,* 57. Brown's book remains the definitive treatment of the "Boston Pamphlet" and the responses it generated.

40. The "Boston Pamphlet" is reprinted in Charles Francis Adams, ed., *The Works of John Adams* (Boston: Little and Brown, 1850), 2: 359–368, and Greene, *Colonies to Nation,* 179–182.

41. "Out of a total of 204 towns listed in a 1761 tax list, only about 120 were represented in the legislature in any year in the late provincial period. . . . The average number of towns responding in six roll call votes taken between 1757 and 1764 was 84, while the total number of towns participating in the six roll calls combined was only 122." [Stephen E. Patterson, *Political Parties in Revolutionary Massachusetts* (Madison: University of Wisconsin Press, 1973), 34.]

42. Richard D. Brown, *Revolutionary Politics in Massachusetts,* 94–9. The original replies are in the Minute Book of the Boston Committee of Correspondence, Bancroft Collection, New York City Public Library; copies are now available on microfilm. The replies were generally recorded in the minutes of their respective towns, but not all of these minutes are extant.

43. Bushman, "Massachusetts Farmers and the Revolution," 80.

44. Bushman, "Massachusetts Farmers and the Revolution," 79–80. Richard D. Brown found that although the overwhelming majority of the replies, like Hubbardston's, were favorable, there was still a wide range. Each reply was unique, proof of "an independence of action which cannot be described as either domination or manipulation by the Boston committee." "Even so," Brown stated, "the diversity was limited, confined within a general agreement about basic political principles. The towns all spoke the same language, used the same conventional phrases of Whig resistance, and shared the same assumptions about political behavior. All agreed on the necessity of defending their rights." [*Revolutionary Politics in Massachusetts,* 120–121.]

It is possible, of course, that these letters reflected only the sentiments of a handful of political activists "spread in a thin layer all over the province," not the true will of the people. (This phrase comes from Richard D. Brown, who actually argues against this hypothesis. [*Revolutionary Politics in Massachusetts*, 94.]) The preeminent historian Arthur M. Schlesinger suggested that "groups of extremists" in each locality wrote the responses and then "engineered" town meetings to get them approved. [Arthur M. Schlesinger, *The Colonial Merchants and the American Revolution, 1763–1776* (New York: Frederick Ungar, 1957; originally published in 1918), 259–260.] Schlesinger seems to have followed the lead of Governor Thomas Hutchinson, whom he quotes uncritically: "Thus, all on a sudden, from a state of peace, order, and general contentment, as some expressed themselves, the province, more or less from one end to the other, was brought into a state of contention, disorder and general dissatisfaction; or, as others would have it, was aroused from stupor and inaction, to sensibility and activity." This notion, that a handful of leaders manipulated the people, has conservative implications: no credence is given to the real grievances of local people. With little evidence to prove or refute this view, Richard D. Brown holds that "it seems safer for the moment to assume that if a town voted, its vote did reasonably express the views of local townspeople." [*Revolutionary Politics in Massachusetts*, 94–5.]

45. For the importance of Boston's leadership with respect to revolutionary thinking at the local level, see also Richard D. Brown, *Knowledge Is Power: The Diffusion of Information in Early America, 1700–1865* (New York: Oxford University Press, 1989).

46. Bushman, "Massachusetts Farmers and the Revolution," 79–81.

47. Lincoln, *History of Worcester*, 232–233; Caleb A. Wall, *Reminiscences of Worcester* (Worcester: Tyler and Seagrave, 1877), 46–7; Nutt, *History of Worcester*, 56–7; MacWade, *Worcester County Elite*, 161; Ellery B. Crane, "A Chapter in the War of the American Revolution," Worcester Society of Antiquity, *Proceedings*, 25 (1909–1911): 186–192; Betty Hobbs Pruitt, ed., *The Massachusetts Tax Valuation List of 1771* (Boston: G.K. Hall, 1978), 372–379.

48. Rice, *Worcester Town Records*, 87, 131, 162, 180.

49. Rice, *Worcester Town Records*, 203.

50. Donald Johnson, in his research of twenty-six selected towns in Worcester County outside the shiretown, found that every one had established a committee of correspondence. [*Worcester in the War for Independence*, 132.]

51. For Chandler and Paine genealogies, see Nutt, *History of Worcester*, 76–8, 200.

52. Johnson, *Worcester in the War for Independence*, 41.

53. The minutes of the American Political Society are housed at the American Antiquarian Society in Worcester. Significant extracts, including the entire rules and regulations, are reprinted in Albert A. Lovell, *Worcester in the War of the Revolution: Embracing the Acts of the Town from 1765 to 1783 Inclusive* (Worcester: Tyler and Seagrave, 1876), 21–6.

54. Rice, *Worcester Town Records*, 215; Boston Committee of Correspondence, Correspondence and Proceedings, Bancroft Collection, New York Public Library, microfilm reel 2, letter 495. Selections of the minutes of the March town meeting appear in Lincoln, *History of Worcester*, 77–8, and Lovell, *Worcester in the War of the Revolution*, 27–9.

55. Rice, *Worcester Town Records*, 214.

56. Charles Hersey, *Reminiscences of the Military Life and Sufferings of Col. Timothy Bigelow* (Worcester: Henry J. Howland, 1860), 8–9. Although Hersey states this incident occurred on March 7, this or a similar confrontation could also have taken place at the May 20 or June 20 meetings.

57. Minutes, American Political Society; reprinted partially in Nutt, *History of Worcester,* 524; Lovell, *Worcester in the War of the Revolution,* 25; Lincoln, *History of Worcester,* 74. Also at the April 4 meeting of the APS, the members voted "that the Committee of Correspondence be directed to notify the committees in the several towns in the county, that the vote for County Treasurer had not been counted at the late Court of General Sessions of the Peace, as had been customary, and warned them of the dangers consequent thereupon, that the people might be on their guard against fraud and deception." The possibility of corruption was very much on their minds.

58. Lincoln, *History of Worcester,* 74–5.

59. Oliver was certainly intimidated. He had already failed to show up for court sessions in Boston and Charlestown. In his memoir he claimed his failure to appear at the Suffolk County session in Boston was due to a snowstorm, but he also admitted that a messenger had told him "that if the chief Justice had gone to Court, he believed that he might have walked the Streets in the Day, but that he would not be safe in the Night." [Douglas Adair and John A. Schutz, eds., *Peter Oliver's Origin and Progress of the American Rebellion* (Stanford: Stanford University Press, 1961), 110.] John Adams wrote in his diary, "I shuddered at the expectation that the mob might put on him a coat of tar and feathers, if not put him to death." [John Adams, *Works,* 2: 328.] Oliver, clearly on the defensive, thought better of making an appearance in faraway Worcester, where he would not enjoy even the limited security of the proximity of British troops.

60. According to the early historian William Lincoln, who presumably had access to oral testimony, the draft was actually written by Nathan Baldwin. [Lincoln, *History of Worcester,* 79.]

61. Rice, *Worcester Town Records,* 224–227.

62. Rice, *Worcester Town Records,* 227–229.

63. Rice, *Worcester Town Records,* 230–233; *Boston News-Letter and Massachusetts Gazette,* June 30, 1774; *Boston Gazette,* July 4, 1774. Spelling here is in accordance with Rice.

64. These letters appear in L. Kinvin Wroth, ed., *Province in Rebellion: A Documentary History of the Founding of the Commonwealth of Massachusetts* (Cambridge: Harvard University Press, 1975), documents 16 and 17, 92–6.

65. Brooke, *Heart of the Commonwealth,* 140.

66. Wroth, *Province in Rebellion,* document 142, 489–494.

67. John Adams, *Works,* 9: 597–598.

68. Wroth, *Province in Rebellion,* document 122, 456–459.

69. For a list of the men elected, and those who were vetoed, see *Boston Gazette,* May 30, 1774.

70. *Boston Gazette,* June 20, 1774.

71. *Boston Gazette,* June 20, 1774.

72. *Boston Gazette,* July 4, 1774.

73. See Walett, "The Massachusetts Council, 1766–1774," 605–627.

74. Both bills were first printed in the *Boston Gazette*, June 6, 1774. The Massachusetts Government Act is reprinted with annotation in Wroth, *Province in Rebellion*, document 148, 506–519. Excerpts from both acts appear in Greene, *Colonies to Nation*, 207–209. For a discussion of how these bills were passed through Parliament, see Bernard Donoughue, *British Politics and the American Revolution* (New York: St. Martin's Press, 1964), 87–101.

75. James Putnam's petition, cited earlier, stated that if the five committee members hadn't themselves voted, the outcome would have been reversed.

76. Wroth, *Province in Rebellion*, document 245, 755–757; Green, *Springfield*, 275–277.

77. *Boston Gazette*, July 4, 1774; Wroth, *Province in Rebellion*, document 166, 545–547.

78. Wroth, *Province in Rebellion*, document 168, 548–549.

79. Gage to Dartmouth, July 27, 1774, *Correspondence*, 1: 364.

3 Intimidation

1. Robert E. Brown, *Middle-Class Democracy*, 341–343.

2. Timothy Paine married John Chandler's sister Sarah, John Murray married Chandler's sister Lucretia, and Abijah Willard's brother Levi married Chandler's sister Katharine. For the land speculation partnership, see MacWade, *Worcester County Elite*, 57.

3. Wroth, *Province in Rebellion*, document 150, 522; John Andrews to William Barrell, August 8, 1774, "Letters of John Andrews of Boston, 1772–1776," Massachusetts Historical Society, *Proceedings*, 8 (1864–1865), 338.

4. The minutes of the August 9–10 Worcester County Convention are reprinted in William E. Lincoln, ed., *The Journals of Each Provincial Congress of Massachusetts in 1774 and 1775, with an Appendix Containing the Proceedings of the County Conventions* (Boston: Dutton and Wentworth, 1838), 627–631, and Wroth, *Province in Rebellion*, document 311, 877–880. In the minutes, Mary's name is recorded as "Sternes," and "Sterne" is inscribed on the gravestones of Thomas and Mary. I have chosen to use the most frequent spelling of their name, "Stearns." [*Inscriptions from the Old Burial Grounds in Worcester, Massachusetts, from 1727 to 1859* (Worcester: Worcester Society of Antiquity, 1878), 59.]

5. Stephen Salisbury to Samuel Salisbury, August 10, 1774, Salisbury Family Papers, Manuscript Collection, American Antiquarian Society, Worcester; cited in Lillian E. Newfield, *Worcester on the Eve of the Revolution* (Clark University: M.A. Thesis, 1941), 87.

6. See Taylor, *Western Massachusetts in the Revolution*, 10–74.

7. Convention of Berkshire County, July 6, 1774, in Lincoln, *Journals of Each Provincial Congress*, 652–655, and Wroth, *Province in Rebellion*, document 310, 873–876.

8. William Williams, Woodbridge Little, and Israel Stoddard to Governor Gage, July 15, 1774, in Wroth, *Province in Rebellion*, document 186, 579–80.

9. Declaration of David Ingersoll, in Wroth, *Province in Rebellion*, document 203, 606–609.

10. John Andrews to William Barrell, August 23, 1774, Andrews, "Letters," 346.

11. Berkshire Committee to Boston Committee, July 25, 1774, in Wroth, *Province in Rebellion*, document 243, 753. Courts had been closed during the Stamp Act crisis, but that was specifically to avoid paying the stamp tax required of all legal transactions. The court closures of 1774 involved a more sweeping goal: to shut down a government that was illegally construed.

12. Boston committee to Berkshire committee, July 31, 1774, Wroth, *Province in Rebellion*, document 251, 767; Boston Committee of Correspondence, Correspondence and Proceedings, Bancroft Collection, New York Public Library, microfilm reel 2, letter 35.

13. J. E. A. Smith, *The History of Pittsfield, Massachusetts, from the Year 1734 to the Year 1800* (Boston: Lee and Shepard, 1869), 194–195.

14. Charles J. Taylor, *History of Great Barrington, Massachusetts* (Great Barrington: Clark W. Bryan, 1882), 288.

15. *Boston Evening-Post*, August 29, 1774. This dispatch was printed in several other newspapers throughout New England.

16. Smith, *History of Pittsfield*, 196.

17. Ingersoll, Declaration, in Wroth, *Province in Rebellion*, document 203, 608–609. Eight so-called "ringleaders" of the Great Barrington crowd were later arrested in Litchfield, Connecticut, but they were soon set free on bond when a crowd threatened to break open the jail. Aaron Burr, who was in Litchfield at the time, wrote on August 17: "[A] mob of several hundred persons gathered at Barrington, and tore down the house of a man who was suspected of being unfriendly to the liberties of the people; broke up the court, then sitting at that place, &c. As many of the rioters belonged to this colony, and the Superior Court was then sitting at this place, the sheriff was immediately dispatched to apprehend the ringleaders. He returned yesterday with eight prisoners, who were taken without resistance. But this minute there is entering town on horseback, with great regularity, about fifty men, armed each with a white club; and I observe others continually dropping in." Aaron Burr to Matthias Ogden, August 17, 1774, Matthew L. Davis, ed., *Memoirs of Aaron Burr* (New York: Harper and Brothers, 1836), 48–9.

18. Gage to Dartmouth, August 27, 1774, Gage, *Correspondence*, 1: 366. The notion that radical action was initiated by farmers of the countryside rather than by the confirmed radicals in Boston seems to have posed a problem for Gage. He added later in the letter: "It is agreed that popular Fury was never greater in this Province than at present, and it has taken its Rise from the old Source at Boston, tho' it has appeared first at a Distance."

19. John Andrews to William Barrell, Andrews, "Letters," 643.

20. Samuel Salisbury to Stephen Salisbury, August 18, 1774, Salisbury Family Papers, American Antiquarian Society; cited in Newfield, *Worcester on the Eve of the Revolution*, 89.

21. Sabine, *Loyalists of the American Revolution*, 2: 11. Sabine does not cite his source for this quotation, but it was presumably contemporary.

22. *Providence Gazette*, August 27, 1774.

23. John Andrews to William Barrell, August 24, 1774, Andrews, "Letters," 346. Leonard's father, Colonel Ephraim Leonard, was a Whig.

24. *Boston Evening-Post*, August 29, 1774.

25. Daniel Leonard to Thomas Gage, August 31, 1774, Wroth, *Province in Rebellion*, document 158, 1: 534–535. The assertion that the "Principals" treated the "main Body" to rum has to be treated cautiously, reflecting a conservative view of mob action. The men might well have been drinking—they often did, whether or not engaging in political action—and some might have treated others, but the hint that the crowd could be bought with liquor seems unfounded, particularly in light of other crowd actions within the following month.

26. An account appearing in the *Boston Gazette* on August 27 agrees in all essentials with Leonard's testimony, save only the part about the rum: "We hear from Taunton, that on the arrival of Daniel Leonard, Esq; at that town, the place of his residence (who has taken the oath, necessary to qualify himself for a Counsellor, and the new plan) the people were greatly exasperated against him, and as it became publicly know that he was in that town, by his going to meeting on Sunday forenoon, a paper was posted up by the meeting-house door, requesting the inhabitants to assemble the next day on the green; Mr. Leonard, it is said, not thinking his situation safe, decamped. The next day the people assembled, but he not being found, the deputy first appeared, and by his conduct so enraged the people, that he thought it prudent to take shelter in Mr. Leonard's house. And we further learn that several shots were fired in the room where he was going to bed, probably to warn him of what he might expect if he persisted in the way he was going on." A different letter, in basic agreement with the other sources, appeared in *Boston Evening-Post*, August 29, 1774.

27. Gage to Dartmouth, August 27, 1774, Gage, *Correspondence*, 1: 365.

28. MacWade, *Worcester County Elite*, 147.

29. *Boston Evening-Post*, August 29, 1774; M. St. Clair Clarke and Peter Force, *American Archives* (Washington, D.C., 1837), 4th Series, 1: 732.

30. For more on the intimidation of Ruggles, see Clarke and Force, *American Archives*, 4th series, 1: 1260–1261; Frank Moore, *The Diary of the American Revolution* (New York: Washington Square Press, 1967), 7.

31. The description of Willard is from Sabine, *Loyalists of the American Revolution*, 2: 429–430.

32. Clarke and Force, *American Archives*, 4th series, 1: 731–732. According to Thomas Gage, "Mr. Willard was grievously maltreated first in Connecticut when he went on Business, and every Township he passed through in his way home in this Province had previous Notice of his Approach, and ready to insult him, Arms were put to his Breast with threats of instant Death, unless he signed a Paper, the Contents of which he did not know nor regard." [Gage to Dartmouth, September 2, 1774, Gage, *Correspondence*, 370.]

33. *Massachusetts Gazette*, Sept. 8, 1774; Declaration of Abijah Willard, August 25, 1774, in Wroth, *Province in Rebellion*, document 153, 527–528; Sabine, *Loyalists of the American Revolution*, 2: 429.

34. American Political Society, Records, August 1 and 18, 1775, Manuscript Collection, American Antiquarian Society in Worcester.

35. *Massachusetts Gazette*, September 15, 1774; *Boston Evening-Post*, September 19, 1774; Lovell, *Worcester in the War of the Revolution*, 41.

36. Rice, *Worcester Town Records*, 234, 238–239; Lovell, *Worcester in the War of the Revolution*, 38; Lincoln, *History of Worcester*, 83.

37. My reconstruction of the order of these three defacements comes from an analysis of the origin document conducted by City Clerk David Rushford and myself.

38. Nutt, *History of Worcester*, 200; Wall, *Reminiscences of Worcester*, 80.

39. Timothy Paine to Thomas Gage, August 28, 1774, Wroth, *Province in Rebellion*, document 154, 528.

40. I have taken these towns, all lying within twenty miles of Worcester, from the list of those which sent militiamen to the court takeover ten days later. [Entry for September 7 in Ebenezer Parkman's Diary, MSS at the American Antiquarian Society in Worcester.]

41. Sources disagree as to the date. Paine himself said initially it was the August 27; later he said August 26. One of the articles printed in the Boston papers places the incident on Saturday, August 27, while others fail to mention a date. I believe the definitive source is the entry in the diary of Ebenezer Parkman, the minister in neighboring Westborough, for August 27: ". . . P.M. am informed that a grt. multitude, above 1500, assembled at Worcester & oblige Hon. Tim. Paine to renounce his Comission as Counsellor &c. and this afternoon they go from Worcester to Rutland, to oblige Col. Murray to do the like; but he is gone to Boston." [Ebenezer Parkman Diary, Manuscript Collection, American Antiquarian Society, Worcester.]

42. Timothy Paine to Thomas Gage, August 28, 1774, Wroth, *Province in Rebellion*, document 154, 528–531.

43. Correspondence Proceedings, Boston, August 29, 1774, Clarke and Force, *American Archives*, 4th series, 1: 745.

44. Newfield, *Worcester of the Eve of the Revolution*, 39.

45. Correspondence Proceedings, Boston, August 29, 1774, Clarke and Force, *American Archives*, 4th series, 1: 745.

46. *Boston Evening-Post*, September 5, 1774. The *Evening-Post* estimated the crowd at 3,000; the account reprinted in *American Archives* states 1,500; that day, Paine said "more than fifteen hundred," while the following day he revised his estimate to "more than Two Thousand." That was a large enough crowd in any case, particularly from a rural area on one day's notice. The only other disagreement among the accounts is that Paine says the people at the common "were drawn up in the form of a hollow square" rather than in two lines. This difference is easy to understand: the ends of the lines might well have collapsed toward the middle as people strained for a view of the principal actor, causing Paine himself to perceive a closed figure.

47. Wall, *Reminiscences of Worcester*, 81–2. Holly Izard, in personal correspondence, explains that Paine "was dressed to his stature, not showing off or being obnoxiously British. A gentleman's attire at the time included a wig, a cravat, ruffled shirt, embellished waistcoat, overcoat, knee breeches, stockings, and buckled shoes."

48. Gage to Dartmouth, September 2, 1774, Gage, *Correspondence*, 1: 370.

49. *Boston Evening-Post*, September 5, 1774.

50. Andrews to Barrell, August 23 and 24, 1774, Andrews, "Letters," 346.

51. In 1864 Lorenzo Sabine wrote, "He abandoned his house on the night of the 25th of August of that year, and fled to Boston, as I find in his own handwriting, in an account-book in the possession of a person of his lineage." [*Loyalists of the American Revolution*, 2: 115.]

52. *Boston Evening-Post*, September 5, 1774.

53. Daniel Murray to John Murray, August 28, 1774, cited in MacWade, *Worcester County Elite*, 152.

54. Sabine, *Loyalists of the American Revolution*, 2: 115.

55. *Boston Evening-Post*, September 5, 1774; *Boston Gazette*, September 5, 1774.

56. Clarke and Force, *American Archives,* 4th series, 1: 1260–1261; Moore, *Diary of the American Revolution,* 7.

57. Worcester's assumption of a leadership role is clear from the assertive tone of the letter calling for a joint meeting: "As we think it necessary the Counties through the Province should adopt as near as possible one form of procedure we take the liberty to propose if you think best that you appoint a meeting of your committee on the 26th day of this month at 2 o'clock PM and request the attendance of the committees of Charleston, Cambridge and as many more of the neighboring towns in that County as will be Convenient and we will depute one or more of our committee to attend. By that means we think there may be a plan of operation agreed upon that will easily be adopted by the Counties of Suffolk, Middlesex and Worcester which in all probability will run through the Province." [Boston Committee of Correspondence, Correspondence and Proceedings, Bancroft Collection, New York Public Library, microfilm reel 2, letter 498; Wroth, *Province in Rebellion,* document 275, 808.]

58. Johnson, *Worcester in the War for Independence,* 63. On August 13 Andrews wrote to Barrell, "It's currently reported that a regiment is to go to Worcester to protect the Court, which is to sit there soon." [Andrews, "Letters," 341.]

59. Boston Committee of Correspondence, Minutes, in Wroth, *Province in Rebellion,* document 213, 688; Boston Committee of Correspondence, Correspondence and Proceedings, Bancroft Collection, New York Public Library, reel 1.

60. Boston Committee of Correspondence, Minutes, in Wroth, *Province in Rebellion,* document 213, 689–692; Boston Committee of Correspondence, Correspondence and Proceedings, Bancroft Collection, New York Public Library, reel 1.

61. Boston Committee of Correspondence, Minutes, in Wroth, *Province in Rebellion,* document 213, 689–692; Boston Committee of Correspondence, Correspondence and Proceedings, Bancroft Collection, New York Public Library, reel 1.

62. *Boston Evening-Post,* August 29, 1774.

63. Andrews to Barrell, August 31, 1774, Andrews, "Letters," 349–350; see also *Boston Evening-Post,* August 29, 1774.

64. George Watson to Gage, August 30, 1774, Wroth, *Province in Rebellion,* document 157, 533. Watson's public resignation appears in the *Massachusetts Spy,* September 22, 1774.

65. Andrew Oliver to Gage, August 25, 1774, Wroth, *Province in Rebellion,* document 152, 525–526.

66. Thomas Hutchinson, Jr., to Gage, August 30, 1774, Wroth, *Province in Rebellion,* document 156, 532–533.

67. Joshua Loring to Thomas Gage, August 31, 1774, Wroth, *Province in Rebellion,* document 160, 537–538.

68. Jones, *The Loyalists of Massachusetts,* 198–200; Sabine, *Loyalists of the American Revolution,* 2: 27.

69. William Pepperell to Gage, August 31, 1774, Wroth, *Province in Rebellion,* document 159, 536.

70. *Boston Gazette,* December 5, 1774; Sabine, *Loyalists of the American Revolution,* 2: 166–176. The November 16 proceedings of the York County Congress, which urged

people to "withdraw all Connection, Commerce and Dealings from him," appears in the *Boston Gazette*, December 5, 1774, and Wroth, *Province in Rebellion*, document 402, 1327–1330.

71. Richard Frothingham, *Life and Times of Joseph Warren* (Boston: Little, Brown, and Co., 1865), 359.

4 Confrontation

1. Andrews to Barrell, August 6 and 7, 1774, Andrews, "Letters," 337–338.
2. Hoerder, *Crowd Action*, 285.
3. Andrews to Barrell, August 26, 1774, Andrews, "Letters," 348.
4. Salem committee to Boston committee, August 25, 1774, Wroth, *Province in Rebellion*, document 281, 816; *Boston Gazette*, August 29, 1774. Note that "other inhabitants" were invited along with merchants and freeholders, in much the same manner as the Boston town meeting had been opened to "the whole body of the people."
5. *Massachusetts Gazette*, August 29, 1774; Wroth, *Province in Rebellion*, document 169, 550.
6. Salem committee to Boston committee, August 25, 1774, Wroth, *Province in Rebellion*, document 281, 817. Portions of this letter appeared with minor variations in the *Boston Gazette*, August 29, 1774. The *Gazette* version added the words "of Voice and Gesture" after "Vehemence."
7. Salem committee to Boston committee, August 25, 1774, Wroth, *Province in Rebellion*, document 281, 818; *Boston Gazette*, August 29, 1774.
8. Andrews to Barrell, August 25 and 26, 1774, Andrews, "Letters," 347.
9. Andrews to Barrell, August 26, 1774, Andrews, "Letters," 347.
10. Andrews to Barrell, August 27, 1774, Andrews, "Letters," 348.
11. Gage to Peter Frye, August 27, 1774, in Wroth, *Province in Rebellion*, document 202, 605.
12. Andrews to Barrell, September 9, 1774, Andrews, "Letters," 357.
13. Proceedings, Convention of Essex County, September 6 and 7, 1774, Lincoln, *Journals of Each Provincial Congress*, 617; Wroth, *Province in Rebellion*, document 317, 901.
14. *Boston Gazette*, September 12, 1774; *Essex Gazette*, September 13, 1774.
15. Andrews to Barrell, August 29, 1774, Andrews, "Letters," 348.
16. See Taylor, *Western Massachusetts in the Revolution*, 54–62.
17. Gage to Dartmouth, August 25, 1774, Gage, *Correspondence*, 1: 364. Williams's letter of resignation was dated August 10; he must have penned it immediately after receiving his official notice of appointment, sent out on August 7.
18. A history of Springfield, written in 1888, states: "We do not know how true it is, but the story has often been told beside Springfield firesides, that the whigs who dominated the town at this exciting time were so outraged at the refusal of John Worthington to join them, that they led him out in a field, formed a ring, and compelled him to kneel, and swear before God that he would renounce his tory views." [Green, *Springfield*, 278.]
19. Hampshire County Congress to Boston Committee of Correspondence, August 31, 1774, Wroth, *Province in Rebellion*, document 314, 883–884.

20. Diary of Reverend Stephen Williams (transcript copy), Richard Salter Storrs Library, Longmeadow, MA, Book 8, 306. Jonathan Judd, Jr., a conservative shopkeeper from Southampton, likewise expressed concern in his diary entry for August 29: "the Heat increases and some from the West have Set out, we hear. Confusion is coming on inevitably." [Jonathan Judd Jr., Diary, v. 2 (1773–1782), Forbes Library, Northampton.]

21. Taylor, *Western Massachusetts in the Revolution*, 64.

22. George Sheldon, *A History of Deerfield, Massachusetts* (Deerfield: Pocumtuck Valley Memorial Association, 1895), 682.

23. John H. Lockwood, *Westfield and Its Historic Influences, 1669–1919* (Springfield: Springfield Printing and Binding, 1922), 1: 515. For estimates of the size of the crowd, see below, notes 25 and 30.

24. Hampshire County Congress to Boston Committee of Correspondence, August 31, 1774, Wroth, *Province in Rebellion*, document 314, 883–886.

25. *Boston Gazette*, September 12, 1774; Wroth, *Province in Rebellion*, document 314, 2: 885–886; Clarke and Force, *American Archives*, 4th series, 1: 747. The estimate of three thousand is also made by Ezra Stiles: "[O]n the 8th Sep. rode from Littlerest to Norwich in Company with Mr. McNeil of Litchfield who gave me very particular & extensive Information of what he was an Eye Witness. He had a singular Opportunity.—He was at Springfield on 30th Augt when he saw three thousand people assembled about the Courthouse and obliged the Judges & all Officers of the Court to promise not to sit & renounce holding any Office under the new Establishment & saw them humble sundry Tories there." [Franklin B. Dexter, ed., *The Literary Diary of Ezra Stiles* (New York: Charles Scribner's Sons, 1901), 1: 479.]

26. James R. Trumbull, *History of Northampton, Massachusetts, from its Settlement in 1654* (Northampton: Gazette Printing Co., 1902), 346–348; Lockwood, *Westfield*, 1: 516–518. Clarke was Hawley's wife's nephew, raised by the Hawleys and trained by his adoptive father to be a lawyer. We do not know the friend to whom this letter was addressed. A brief passage from Clarke's letter is cited in Charles Tilly, "Collective Action in England and America, 1765–1775," Richard M. Brown and Don E. Fehrenbacher, *Tradition, Conflict, and Modernization: Perspectives on the American Revolution* (New York: Academic Press, 1977), 65.

Trumbell notes that "uncle Catlin" was "Major Catlin of Deerfield, a noted tory." Caleb Strong of Northampton weathered the Revolution to become a United States Senator, a leading Federalist, and a Governor of Massachusetts. Jonathan Bliss, a powerful conservative attorney from Springfield and one of the seventeen Tory "rescinders," emigrated to New Brunswick, Canada, during the war. Moses Bliss, also a lawyer from Springfield, stayed at home and retained his standing in the community as deacon of the First Congregational Church. Captain James Merrick came from the wealthiest family in Monson. "O. Warner" was probably Oliver Warner of Hadley, and "Mr. Stearns" probably Jonathan Stearns of Northampton. [Thanks to Stephen Meunier of the Connecticut Valley Historical Museum for helping track these people down.]

27. Worthington's humiliation might have been exaggerated in the local folklore. See above, note 18.

28. Reverend Stephen Williams did report that on the evening of August 31, his son Samuel and "Seargt G. Colton" were approached and forced "to Sign Something, I know not what." Even so, had there been violence, Reverend Williams would have been the first to report it, which he did not. [Williams, Diary, 8: 309.]

29. Williams, Diary, 8: 309.

30. Jonathan Judd, Jr., Diary, v. 2 (1773–1782), Forbes Library, Northampton. The number "4,000" is difficult to decipher. The significant digit is not nearly so angular as Judd's other "fours," while it does resemble his "twos." According to common syntax, however, it would more likely be "4" because it appears after "3." Since it has always been translated that way, I will continue to do so. In any case, the number is only an estimate, and hearsay at that. All reports agree that the Springfield crowd numbered somewhere in the thousands, rivaling the large crowds of more populous Boston.

31. The proceedings of the Middlesex County Convention of August 30–1, 1774, appear in Lincoln, *Journals of Each Provincial Congress*, 609–614; and Wroth, *Province in Rebellion*, document 315, 886–893. All quotations below are from these proceedings.

32. The proceedings of the Worcester County Convention of August 30–1, 1774, appear in Lincoln, *Journals of Each Provincial Congress*, 631–635; and Wroth, *Province in Rebellion*, document 316, 894–897. All quotations below are from these proceedings, unless otherwise noted.

33. American Political Society, Records, American Antiquarian Society, Worcester.

34. Salisbury Family Papers, American Antiquarian Society, Worcester. Some of these letters are cited in Newfield, *Worcester on the Eve of the Revolution*, 86.

35. Lincoln, *History of Worcester*, 88.

36. *Massachusetts Spy*, August 25, 1774.

37. Gage to Dartmouth, August 27, 1774, Gage, *Correspondence*, 1: 366.

38. *Boston Gazette*, September 5, 1774.

39. *Boston Gazette*, September 5, 1774. The court records are reprinted in Wroth, *Province in Rebellion*, document 333, 1047–1068.

40. *Boston Gazette*, September 5, 1774.

41. Gage to Dartmouth, September 2, 1774, Gage, *Correspondence*, 1: 370. According to Andrews, Gage himself confined the councilors to Boston, fearing they might succumb to pressure and resign if they ventured into the countryside: "Governor wont let [them] go home, least they should be prevail'd on to comply." [Andrews to Barrell, September 4, 1774, Andrews, "Letters," 354.]

42. Council Proceedings, August 31, 1774, Wroth, *Province in Rebellion*, document 151, 525.

43. Gage to Dartmouth, September 2, 1774, Gage, *Correspondence*, 370.

44. *Boston Evening-Post*, September 5, 1774, and *Boston Gazette*, September 5, 1774. These two articles are nearly identical, differing only in a few minor details.

45. *Boston Evening-Post*, September 5, 1774; *Boston Gazette*, September 5, 1774.

46. *Boston Gazette*, September 5, 1774; Wroth, *Province in Rebellion*, document 201, 604. Brattle would later claim that this letter was in response to a request by Gage to inventory the stores under his charge.

47. Andrews to Barrell, September 1, 1774, Andrews, "Letters," 351.

48. Andrews to Barrell, September 2, 1774, Andrews, "Letters," 351.

49. Andrews to Barrell, September 2, 1774, Andrews, "Letters," 351.

50. Joseph Warren to Samuel Adams, September 4, 1774, Samuel Adams Papers, Bancroft Collection, New York Public Library; reprinted in Frothingham, *Joseph Warren*, 356; Hoerder, *Crowd Action*, 288; *Boston Evening-Post*, September 5, 1774; *Boston Gazette*, September 5, 1774. At the time, friends and family of Sewall claimed the firing was unintentional; later, when petitioning the British for claims because he was a loyalist, Chipman claimed it was intentional.

51. Andrews to Barrell, September 2, 1774, Andrews, "Letters," 351.

52. *Boston Evening-Post*, September 5, 1774; *Boston Gazette*, September 5, 1774; Andrews to Barrell, September 2, 1774, Andrews, "Letters," 351.

53. Andrews to Barrell, September 2, 1774, Andrews, "Letters," 352.

54. *Boston Gazette*, September 5, 1774; Wroth, *Province in Rebellion*, document 164, 542–543; Sabine, *Loyalists of the American Revolution*, 2: 130–131. Oliver's statement was intended for a public audience.

55. Andrews to Barrell, September 2, 1774, Andrews, "Letters," 352.

56. Joseph Warren to Samuel Adams, September 4, 1774, Samuel Adams Papers, Bancroft Collection, New York Public Library; reprinted in Frothingham, *Joseph Warren*, 356.

57. *Boston Gazette*, September 5, 1774.

58. *Boston Evening-Post*, September 5, 1774; *Boston Gazette*, September 5, 1774.

59. Thomas Young to Samuel Adams, September 4, 1774, Samuel Adams Papers, Bancroft Collection, New York Public Library. According to another eyewitness, Danforth actually had to read his statement twice so that all could hear. After each reading, a vote was taken to see if his declaration would suffice. [Hoerder, *Crowd Action*, 289.]

60. Joseph Warren to Samuel Adams, September 4, 1774, Samuel Adams Papers, Bancroft Collection, New York Public Library; reprinted in Frothingham, *Joseph Warren*, 356.

61. Edward Hill to John Adams, September 4, 1774, Butterfield, *Adams Family Correspondence*, 1: 149.

62. Hoerder, *Crowd Action*, 289.

63. Hoerder, *Crowd Action*, 290.

64. Warren to Sam Adams, September 4, 1774, Samuel Adams Papers, Bancroft Collection, New York Public Library; Frothingham, *Joseph Warren*, 356; *Boston Evening-Post*, September 5, 1774; *Boston Gazette*, September 5, 1774. Customs commissioner Benjamin Hallowell, who rode through Cambridge on Friday, noted that "the attack upon the Attorney Generals House the Night before, was disapproved of by every considerate person in that town, that there was only boyes and Negroes Concerned." [Benjamin Hallowell to Gage, September 8, 1774, Wroth, *Province in Rebellion*, document 204, 610.]

65. Hoerder, *Crowd Action*, 289. Andrews wrote, "It is worthy remark that Judge Lee observ'd to 'em, after he had made his resignation, that he never saw so large a number of people together and preserve so peaceable order before in his life." [Andrews to Barrell, September 3, 1774, Andrews, "Letters," 353.]

66. Thomas Young to Samuel Adams, September 4, 1774, Samuel Adams Papers, Bancroft Collection, New York Public Library.

67. Hoerder, *Crowd Action*, 290.

68. Benjamin Hallowell to Gage, September 8, 1774, Wroth, *Province in Rebellion*, document 204, 609–612.

69. Andrews to Barrell, September 2, 1774, Andrews, "Letters," 352–353.

70. *Boston Evening-Post*, September 5, 1774; *Boston Gazette*, September 5, 1774.

71. Gage to Dartmouth, September 2, 1774, Gage, *Correspondence*, 1: 372.

72. For Oliver's resignation and accompanying statement, see *Boston Evening-Post*, September 5, 1774; *Boston Gazette*, September 5 and 12, 1774; *Massachusetts Spy*, September 8, 1774; Clarke and Force, *American Archives*, 4th series, 1: 764–766; Sabine, *Loyalists of the American Revolution*, 2: 130–133. Additional sources for the Cambridge incident can be found in Clarke and Force, *American Archives*, 4th series, 1: 761–770.

73. Stiles, *Diary*, 481. The observer was "Mr. McNeil" discussed on page 128.

74. Andrews to Barrell, September 6, 1774, Andrews, "Letters," 355. Benjamin Church came in with a lower estimate, but he was including only those from Springfield and closer who "had risen in one body armed & equipped & had proceeded on their march as far as Shrewsbury on their way to Boston to the Number of Twenty Thousand." [Church to Sam Adams, September 4, 1774, Samuel Adams Papers, Bancroft Collection, New York Public Library.]

75. Lincoln, *History of Worcester*, 87.

76. Williams, Diary, Book 8, 311–313. Williams soon learned that "not one man . . . was killed."

77. Stiles, *Diary*, 479.

78. Stiles, *Diary*, 479–481. There are other firsthand accounts as well, although not so extensive. Ebenezer Parkman, a minister from Westborough, wrote in his diary on September 2: "It is a day of peculiar Anxiety & Distress! Such as we have not had— . . . Breck is emplyd in ye night to cast Bullets." The following day he added, "My son Breck with provisions, Bread, Meat &c Coats, Blankets for it was rainy, rides down towards Camb. . . . Mr. Saml Winthrop computed there were about 7000 of ye country pp had gathered into Cambridge on this occasion." [Ebenezer Parkman, Diary, Manuscript Collection, American Antiquarian Society, Worcester.]

79. Adams, *Diary and Autobiography*, 2: 160. The same theme was expressed by Joseph Warren: "The people from Hampshire County crowded the county of Worcester with armed men; and both counties received the accounts of the quiet dispersion of the people of Middlesex with apparent regret, grudging them the glory of having done something important for their country without their assistance." [Warren to Samuel Adams, September 4, 1774, Samuel Adams Papers, Bancroft Collection, New York Public Library; reprinted in Frothingham, *Joseph Warren*, 356.]

80. Andrews to Barrell, September 6, 1774, Andrews, "Letters," 355.

81. Ebenezer Parkman, Diary, entry for September 7, 1774, Manuscript Collection, American Antiquarian Society, Worcester. "Chauxitt," or Chocksett, part of Lancaster, became the town of Sterling in 1781. [William F. Galvin, "Historical Data Relating to Counties, Cities, and Towns in Massachusetts," 1997.] I am indebted to Peter Viles for this reference.

82. Parkman totals these figures at 4,722, an understandable error in addition.

83. For the other size estimates, see note 90.
84. American Political Society, Records, American Antiquarian Society.
85. The account from an unidentified Tory, cited in note 90, seems to corroborate this observation: ". . . about one thousand of them had fire-arms . . ." At first glance this would seem to lend support to Michael Bellesiles's contention that only a fraction of men of those times possessed firearms. [*Arming America: The Origins of a National Gun Culture* (New York: Alfred A. Knopf, 2000).] I read the evidence differently. If some of the *companies* had arms and others did not, as Parkman states, that would account for the partial arming of the militiamen. It would also argue against Bellesiles, since if only a "few" companies had arms, and there were about one thousand men in arms, most of the militiamen in those companies must have been armed. The various appeals throughout the summer and fall also seem to suggest that most of the men had access to guns; it was the quantity of powder and shot that were at issue. Certainly, John Andrews seemed to think that men throughout the countryside were armed when he wrote on August 26, "every male above the age of 16 possessing a firelock with double the quantity of powder and ball enjoin'd by law." ["Letters," 347.]
86. Parkman wrote, "The Court House was filled with Committees of Correspondence from each Town, & the Door fastened & guarded." He might have been blending the occupation of the courthouse with the County Convention being held across the street at Timothy Bigelow's house, but the courthouse did have to be barricaded to prevent the judges from entering and it stands to reason that the local men from the town of Worcester would play a major role in that occupation. My supposition that men from Spencer might also be involved is admittedly conjectural, based on Parkman's observation that only the men from Spencer and Worcester did not conform to the order on his list as they stood along Main Street later that day.
87. Proceedings of the Worcester County Convention, in Lincoln, *Journals of Each Provincial Congress*, 635; Wroth, *Province in Rebellion*, document 318, 905. Unless otherwise noted, my account of the events on September 6 and 7 in Worcester is based on these proceedings.
88. Stephen Salisbury to Samuel Salisbury, September 7, 1774, Salisbury Family Papers, American Antiquarian Society, Worcester.
89. Lincoln, *Journals of Each Provincial Congress*, 637; Wroth, *Province in Rebellion*, document 318, 907–908.
90. This account comes from an anonymous letter addressed to the Provincial Congress of Massachusetts and published in various newspapers, including the Boston *Weekly News-Letter*, February 23, 1775, and New York's *Rivington's Gazette*, March 9, 1775. It has been reprinted in Clarke and Force, *American Archives*, 4th series, 1: 1261; Moore, *Diary of the American Revolution*, 8. Former Chief Justice Peter Oliver obviously relied on this account when he wrote: "A Mob of 5000 collected at Worcester, about 50 Miles from Boston, a thousand of whom were armed. It being the Time when the Court of Common Pleas was about sitting, the Mob made a lane, & compelled ye. Judges, Sheriff, & Gentlemen of the Bar, to pass & repass them, Cap in Hand, in the most ignominious Manner; & read their Disavowall of holding Courts under the new Acts of Parliament, no less than Thirty Times in the Procession." [Douglas Adair and John A. Schutz, eds., *Peter Oliver's*

Origin and Progress of the American Rebellion (Stanford, CA: Stanford University Press, 1967), 153.]

William Lincoln, who still had access to the oral testimony of elderly informants who had participated in the event, gave a similar account: "On the invitation of the convention, the people of the county had assembled to the number of about six thousand. The companies of the several towns were under officers of their own election, and marched in military order. Having been formed in two lines, when the arrangements were completed, the royalist justices, and officers, were compelled to pass through the ranks, pausing at several intervals, to read their declarations of submission to the public will. At evening, finding that no troops were on their way to sustain the judicial tribunals, whose constitution had been corrupted by the act of parliament, the great assembly dispersed peacefully." [*Journals of Each Provincial Congress,* 635.]

The Boston newspapers, overwhelmed with stories of the Powder Alarm mobilization, crowd actions, and forced resignations, gave little play to the Worcester court closure. In a listing of events which included twelve hundred men marching from Hartford, two thousand from Plymouth going after one of the councilors, and three hundred in Weston hounding Colonel Elisha Jones (they "made his Mightiness walk through their Ranks with his hat off and express his sorrow for past Offences"), the *Boston Gazette* reported on September 12: "We hear that near 6000 Men assembled at Worcester, on Monday and Tuesday last, who prevented the Inferior Court from sitting there." The ubiquitous nature of the revolution of 1774 precluded a full telling of the story, then as well as now.

91. Lincoln, *Journals of Each Provincial Congress,* 637; Wroth, *Province in Rebellion,* document 318, 907.

92. Davis, *Confiscation of John Chandler's Estate,* 224.

93. Stephen Salisbury to Samuel Salisbury, September 7, 1774, Salisbury Family Papers, American Antiquarian Society.

94. Lincoln, *History of Worcester,* 87; Johnson, *Worcester in the War for Independence,* 59. The six men—David Moore, Samuel Moore, John Moore, Ignatious Goulding, Micah Johnson, and Robert Blair—returned two or three weeks later, "when their apprehensions subsided." It is unclear whether these men fled following Timothy Paine's resignation ten days before or in the wake of the court closure of September 6. Today, the road leading from Worcester to Stone House Hill is called Tory Fort Lane.

95. Lincoln, *Journals of Each Provincial Congress,* 637; Wroth, *Province in Rebellion,* document 318, 907.

5 Consolidation

1. It doubtless felt a bit strange for patriots to be hiring back some of the men they had just deposed, but Timothy Paine and the others who had just been humiliated by their neighbors would not dare to exert any authority beyond the most routine of duties. Until he could be replaced in a formal and orderly fashion, Paine would continue to record wills, admonish thieves, or follow any other instructions the patriots gave him. This revolution, after all, was not as much concerned with personalities as with the structure of gov-

ernment, its basic underpinnings. It was not some knee-jerk insurrection in which power-hungry insurgents usurped control of the governmental apparatus to place themselves in control, but a conscious, well-conceived attempt to regain the people's franchise and place it on a more solid footing. The careful measures taken to establish interim procedures demonstrated the serious, deliberative nature of the rebels' business.

2. Andrews to Barrell, September 5, 1774, Andrews, "Letters," 355.

3. Two meetings between the Boston selectmen and Gage, on September 5 and 9, were covered in the *Boston Gazette*, September 12, 1774.

4. Andrews, "Letters," 354–359.

5. Andrews, "Letters," 356–357.

6. Andrews, "Letters," 359–360.

7. Andrews, "Letters," 362.

8. Gage to Dartmouth, September 12, 1774, Gage, *Correspondence*, 1: 374.

9. Abigail Adams to John Adams, September 14, 1774, Butterfield, *Adams Family Correspondence*, 1: 152.

10. Andrews to Barrell, September 9, 1774, Andrews, "Letters," 357–358. Governor Gage agreed with Adams and Andrews: "People are daily resorting to this Town for Protection, for there is no Security to any Person deemed a Friend to Government in any Part of the Country; even Places always esteemed well affected have caught the Infection, and Sedition flows copiously from the Pulpits. The Commissioners of the Customs have thought it no longer safe or prudent to remain at Salem, considering the present distracted State of every Part of the Province, and are amongst others come into the Town, where I am obliged likewise now to reside on many Accounts." [Gage to Dartmouth, September 12, 1774, Gage, *Correspondence*, 1: 374.]

11. Abigail to John Adams, September 14, 1774, Butterfield, *Adams Family Correspondence*, 1: 152.

12. *Boston Gazette*, September 12, 1774; Sabine, *Loyalists of the American Revolution*, 1: 592.

13. Declaration of Benjamin Read, September 14–15, Israel Williams Papers II, Massachusetts Historical Society. See also related declarations from William Read, James Hunt, and Seth Tubbs. For an excellent discussion of this incident, see Nobles, *Divisions Throughout the Whole*, 171–176.

14. Clarke and Force, *American Archives*, 4th Series, 1: 1263; Moore, *Diary of American Revolution*, 11; Nobles, *Divisions Throughout the Whole*, 169; Sheldon, *History of Deerfield*, 698; Daniel W. Wells and Reuben F. Wells, *A History of Hatfield, Massachusetts* (Springfield: F. C. H. Gibbons, 1910), 187.

15. Robert A. Gross, *The Minutemen and Their World* (New York: Hill and Wang, 1976), 55. This version of the story was passed down by a great-grandson of one of the patriots.

16. *Boston Gazette*, November 28, 1774. The letter was dated September 19.

17. In the early part of September, close to half the space in Boston's newspapers was taken up by resignations and recantations. The comparison with McCarthyism is not incidental. However democratic, this revolution was carried on by and for the majority, with little attention given to minority rights. The comparison with the Salem witch trials is not incidental either. The majoritarian democracy practiced during the revolution of 1774 was firmly rooted in the New England tradition of forced compliance with community norms.

18. *Boston News-Letter and Massachusetts Gazette,* September 22, 1774; Proceedings, Essex County Convention, September 6–7, 1774, Lincoln, *Proceedings of Each Provincial Congress,* 616; Wroth, *Province in Rebellion,* document 317, 898–904.

19. Lincoln, *Proceedings of Each Provincial Congress,* 616–618.

20. *Boston News-Letter and Massachusetts Gazette,* September 15, 1774; Proceedings, Suffolk County Convention, September 6–9, 1774, Lincoln, *Proceedings of Each Provincial Congress,* 601. Both the rough and final drafts of the Suffolk Resolves appear in Wroth, *Province in Rebellion,* documents 319 and 320, 910–921.

21. Lincoln, *Proceedings of Each Provincial Congress,* 602–605.

22. "Extracts from the Journals of the Continental Congress," Lincoln, *Proceedings of Each Provincial Congress,* 727. Gaining the official endorsement of the Continental Congress for the Suffolk Resolves was a strategic move by radical patriots, intended to sidestep the proposals of Joseph Galloway. Galloway and other moderates were forced to vote in favor of the Resolves in order not to appear unpatriotic.

23. John Adams, *Diary and Autobiography of John Adams,* 2: 134–135.

24. Proceedings of the Middlesex County Convention, September 13, 1774, Wroth, *Province in Rebellion,* document 322, 922–924; *Boston Gazette,* September 12 and 19, 1774; *Boston Evening Post,* September 19; Gross, *Minutemen and their World,* 53–4.

25. For the Cumberland Convention of September 21–22, see Lincoln, *Proceedings of Each Provincial Congress,* 655–659; Wroth, *Province in Rebellion,* document 324, 931–937. For the Dukes Convention of November 9, see Wroth, *Province in Rebellion,* document 400, 1317–1321. For the York Convention of November 16, see Wroth, *Province in Rebellion,* document 402, 1327–1330; *Boston Gazette,* December 5, 1774.

26. Proceedings, Bristol County Convention, September 28–29, Lincoln, *Proceedings of Each Provincial Congress,* 626–627; Wroth, *Province in Rebellion,* document 329, 958–963. See also Wroth's introductory essay, *Province in Rebellion,* 69.

27. Proceedings, Barnstable County Meeting, September 27–28, 1774, in Wroth, *Province in Rebellion,* document 327, 947–953; *Boston Gazette,* October 31, 1774.

28. Proceedings, Plymouth County Convention, September 26–27, in Lincoln, *Proceedings of Each Provincial Congress,* 621–625; Wroth, *Province in Rebellion,* document 326, 941–947.

29. George Watson and Pelham Winslow to Thomas Gage, October 6, 1774, Wroth, *Province in Rebellion,* document 356, 1215. Watson and Winslow estimated the crowd at two thousand; John Andrews, based on hearsay, called it four thousand. [Andrews to Barrell, October 6, 1774, Andrews, "Letters," 373.]

30. *Boston Gazette,* October 31, 1774; Proceedings, Plymouth County Convention, October 4, Wroth, *Province in Rebellion,* document 399, 1314–1317.

31. Watson and Winslow to Gage, October 6, 1774, Wroth, *Province in Rebellion,* 1216.

32. Andrews to Barrell, October 6, Andrews, "Letters," 373–374.

33. The proceedings of the Worcester County Convention of September 20–21 were printed in the *Massachusetts Spy,* October 6, 1774, and reprinted in Lincoln, *Proceedings of Each Provincial Congress,* 640–646, and Wroth, *Province in Rebellion,* document 323, 924–930.

34. Lincoln, *Proceedings of Each Provincial Congress,* 642.

35. Gage to Dartmouth, September 12 and 25, Gage, *Correspondence*, 1: 374, 376. Gage, Proclamation Dissolving the General Court, September 28, 1774, in Wroth, *Province in Rebellion*, document 172, 554.

36. Rice, *Worcester Town Records*, 244; Lincoln, *History of Worcester*, 91–2; Lovell, *Worcester in War of Revolution*, 50; Nutt, *History of Worcester*, 538. These instructions, of course, originated in the American Political Society, which approved them the day before the town meeting. [American Political Society, Records, October 3, 1774.]

37. Lincoln, *Journals of Each Provincial Congress*, 6.

38. Wroth, *Province in Rebellion*, 80.

39. Lincoln, *Journals of Each Provincial Congress*, 23.

40. Lincoln, *Journals of Each Provincial Congress*, 28–9. Italics appeared in the official minutes.

41. Lincoln, *Journals of Each Provincial Congress*, 30.

42. Lincoln, *Journals of Each Provincial Congress*, 38–9. In fact, although the towns were more than willing to withhold payments from the old receiver-general, most would prove lethargic when it came to handing over their money to a fledgling Congress that could only "recommend" the payment of taxes.

43. Lincoln, *Journals of Each Provincial Congress*, 32–4.

44. Gage, *Correspondence*, 1: 377–378.

45. Gage, *Correspondence*, 1: 379.

46. Gage, *Correspondence*, 1: 380–381. Gage saw clearly that the Massachusetts Government Act was to blame for the rebellion he could not supress. In a similar vein, a letter to the *London Chronicle* on November 18, 1774, stated: "The late Act for the better regulating the civil government of this province has, . . . in effect, dissolved the Government. The people will never acknowledge the new counsellors. Several of them refused to take their places. The people in different parts of the country have obliged some others to resign; so that there are none now but what are in Boston. A stop is also put to the holding the courts of justice upon the new plan. Thus we have neither legislative nor executive powers left in the province. There are but two possible ways to restore order and good government here: one is, by repealing the Acts which have been the sole occasion of these commotions; and this, I firmly believe, would quickly end them. The other, by laying the country waste by fire and sword, and extirpating the present inhabitants, leaving none to be governed, if that can be called restoring government. Any hostile measures short of this will never answer the end." [Frothingham, *Joseph Warren*, 373.]

47. Gage, *Correspondence*, 1: 383.

48. *Boston Evening-Post*, November 7, 1774; Wroth, *Province in Rebellion*, document 352, 1207–1209. The notice was in two parts, dated October 31 and November 2. The first notice instructed sheriffs, constables, and collectors to pay all money to him; the second notice stated specifically that they should pay no money to Henry Gardner.

49. *Boston Evening-Post*, November 14, 1774; Wroth, *Province in Rebellion*, document 353, 1209–1212.

50. Gage, *Correspondence*, 1: 383. For the strength of the British army in Boston, see John Shy, *Toward Lexington: The Role of the British Army in the Coming of the American Revolution* (Princeton: Princeton University Press, 1965), 413, 419.

51. Gage, *Correspondence*, 2: 659.

52. Gage, *Correspondence*, 1: 387.

53. Jonathan Judd, Jr., Diary, September 7, 1774. Richard D. Brown, who began his study
    with an emphasis on the leadership of the Boston Committee of Correspondence, con-
    cluded that "activity at the local level proved decisive." By the end of summer, the towns
    themselves "constituted the sole effective government in the province," he wrote. "All
    power derived directly and immediately from the people. At the level of day-to-day be-
    havior, a republic had been established in Massachusetts." [*Revolutionary Politics in Mass-
    achusetts*, 236.]

6 Battle Lines

1. Gage, *Correspondence*, 2: 654.

2. John Pitt to Samuel Adams, October 16, 1774, Samuel Adams Papers, Bancroft Collection, New York Public Library. This theme would be echoed time and again during the
   fall of 1774. On November 21, Joseph Warren wrote to Josiah Quincy, Jr., that Bostonians were still hopeful of a reconciliation. "It will require, however, a very masterly policy to keep the province, for any considerable time longer, in its present state. The town
   of Boston is by far the most moderate part of the province." [Josiah Quincy, *Memoir of
   the Life of Josiah Quincy Jun. of Massachusetts* (New York: Da Capo, 1971; originally
   Boston: Cummings, Hillard, and Co., 1825), 206; also reprinted in Frothingham, *Joseph
   Warren*, 395.]

3. Thomas Young to Samuel Adams, September 4, 1774, Samuel Adams Papers, Bancroft
   Collection, New York Public Library; cited in Richard D. Brown, *Revolutionary Politics
   in Massachusetts* (Madison: University of Wisconsin Press, 1973), 232.

4. Stephen E. Patterson, *Political Parties in Revolutionary Massachusetts*, 118.

5. Joseph Warren to Samuel Adams, September 12, 1774, Samuel Adams Papers, Bancroft
   Collection, New York Public Library; reprinted in Frothingham, *Joseph Warren*,
   375–376.

6. Joseph Warren to Samuel Adams, September 4, 1774, Samuel Adams Papers, Bancroft
   Collection, New York Public Library; reprinted in Frothingham, *Joseph Warren*, 358.

7. Harry A. Cushing, ed., *The Writings of Samuel Adams* (New York: G. P. Putnam's Sons,
   1907), 3: 157; Frothingham, *Joseph Warren*, 377.

8. Samuel Adams, *Writings*, 3: 159; Frothingham, *Joseph Warren*, 378.

9. See my treatment in *A People's History of the American Revolution: How Common People
   Shaped the Fight for Independence* (New York: The New Press, 2001), 12–18.

10. According to Stephen Patterson, "My study of Massachusetts suggests that the Boston
    crowd, while it possessed an identity, was unable to rationalize its purpose or to separate
    itself wholly from the ideas and goals of republican leaders. Rural people, however, . . .
    were able to formalize and synthesize their revolutionary purpose, and to establish a di-
    rection different from, if not contrary to, that of the early revolutionary leadership." [*Po-
    litical Parties*, 58.] Other historians to contrast the new leadership of country radicals
    with the old leadership of Boston patriots include Merrill Jensen, *The Founding of a Na-
    tion: A History of the American Revolution, 1763–1776* (New York: Oxford University

Press, 1968), 553–567; and Richard D. Brown, *Revolutionary Politics in Massachusetts*, 231–236.

11. Wroth, *Province in Rebellion*, 80.

12. For an excellent treatment of this subject, see Johnson, *Worcester in the War for Independence*, 16–23.

13. Rice, *Worcester Town Records*, 216.

14. Lincoln, *Journals of Each Provincial Congress*, 57–8.

15. Patterson, *Political Parties in Revolutionary Massachusetts*, 113–114; Jensen, *The Founding of a Nation*, 561.

16. Andrews to Barrell, September 25, 1774, Andrews. "Letters," 367–368. Writing to Samuel Adams on September 29, Joseph Warren stated that the Boston tradesmen, although pressed for money, refused to work for the British because of "a great aversion to do anything displeasing their brethren in the country." [Frothingham, *Joseph Warren*, 381.]

17. Andrews to Barrell, October 1, 1774, Andrews. "Letters," 371–372.

18. Andrews, "Letters," 373. The letter continued: "This day a deputation of twelve came to town with a *very* spirited remonstrance from the *body* of Worcester County, which consists of five and forty towns; where they have incorporated *seven regiments* consisting of a thousand men each, chose their officers, and turn out twice a week to perfect themselves in the military art—which are call'd *minute men*, i.e., to be ready at a minute's warning with a fortnight's provision, and ammunition and arms."

19. Andrews, "Letters," 380–381.

20. Benjamin Church to Sam Adams, September 29, 1774, Samuel Adams Papers, Bancroft Collection, New York Public Library.

21. Quincy, *Memoir*, 186–187.

22. Wroth, *Province in Rebellion*, 81–2.

23. Although the farming regions of Massachusetts were well represented in the Provincial Congress, the most radical of the country revolutionaries were not even there. Historian L. Kinvin Wroth has pointed out that most of those elected to the Provincial Congress were well-to-do men not very representative of their constituencies. Twenty-two percent were merchants, lawyers, or doctors—far above the statistical norm for a rural society. According to the 1771 tax assessments, 60 percent ranked among the wealthiest 10 percent of their towns, and virtually all ranked in the top half. About 85 percent had previously held public office; more than 70 percent of the former representatives to the General Court had been elected to serve their communities in this new capacity. [Wroth, *Province in Rebellion*, 80–1.] The local revolutionaries who had closed the courts, for whatever reasons, had turned to many of their old leaders when it came time to put together some semblance of a new government. Perhaps it was their desire not to be perceived as a "mob"; perhaps they didn't want to rock the boat any more than necessary; perhaps they reasoned that previous experience would serve as an asset in the tasks ahead. In any case, the Massachusetts Revolution of 1774 signified more a change in governmental structure than in representational leadership.

24. Wroth, *Province in Rebellion*, document 347, 1200–1202; Lincoln, *Journals of Each Provincial Congress*, 68.

25. Gage to Dartmouth, December 15, 1774, Gage, *Correspondence*, 1: 388.

26. Andrews, "Letters," 390.

27. Andrews, "Letters," 391.

28. For a clear account of the seizure of Fort William and Mary, see David Hackett Fischer, *Paul Revere's Ride* (New York: Oxford University Press, 1994), 52–8. For the full array of source documents, see Charles L. Parsons, "The Capture of Fort William and Mary, December 14 and 15, 1774," *New Hampshire Historical Society Proceedings*, 4 (1890–1905), 18–47.

29. Gage to Dartmouth, January 27, 1775, Gage, *Correspondence*, 1: 391.

30. Wroth, *Province in Rebellion*, document 671, 1969. Dr. Benjamin Church, listed as a member of the Committee of Safety, was the likely source of this intelligence. Three days earlier, an intelligence report stated that "Twelve pieces of Brass Cannon mounted, are at Salem and lodged near the North River, on the back of town." [Wroth, *Province in Rebellion*, document 670, 1968.]

31. Henry Steel Commager and Richard B. Morris, *The Spirit of 'Seventy-Six: The Story of the American Revolution as Told by Participants* (Indianapolis: Bobbs-Merrill, 1958), 63–5.

32. Rice, *Worcester Town Records*, 249–253.

33. Lincoln, *Journals of Each Provincial Congress*, 649; Wroth, *Province in Rebellion*, document 447, 1438.

34. Lincoln, *Journals of Each Provincial Congress*, 650–651.

35. *Massachusetts Gazette and Boston Weekly News-Letter*, April 13, 1775.

36. American Political Society, Records, meetings of December 5, 1774; February 26, March 11, April 1, May 6, and May 20, 1776. May 20 was the last meeting. Twice it was moved to dissolve the Society, but both times the motion failed. Although the May 20 meeting was adjourned to "the first Monday in June at five o'clock at the Hous of Mrs. Starns," it seems from the blank pages in the record book that the APS never reconvened.

37. Wroth, *Province in Rebellion*, document 800, 2182–2183. The note, dated March 24, was not published until June 7.

38. Timothy Bigelow to William Henshaw, March 1, 1775, Henshaw Family Papers, Box 1, Folder 3, American Antiquarian Society. Three weeks later, in the face of patriot pressure, Wheeler was forced to apologize for his wavering. His recantation of March 21 is also in the Henshaw Family Papers, which serve as an excellent source for the military preparations in Worcester County. Wheeler had been chairman of the APS for the meeting of April 4, 1774.

39. Wroth, *Province in Rebellion*, document 458, 1555.

40. Dr. Robert Honyman, *Colonial Panorama, 1775*, Philip Padelford, ed., (San Marino, CA: Huntington Library, 1939), 49.

41. These reports, the best sources we have for the debates in the Provincial Congress, are reprinted in Wroth, *Province in Rebellion*, documents 670–695, pages 1967–1995. Dr. Benjamin Church, one of the informants, served on the all-important Committee of Safety. See also Allen French, *General Gage's Informers* (New York: Greenwood Press, 1968).

42. James Warren to John Adams, February 20, 1775, *Warren-Adams Letters* (Boston: Massachusetts Historical Society, 1917), 1: 41.

43. Gage to Dartmouth, February 20, 1775, Gage, *Correspondence,* 1: 393.
44. Lincoln, *Journals of Each Provincial Congress,* 89–90. Only one of the five, the members stipulated, could be from Boston.
45. Joseph Hawley to Thomas Cushing, February 22, 1775, Lincoln, *Journals of Each Provincial Congress,* 749–750.
46. Wroth, *Province in Rebellion,* document 454, 1551–1552.
47. Spy report of March 30, 1775, Wroth, *Province in Rebellion,* document 679, 1976.
48. Andrews to Barrell, March 18, 1775, Andrews, "Letters," 401.
49. Dartmouth to Gage, January 27, 1775, Gage, *Correspondence,* 2: 179.
50. See Andrews to Barrell, January 4, 7, and 8, Andrews, "Letters," 393.
51. Dartmouth to Gage, January 27, 1775, Gage, *Correspondence,* 2: 179–183. Wroth, *Province in Rebellion,* document 661, 1948–1953.
52. *Boston Gazette,* April 3, 1775. Parliament also added to the repressive Coercive Acts by restricting the productive Newfoundland fisheries to the British trade.
53. Lincoln, *Journals of Each Provincial Congress,* 136.
54. Spy report of April 9, 1775, Wroth, *Province in Rebellion,* document 682, 1980; French, *General Gage's Informers,* 19–21.
55. Lincoln, *Journals of Each Provincial Congress,* 121–129.
56. Lincoln, *Journals of Each Provincial Congress,* 135.
57. Lincoln, *Journals of Each Provincial Congress,* 135. "The recorded vote may have been accurate," Stephen Patterson has observed, "but it did not indicate how many opponents of the plan absented themselves while the vote was being taken." [*Political Parties in Revolutionary Massachusetts,* 117.] But even if some members did "absent themselves," their unwillingness to have their opposition recorded indicates that the political momentum had shifted toward full-scale preparation for war.
58. Spy report of April 15, 1775, Wroth, *Province in Rebellion,* document 683, 1981; French, *General Gage's Informers,* 23–4. This was undoubtedly Timothy rather than Joshua, since Timothy was at that point the town's representative to the Provincial Congress. Also, the issues at hand were military, Timothy's special area of interest and expertise.
59. Spy report of April 18, 1775, Wroth, *Province in Rebellion,* document 684, 1983.
60. Lincoln, *Journals of Each Provincial Congress,* 141–143.
61. James Warren to Mercy Warren, April 7, 1775, *Warren-Adams Letters* (Boston: Massachusetts Historical Society, 1917), 1: 45.
62. *Massachusetts Gazette and Boston Post-Boy,* April 3–10, 1775.
63. Andrews, "Letters," 402.
64. Lincoln, *Journals of Each Provincial Congress,* 142–143.
65. Lincoln, *Journals of Each Provincial Congress,* 146.
66. In addition to the report cited in note 67, a complete journal survives from a mission undertaken in late February and March: "General Gage's Instructions, of 22d February, 1775, to Captain Brown and Ensign D'Bernicre," and "Narrative, &c.," Massachusetts Historical Society, *Collections* 4 (1916): 204–218. Brown and D'Bernicre were instructed to investigate main roads and alternate routes, fording places, passes through the hills; they were to determine whether towns were "capable of being made defencible"; they were to explore the possibilities for obtaining "provisions, forage, straw, &c. the number

of cattle, horse, &c. in the several townships of Suffolk and Worcester Counties." The prospects for an invasion of Worcester did not look promising, for the populace was too aroused. While in Worcester the spies were sheltered in the tavern of William "Tory" Jones, just south of the meeting house and common. The Worcester part of the journal is reprinted in Lincoln, *History of Worcester*, 95–6.

67. This version of Howe's journal, taken from an 1827 printing and intended for an American audience (Howe claims to have joined the patriots after he completed his mission), is reprinted in D. Hamilton Hurd, *History of Middlesex County, Massachusetts* (Philadelphia: J. W. Lewis and Co., 1890), 579–584.

7 The End of Revolution

1. Lincoln, *History of Worcester*, 97.
2. Lincoln, *History of Worcester*, 98; Nutt, *History of Worcester*, 558–559.
3. Lincoln, *Journals of Each Provincial Congress*, 370.
4. Lincoln, *Journals of Each Provincial Congress*, 475.
5. The exact number remains unclear. William Lincoln, who wrote at a time when oral testimony could still be obtained, claims that "among the volunteers, under the command of Arnold, who engaged in the winter march through the wilderness, were Major Timothy Bigelow, Capt. Jonas Hubbard, and twelve soldiers from Worcester." [Lincoln, *History of Worcester*, 101.] But Lincoln mentions only two others by name, and his word was not always reliable, as we see in the text below. Charles Nutt, writing in the early twentieth century, listed nine men from Worcester by name. [Nutt, *History of Worcester*, 564.] The records of the seventeen-volume *Massachusetts Soldiers and Sailors of the Revolutionary War*, published in 1898, do not show several of these soldiers as participating in the Quebec expedition, but these records must be incomplete: there is no mention that John Pierce was on the expedition, despite his extensive journal.
6. The journal, not made public for a century and a half, is reprinted in Kenneth Roberts, *March to Quebec: Journals of the Members of Arnold's Expedition* (Garden City: Doubleday and Co., 1947), 653–711.
7. Roberts, *March to Quebec*, 701.
8. A list of casualties and prisoners from Hubbard's Company appears in Roberts, *March to Quebec*, 36. Roberts took this list from one of the participants, Joseph Ware, whose journal was published in the *New England Historical and Genealogical Register* 6 (1852). Nutt lists "Corp. Nathaniel Heywood" as "killed" on page 564, but on page 150 he states that "Heywood, Lieut. Nathaniel" served again in New York in 1777. Heywood does not appear on Ware's list.
9. Roberts, *March to Quebec*, 36; Nutt, *History of Worcester*, 564. Two of the men from Worcester (John Hall and John McGuire) were said to have joined the British army in order to gain their freedom.
10. Rice, *Worcester Town Records*, 280.
11. See Nutt, *History of Worcester*, 561, for the list of men answering the alarm of August 28, 1777.
12. The list of members of the American Political Society, from the APS Minutes at the

American Antiquarian Society in Worcester, are reprinted in Lovell, *Worcester in War of Revolution*, 24. For the names of those who marched towards Concord, see Nutt, *History of Worcester*, 557–558; Lincoln, *History of Worcester*, 98.

13. Rice, *Worcester Town Records*, 278, 294–295, 305.

14. Rice, *Worcester Town Records*, 342, 344–345.

15. Rice, *Worcester Town Records*, 377–386.

16. The list of recruits appears in Nutt, *History of Worcester*, 562. Twelve of twenty-one appear in *Massachusetts Soldiers and Sailors*, and ten of these listings record occupations according to Worcester County Superintendent Seth Washburn's "descriptive list of men serving for Worcester according to the resolves of December 2, 1780." One, Jupiter, was "reported a Negro," while I infer from the customary usage of the time that Cato (no last name) was also African American. (Fourteen men called Cato are listed in *Massachusetts Soldiers and Sailors*, but none from Worcester.)

17. "List of Voters for the Year 1779 in Worcester," Worcester Society of Antiquity, *Proceedings*, 16 (1899): 451–452. The right to vote, at that time, was still determined by property qualifications. The 1779 voters lists, totaling 218 names, includes eight women (property-owning widows and Mary Chandler, John Chandler's wife) and eleven estates. Dead people could still vote, but the poor could not.

18. Rice, *Worcester Town Records*, 315–317.

19. Although most former Tories remained at home, politically muted, several of the most vocal Tories had by this time left the country. The property of the exiles was confiscated to help finance the war effort. On May 29, 1775, the town meeting had instructed David Bancroft, its representative to the Provincial Congress, "that the Estates of our Domestick Enemies may be secured for the Publick use." [Rice, *Worcester Town Records*, 266.] By 1777 most of the property vacated by Tory émigrés was being administered by government agents; in 1778, 309 of those who had left (including John Chandler, John Murray, James Putnam, Timothy Ruggles, Abijah Willard, and several of their sons) were legally banished; in 1779 the estates of these men were finally confiscated and sold off to finance the war effort. [The Banishment Act, including a complete list of those affected, and the two Confiscation Acts are reprinted in James H. Stark, *The Loyalists of Massachusetts* (Boston: James H. Stark, 1910), 137–144. For a detailed study of the largest estate in Worcester County, see Davis, *Confiscation of John Chandler's Estate*.] Much of John Chandler's estate wound up in the hands of prominent patriots—men like the printer, Isaiah Thomas, and the new probate judge, Levi Lincoln. [Newcomer, *Embattled Farmers*, 151.]

20. Rice, *Worcester Town Records*, 349, 401.

21. Lincoln, *Journals of Each Provincial Congress*, 566. The "lunatic," Daniel Adams of Boston, was the subject of two separate resolutions in June 1775.

22. " . . . 3. No member shall speak more than twice to one question, without first obtaining leave of Congress; nor more than once until others have spoken that shall desire it. . . . 8. No member shall nominate more than one person for a committee, provided the person so nominated be chosen. 9. No member shall be obliged to be upon more than two committees at time, nor chairman of more than one." [Lincoln, *Journals of Each Provincial Congress*, 164–165.]

23. Rice, *Worcester Town Records,* 264–266.

24. Lincoln, *Journals of Each Provincial Congress,* 230.

25. Lincoln, *Journals of Each Provincial Congress,* 359.

26. Lincoln, *Journals of Each Provincial Congress,* 757.

27. Taylor, *Western Massachusetts in the Revolution,* 82–3.

28. Taylor, *Western Massachusetts in the Revolution,* 81.

29. The Pittsfield petition is reprinted in Oscar and Mary Handlin, eds., *The Popular Sources of Political Authority: Documents on the Massachusetts Constitution of 1780* (Cambridge: Harvard University Press, 1966), 61–4.

30. Handlin and Handlin, *Popular Sources,* 92.

31. The responses are reprinted in Handlin and Handlin, *Popular Sources,* 101–166.

32. Handlin and Handlin, *Popular Sources,* 164–166.

33. Handlin and Handlin, *Popular Sources,* 175.

34. Taylor, *Western Massachusetts in the Revolution,* 89; Handlin and Handlin, *Popular Sources,* 254.

35. Taylor, *Western Massachusetts in the Revolution,* 91.

36. Handlin and Handlin, *Popular Sources,* 367.

37. Handlin and Handlin, *Popular Sources,* 370–373.

38. Taylor, *Western Massachusetts in the Revolution,* 98. The Berkshire Constitutionalists are also discussed in Theodore M. Hammett, *The Revolutionary Ideology in its Social Context: Berkshire County, Massachusetts, 1725–1785* (Brandeis University: Ph.D. Thesis, 1976), 123–141.

39. The Constitution of 1780 is reprinted in Handlin and Handlin, *Popular Sources,* 441–472; and Ronald M. Peters, Jr., *The Massachusetts Constitution of 1780: A Social Compact* (Amherst: University of Massachusetts Press, 1978), 195–224.

40. Charles Hersey, *Reminiscences of the Military Life and Sufferings of Col. Timothy Bigelow* (Worcester: Henry Howland, 1860), 15, 19. Hersey stated he heard these tales in his youth, directly from revolutionary veterans.

41. Hersey, *Timothy Bigelow,* 22.

42. *Massachusetts Soldiers and Sailors,* 2: 26–7. Ellery Crane, who passed on Hersey's stories unquestioningly, reported that according to "Heitman's Register," Bigelow had "retired January 1, 1781." ["A Chapter in the War," 196.] Crane failed to address the apparent inconsistency of a soldier who had just "retired" being "everywhere all the time" during a subsequent battle. It is possible, however, that Bigelow returned to active duty and did fight at Yorktown after he was acquitted of the charges against him. Crane, probably following Hersey, states that Bigelow went on to serve on the Hudson, at Providence, and finally at the arsenal in Springfield before leaving the military for good.

43. I am indebted to Kenneth Moynihan for calling my attention to this reference.

44. John Joseph Henry, "Campaign Against Quebec," Roberts, *March to Quebec,* 379. Henry's memoir was first published in 1812.

45. Robert A. Feer, *Shays's Rebellion* (New York: Garland, 1988; reprint of Ph. D. thesis, Harvard University, 1958), 47–8.

46. Rice, *Worcester Town Records,* 401–402.

47. Rice, *Worcester Town Records,* 409.

48. Rice, *Worcester Town Records*, 423–424.

49. David P. Szatmary, *Shay's Rebellion: The Making of an Agrarian Insurrection* (Amherst: University of Massachusetts Press, 1980), 19–36.

50. Szatmary, *Shays' Rebellion*, 29–31. For the dramatic increase in lawsuits in Worcester County, see also Feer, *Shays' Rebellion*, 60.

51. Szatmary, *Shays' Rebellion*, 33. For more on the colorful Whiting, see Stephen T. Riley, "Dr. William Whiting and Shays' Rebellion," *Proceedings of the American Antiquarian Society* (October 1956): 119–166.

52. Feer, *Shays' Rebellion*, 73–4.

53. Feer, *Shays' Rebellion*, 95, 176–179; Szatmary, *Shays' Rebellion*, 39.

54. Feer, *Shays' Rebellion*, 110.

55. Feer, *Shays' Rebellion*, 180–211. Curiously, Szatmary [*Shays' Rebellion*, 58–9] devotes but a single paragraph to the court closures of the late summer of 1786 in Massachusetts—the clear beginning of "Shays' Rebellion." Like other historians, he misses much of the point by failing to draw the obvious parallels with the court closures of 1774, which were obviously in the minds of the insurgents.

56. The term "Shays' Rebellion" misleadingly suggests that Daniel Shays either initiated the insurrection or exerted some kind of controlling influence over it. Neither is the case. Shays was not even present at the first court closure, nor at some of the later ones. He seems to have risen to a leadership position because of his military experience: he had been a captain during the Revolution. The insurgents, recognizing they were in an armed confrontation, called upon him to make military decisions, not to represent them politically. He filled an important role, but we should be careful to note that he in no way owned the movement, as the term "Shays' Rebellion" implies. Shays himself recognized this when he said to General Rufus Putnam: "I at their head! I am not . . . I never had any appointment but that at Springfield, nor did I ever take command of any men but those of the county of Hampshire; no, General Putnam, you are deceived, I never had half so much to do in the matter as you think." [Feer, *Shays's Rebellion*, 212.] The term "Shays' Rebellion," I suspect, is commonly accepted for two reasons: innocently, it is convenient, substituting the name of an individual for a complex social movement; not so innocently, it is intended to belittle the significance of the insurgents, connoting a mass of people unquestioningly following their leader rather than acting for reasons of their own. Implicitly, it steers us away from the real grievances of the insurgents. This problem is magnified when the rebellious farmers are labeled "Shaysites," as if they were in some type of cult. The failure to recognize the true importance of the farmers' rebellion of the mid-1780s is due in part to the general acceptance of this simplistic but misleading nomenclature; it is also due to the failure to acknowledge its connection with the very successful rebellion waged twelve years earlier by many of the very same people.

57. Szatmary, *Shays' Rebellion*, 86–7.

58. Kenneth J. Moynihan, "Meetinghouse vs. Courthouse: The Struggle for Legitimacy in Worcester, 1783–1788," in Martin J. Kaufman, ed., *Shays' Rebellion: Selected Essays* (Westfield, MA, 1787), 45.

59. Albert Farnsworth, "Shays's Rebellion," *Massachusetts Law Quarterly* 12 (1927): 34. I am indebted to Kenneth Moynihan for calling my attention to this reference.

60. Crane, "Chapter in the War," 192.

61. Nutt, *History of Worcester*, 488; Charles Martyn, *The Life of Artemas Ward* (New York: Artemas Ward, 1921), 300.

62. Thomas gave no special attention to Bigelow, despite the fact that Timothy Bigelow had helped move Thomas's press to Worcester back in April 1775, allowing Thomas to work out of his own home until he could set up on his own.

63. Worthington had decided to stay at home and try to work within the new order. For four years he did what the revolutionaries told him to do, and by 1778 he was once again serving as moderator of the town meeting. [Green, *Springfield*, 294; Nobles, *Divisions Throughout the Whole*, 178–179.] Israel Williams, on the other hand, was unable to come to an accommodation with the patriots. In May 1775, shortly after the fighting commenced, he was forced to sign another declaration showing "his Readiness to Join his Countrymen," and later that year the Hatfield Committee of Correspondence, along with some officers of the country militia, suggested that Williams join his fellow Tories who had already moved to Boston: "Your Conduct has been from first to last one continued Series of Treason and Rebellion at your County and you have been and are Still an open avowed Enemy to your Country. . . . the People throughout the Province know you and all your Machinations and movements and think Death too mild a Punishment for you." [Nobles, *Divisions Throughout the Whole*, 177.] Still, Williams stayed on. A year later, accused of importing British goods and writing a friendly letter to the hated Thomas Hutchinson, Williams was arrested and confined. He remained in jail for over three years, spending his seventieth birthday behind bars. He wrote petition after petition to secure his freedom, but all to no avail. Rejected even by his church, the greatest of all "river gods" had become a prisoner and social outcast. He never regained any sort of power, nor even acceptance by his neighbors. Israel Williams died in oblivion in 1788, eight years after his release from prison. [Nobles, *Divisions Throughout the Whole*, 178; Newcomer, *Embattled Farmers*, 64–5.]

64. Brooke, *Heart of the Commonwealth*, 212.

65. Brooke, *Heart of the Commonwealth*, 212.

Epilogue: Why the Story Has Not Been Told

1. See, for instance, David Hackett Fischer's discussion of how the actions of various messengers congealed into the tale of Paul Revere, the lone midnight rider. [*Paul Revere's Ride* (New York: Oxford University Press, 1994).] See also my discussion on Daniel Shays and "Shays' Rebellion," chapter 7, note 56. Often, apologists for the status quo try to discredit revolutions or insurrections by claiming they are led by a few individuals who are stirring up the trouble—outside agitators, union organizers, or carpetbaggers from the North. The people, if left to themselves, would not rebel. For established governments, this top-down view of political or social unrest has an additional benefit: "ringleaders" can be isolated and punished.

2. Joseph Hawley, the Northampton "river god" who became a player among pre-Revolutionary Whigs, has left more of a name for himself among political historians. But there is no indication he exercised much influence over the court closures in Hamp-

shire County, and he certainly wasn't involved in the various mobbings of his political adversary, Israel Williams. In the consolidation phase of the Revolution, after governmental powers had been usurped, he counseled caution at every turn. Hawley, the best known of the lot, was hardly a firebrand.

3. In 1955 Robert E. Brown concluded that because the rebels were "middle-class," there had been no "revolution" at all. [*Middle-Class Democracy and the Revolution in Massachusetts, 1691–1780.*] In colonial Massachusetts, Brown estimated 97 percent of the adult males in Worcester met the minimal property qualifications for enfranchisement; the figure was lower provincewide, but on average more than three of every four adult males could vote. [48–51.] Brown correctly surmised that the threat of losing their franchise propelled the people of Massachusetts to fight, but he argued that this could not be construed as a "revolution" since the people were attempting only to preserve the existing order. "The problem was not one of attaining a democratic society," Brown wrote, "but of keeping the democracy they had." [351.] Brown was reacting specifically to the Progressives, who tried to claim the American Revolution involved internal class conflict in the colonies. By examining tax records, he found that rebel leaders were "substantial, middle-class property owners," not "radical, lower-class proletarians." [334.] He also found that most of the men whom the patriots chose to represent them in the new government had served in the General Court for years. [330–333.] Furthermore, since many of the elections were near unanimous, Brown concluded there was little internal conflict of any sort. [353.] With no change of leadership, with "rebels" who were well-to-do, and with undisputed elections, Brown maintained that the term "revolution" should not be applied to the American War of Independence.

Brown's arguments, plausible at first sight, were based on faulty assumptions. To determine the character of a mass movement by the economic standing of its so-called leaders can be misleading—particularly if the movement is essentially leaderless, as this one was. We cannot infer anything from the economic status of representatives to the General Court, for these men were not "representative" of the patriots in any statistical sense. (It is little wonder the members of the General Court were well off: in those days, nobody else could afford the time to serve.) The people did not have a problem with their representatives but with governmental structures they hoped to change. Colonial Massachusetts had been governed not only by town meetings but by royal governors and elite office-holders who served at the pleasure of the Crown. Two strands of government—democratic and deferential—existed side-by-side in precarious balance. When the Massachusetts Government Act tipped the scales in one direction, the citizens decided it was time to move the opposite way. In dramatic fashion, which Brown failed to acknowledge, they deposed not their own representatives but the British-appointed elite, and they altered their government to exclude all authority not based directly on the will of the people. This was truly revolutionary—particularly since almost all the people were behind it. Perhaps Brown's most erroneous assumption was that unanimity implied the absence of revolution. Quite the contrary: the more unanimous, the stronger the revolution. Timothy Paine did not resign his seat on the Council because five "substantial, middle-class property owners" came to his home and asked him to; he resigned because there were two thousand people waiting outside.

The new social history, starting in the late 1960s and reaching its zenith in the 1970s, challenged Robert Brown's view of late colonial Massachusetts as "middle class." Local studies of Dedham, Andover, Concord, and rural Suffolk County suggested that New England society just prior to the Revolution showed signs of "economic polarization and potential class conflict." [Kenneth Lockridge, "Land, Population, and the Evolution of New England Society," *Past and Present* 39 (1968), 68. These local studies are cited in chapter 2, note 1.] "The disturbing social and economic changes did not 'cause' the townspeople's rebellion against the new British moves," said Robert Gross in his landmark book on Concord, "but the continuing decay in their fortunes added special poignancy to their fears." [Gross, *Minutemen and Their World,* 107.] Bruce Merritt, in his study of Deerfield, concluded that "social conflict lay at the heart of the revolutionary turmoil." [Bruce G. Merritt, "Loyalism and Social Conflict in Revolutionary Deerfield, Massachusetts," *Journal of American History* 57 (1970): 279.] At issue was not simply wealth but occupation: Whigs were mostly farmers, while Tories were primarily professionals or involved with commercial interests.

These scholars, inheriting something of the Progressive tradition, searched for evidence of internal conflict in the American Revolution. It seems they would have gleaned onto a revolution of common farmers and artisans—but they didn't. Unable to determine whether or not the men who closed the courts were poor farmers (since we do not even know most of their names, we cannot consult tax lists to find their economic standing), they saw no particular reason to delve into a subject that held little prospect of revealing class conflict.

John L. Brooke, in his study of Worcester County [*The Heart of the Commonwealth: Society and Political Culture in Worcester County, Massachusetts, 1713–1861*], was not impressed with the attempts of Progressives and new social historians to read class conflict into the revolutionary turmoil on the local level. "Rather than a radical leveling," he wrote, "the events of late August and early September [1774] point to a successful maintenance of the status quo by the Whig gentry." [148.] To support this conclusion, Brooke showed that the justices of the peace appointed by the revolutionary government were "a strikingly familiar group," many of whom had held office or been politically active before the Revolution. "[T]he opening phases of the Revolution were continuous with recent provincial experience, rather than making a fundamental break with the past," he concluded. [155–157.]

Brooke was partially correct: the court closures produced no radical leveling of society. But they did have profound revolutionary consequences, which he failed to see because of his focus on so-called leaders and office holders. This was not a *junta,* which substituted one group of officials for another; this was a *revolution,* which redefined the basis of political authority. The patriots of Worcester had been complaining about royal patronage for a decade—and on September 6, 1774, they ended it forever. Although they returned many of same men into office, they made it perfectly clear that all public officials, even "the most dignified servants," were entirely "dependant on the people for their existence as such." [Lincoln, *Journals of Each Provincial Congress,* 633.] Never were a people more suspicious of the abuse of political power. After ridding themselves of British authority, the patriots of Worcester pushed for a new government with frequent elections, no plural office holding, and a host of other measures that would have ensured that power remain in the hands of the voters.

4. David Hatchett Fisher aptly labels this view of Lexington and Concord "The myth of injured innocence." [*Paul Revere's Ride,* 327–328.]

5. Dartmouth to Gage, January 27, 1775, Gage, *Correspondence,* 2: 179.

INDEX